O. & M. AND MANAGEMENT SERVICES

O. & M. and Management Services

Services

A PRACTICAL GUIDE

J. C. DENYER

Senior Lecturer at South-west London College
Examiner to the Institute of Administrative Accounting
and Data Processing
Council Member of the Society of Management Information Technology

MACDONALD AND EVANS
8 John Street, London WC1N 2HY

MACDONALD & EVANS LTD.
8 John Street, London WC1N 2HY

First published January 1976

©
MACDONALD AND EVANS LIMITED
1976

ISBN: 0 7121 1515 3 (Hard case)
ISBN: 0 7121 1520 X (Paperback)

Printed in Great Britain by
Richard Clay (The Chaucer Press), Ltd.,
Bungay, Suffolk

PREFACE 24/11/80

It has become obvious in recent years that business efficiency has lagged behind technological development. No doubt a great deal of this is due to lack of efficiency in the office but office efficiency is related to overall management efficiency. It is difficult to separate the two.

Organisation & Methods has now grown into Management Services, an area more concerned with assessing management efficiency, and not merely office efficiency. The expansion of Management Services in local and central government and in business proves the importance of this process.

In this book, the reader is assumed to have a basic knowledge of office machines and systems; the author's previous book, *Office Management*, is aimed at providing the rudiments. To assess, and where possible, increase efficiency, requires considerable further study.

It is necessary to examine the relationship of office efficiency to overall management efficiency and to examine the main quantitative techniques involved. However, this book does not intend to give examples of systems or machine applications but rather to give general principles of their examination and introduction. Organisation & Methods check lists are appended to the end of relevant chapters and case studies of interest are included where applicable.

There are so many different theories of management that this book intends to provide a background only to the most important and acknowledged theories.

Some writers seem to think that office efficiency rests entirely with organisation and systems, but it is suggested that personnel and machines are just as important, in fact, essential to the proper working of systems. Relevant chapters have therefore been included on these aspects.

Since management and office efficiency have counterparts in all spheres of human activity, the term "enterprise" has been used in referring to any kind of concern in government, hospital administration, business, etc.

Part One is introductory; Part Two deals with details of office efficiency. Further Parts deal with management elements, Organisation & Methods techniques, operational research, electronic data processing and work control.

As this book cannot be more than an introduction to the subject a bibliography is included, and also a list of British Standard specifications on items relevant to office management.

J.C.D.

CONTENTS

PART TWO: OFFICE EFFICIENCY

PART THREE: ELEMENTS OF MANAGEMENT

PART FIVE: OPERATIONAL RESEARCH

PART SIX: E.D.P.

PART SEVEN: CONTROL OF WORK

LIST OF ILLUSTRATIONS

Part One: Introduction

Chapter 1 Efficiency   2H/11/80
9/2/81

Introduction

The main objective of Organisation & Methods (O. & M.) is maximum office efficiency. Few would question this statement, but when it comes to a precise interpretation of what is meant by "efficiency," a number of definitions are possible.

To one person, to increase efficiency simply means to reduce overhead costs to the bare minimum, with the result that management may be starved of essential information.

Another person might take the similarly short-sighted view—what might be called the professional accountant's view—that if the running costs of an office are *x* per cent lower than those of other businesses, then it must be an efficient office. While not denying that reduced over-heads may result in increased profit, if this also results (as it often does) in a reduced customer service and a tense, overworked staff with a high labour turnover, it is doubtful whether true efficiency has been achieved.

Some people view efficiency as being in direct proportion to the number of staff employed in a business: if the business is continuing at its existing size and manages to retain its staff without a high labour turnover, it is assumed to be efficient.

To others again, efficiency has become synonymous with work study investigation, and with everyone subsequently working at top speed without pausing for breath. Efficiency experts have for this reason tended to earn themselves a bad reputation, particularly as the results are often that staff begin to leave and more mistakes tend to occur, usually compounded of inexperience, bad training and bad supervision.

Undoubtedly the office function should be performed as cheaply as possible. The real meaning of efficiency could therefore be said to be the achievement of the *purpose* of the particular office at the lowest possible cost. There are many offices with very expensive equipment (perhaps a computer) and a multitude of staff, which never fully achieve the purpose for which they were set up, partly because the purpose has never been clearly defined and partly because, even if aware of it office managers often lack the knowledge and ability to ensure that it is achieved.

1

✓   Achieving the purpose of an office is so important that it is often
worth spending more money in order to ensure that it is achieved. It
should always be borne in mind, however, that the spending of more
money does not necessarily by itself mean the achievement of the purpose, a subject which is discussed in later chapters.

Function of the office

The function of the office within any organisation is often crucial. In a
business, it is usually *secondary* to the main object of the business,
which may be manufacturing, trading, etc. Nevertheless, the making of
a profit from such buying and selling activities is of paramount importance, and for this reason the office can be said to be *complementary*
inasmuch as the other activities of the business which contribute to
making the profit could not be carried on without the aid of the office.
✓ Manual workers require their wages to be calculated and paid out;
factory workers require raw material to be purchased; the sales department has to sell the goods in which the business trades.
✓   The office is also important because it exercises a *controlling* influence
over the business. One only has to think of budgetary control, stock
control, production control and so on to realise the importance of this
function of the office.
✓   Finally, the office is important because it assists in the general
management of the business, which is discussed further in a later chapter.
✓   To perform these activities, the office *receives* information, *records*
information, *arranges* and *analyses* information, and *gives* information.
This is the basic function of all offices, and it is important that it should
do so efficiently, thus giving the maximum assistance in the management
of the enterprise.

Assessing efficiency

If achieving the purpose of an office in the most economical way is the
true meaning of efficiency, it should be easy to assess the efficiency of
any particular office.
  Unfortunately, this is not an easy task, because:

  (*a*) there is not always complete agreement on the precise purpose
of an office;
  (*b*) how does one know what is the limit of economy without
sacrificing service?
  (*c*) there are degrees of efficiency, which vary with the particular
management philosophy being adopted; and

(*d*) modern office management, particularly in the large concern, has become such a complicated affair, that some simple test in order to assess efficiency is almost impossible to introduce.

Some businessmen are content with a negative assessment of efficiency, *i.e.* if there is absence of clerical mistakes, absence of complaints from customers, absence of undue delays in dealing with letters, etc. then the office is assumed to be efficient. But, of course, it might not be achieving what it should be, and its cost might be double what it should be—in other words, it is really inefficient.

This is not to say that such an assessment is invalid, but the converse might not apply, because the express purposes of any office system should include "accuracy," with no delays in finding files, etc. It should also achieve all this at the lowest cost.

As mentioned above, "costs" can never be the sole criteria of efficiency in the office, and in an inefficient office, there are often hidden costs which are not apparent at the superficial glance. Thus, an otherwise efficient office may have a high labour turnover, resulting in high costs of recruiting and training new staff, and it is doubtful if the work will be very accurate, almost always having to be performed by inexperienced staff.

Positive checks

Negative checks are useful, but do not in themselves indicate a positive efficiency; what other measurements can be used?

It is suggested that if the elements of office work can be analysed, then a positive checking can be performed on each of these elements, *i.e.*, purpose, method and systems, personnel, organisation, environment and machines and equipment.

These elements of office efficiency are dealt with in greater detail in later chapters, but it cannot be assumed that even if proper attention is given to them all, an efficient office will automatically result!

In the first instance, there is the question of proportion. When in one office, machines are not really applicable, emphasis should be laid on (say) systems and personnel. The larger the staff of an office, the more likely there is to be something wrong with the organisation, no matter what marvellous systems and machines it possesses.

It is not pretended that the above list includes all the ingredients of efficiency, because a great deal will depend on management policies in various directions. Often, wrong policies result in all manner of inefficiencies, *e.g.*, the supplying and charging for empty boxes instead of using non-returnables, the expense of keeping unnecessary records, and thereby creating unnecessary costs.

Office administration and management

The relationship of office administration to general management is important, because the office is a part of, and definitely assists, management. Secondly, the relative efficiency of an office is affected by the policies of top management.

Thus, if top management decides to change its pricing policies at least once a week, then it must expect to have complications, if not delays and mistakes in office work. Similarly, if management decides it would rather have a high labour turnover than offer internal promotion, then it must expect to have lowered office efficiency, resulting from constantly-changing staff and work being performed by inexperienced people.

Where management is concerned with running a whole business, including various shops or factories, office administration is more concerned with implementation and interpretation of management policies. And if top management policy is faulty, no increase in office efficiency will compensate for it. Some years ago, the author was concerned with the assessment of the efficiency of a particular business, and it was discovered that the proprietors were simply drawing more out of the business than the profits justified. Far from building up capital reserves, they were actually eroding their capital, yet they had requested an efficiency audit!

Again, if top management starves the business of working capital so that there are never sufficient stocks to supply most of the customers' wants, then office work will be created because of the need to answer telephone calls, and write letters about delayed deliveries, the sending of substitutes, etc.

In addition to faults in basic policies of management, there might even be faulty policies directly concerning the office. The directors of a nationally-known food concern insisted on a computer being installed regardless of whether it would be suitable to the company's requirements. Indeed, in a recent survey, it was reported that 60 per cent of business concerns installed computers, and *then* considered what use could be made of them!

Management efficiency

Management efficiency is examined more closely in Chapter 12, so that all that needs to be looked at here is the difference between management and office efficiency. It is possible to have an efficient management (in terms of profitability, good policies, etc.) and yet have an inefficient office. In fact, some of the biggest and most profitable concerns have been shown to be the most inefficient in their office operations. Conversely, even if the office is most efficient, it will not in itself make for an efficient business, because however efficient the office might be, if top management policies are bad, then the whole enterprise will be inefficient.

Large-sized units might give economies of scale and make the best use of specialists, but there is all too often lack of co-ordination, bad organisation, and waste of staff time (particularly that of private secretaries). Although small units may have better morale, more informal operations, and greater sensitivity to change, their office efficiency is often low because of ignorance and the lack of expertise that the larger concerns possess. Probably the most efficient management is in the enterprises of medium size; in America, when efficiency of different-sized business concerns were assessed, the fifth from the top in size was assessed as being the most efficient.

Chapter 2 Organisation & Methods

O. & M. can be defined as the scientific inquiry into office management, with a view to increasing its efficiency. Other definitions have included the following:

1. The objective and analytical study of administrative practices carried out by full-time specialists in order to increase effectiveness in organisation and administration.
2. The study, analysis and improvement of organisation and systems which service, control and co-ordinate the operations of an enterprise.
3. The review and improvement of the organisation and methods of clerical work.
4. Clerical work study.
5. Organised common sense.

It will be seen that there is quite a difference in these definitions, and in fact there are no clear limits as to what it can include, except that it is concerned with anything connected with efficiency and clerical work.

There are many who dislike the term "O. & M.," because, of course, the two elements included in the term are not the only things that contribute to efficiency. But although some prefer the term "work study," this is usually more applicable to manual work, although its techniques can apply just as much in the office.

In fact, a few years ago, the Treasury O. & M. *Bulletin* was thinking of changing its title, and in the event (since everyone knows something of what is meant by O. & M.), changed it to "*Management Services in Government incorporating the* O. & M. *Bulletin.*"

Necessity for O. & M.

There are many reasons why O. & M. is necessary:

1. In the first place, there is possibly an acute shortage of experts in office management, partly because business managers who may be excellent salesmen, engineers, etc., think that in practice

6

achieving efficiency is only a matter of common sense. Consequently, the methods, systems and forms used are far from efficient.

2. The quality of office work is not easy to assess; it is not immediately visible, as are products coming out of a machine. The product of office work is usually information on various pieces of paper (and it is sometimes thought that the more the information—and the more pieces of paper—the better is the office!).

3. Perhaps a vital factor also is that systems and forms having once been created by a particular manager, thereafter seem to be regarded as sacrosanct. Very often criticism of such systems and forms is seen as personal criticism of the manager concerned.

4. In large business concerns, many people already know the basic defects in organisation and systems, but dare not say it out loud. It is the duty of O. & M. to identify the defects and put them on paper.

5. When a business grows from a small one-man concern to a very large one, attention is given to broad management policies, but it is not realised how out of keeping many of its office systems still are with the increased size of the business.

6. Even if there has been no growth in the business, the same old systems and forms are used, just because they have always been used, and because they have worked fairly well in the past.

7. There is often a failure to give one person overall authority and responsibility for improving offices throughout a concern. Like any other functional appointment, the O. & M. expert is viewed as an outsider who is likely to interfere and upset the running of any department he is concerned with.

8. Some managers also fail to accept that office management is a specialist subject, and think that office efficiency is the job of the local supervisors.

While O. & M. may be necessary, it is not always employed, and often only exceptional circumstances induce a company to employ such an expert:

1. When overhead costs are mounting at an exorbitant rate.

2. When management consultants are employed perhaps to improve profitability, and include in their report a section recommending that the company should also look into its administrative methods.

3. When installing a computer it is always necessary to carry out the equivalent of an O. & M. overhaul of the office administration and its methods.

4. When, owing to high labour turnover and increased complaints from customers, it is evident that the office has become inefficient.

✓ Advantages of O. & M.

Whether O. & M. be practised by one person in a small business, or by a huge department in a large international concern, the advantages are the same:

1. A fresh independent view is brought to bear on deficiencies which are often unapparent to the sometimes rather blinkered eyes of the line managers.
2. The O. & M. officer has time to investigate inefficiency in all its aspects, unlike the local supervisor who may be only just able to keep up with the flow of work.
3. The O. & M. officer is not bounded by departmental consider- ations; neither is he biassed in favour of any one department.
4. Equally, he can see the relevance of a system in one department to what is happening in another; in other words, he can take a broad *company* viewpoint.
5. He brings his experience of other departments and perhaps other businesses with him which may be of help in solving problems of any particular department.
6. He is a trained investigator, and knows the different methods of obtaining all the information required.
7. He is the expert, and should know all the alternative methods of performing office work.
8. Through his functional responsibility, he can exercise a co- ordinating influence on the whole concern.
9. Because of his independence, he can give management advice on how office efficiency can be improved, particularly in the reduc- tion of paperwork.

Let it be clear that the O. & M. officer is a functional officer, and his job is to give advice to management; he cannot install any new system or methods without approval of management. However, it would be a foolish management which employed an expensive functional officer and then failed to take his advice!

Difficulties

There are many difficulties in setting up and in running an O. & M. department, the outstanding ones being:

1. Difficulty of assessing the existing systems. No spot check can be a fair measurement of the work or of its volume. What seems to be an over-staffed section on Monday may well seem an under-staffed section on Friday.

2. It is often difficult to assess some kinds of clerical work altogether. The duties of some jobs are so complicated and diffuse that it is almost impossible to reduce them to a neat summary.

3. The line officers view the O. & M. inquiry as a fault-finding exercise, and resent it.

4. The staff, fearing possible redundancy, fail to co-operate and give false impressions of the work they perform.

5. What seems feasible in theory is not always practicable, for various external factors may change the operation of office functions, the full effect of which is not always apparent.

6. Non-co-operation of top managers, who view the O. & M. officers as extraneous, expensive busybodies.

7. As mentioned previously, office efficiency is very much affected by business policies, and although an O. & M. officer can make recommendations about policies, it may be thought that he is going outside his terms of reference, instead of concentrating on office activities.

8. Looking at office work from outside the department it must be recognised that the O. & M. officer is a layman, and therefore may find it difficult to grasp the qualitative and discretionary elements in the work.

9. Although his training should prepare him for the unfamiliar, there may be difficulties when it comes to assessing office work where the main function is technical, such as the work related to architects, chemists, etc.

10. The need to understand the relevance and necessity of tradition in the practice or profession.

11. The factory floor has inspectors (and often also work study officers) whose job it is to see to the efficiency of production, and whose work has become accepted (with certain exceptions) by the workers. But in the office, it is a comparatively new development and is still not fully accepted.

12. Related to this is the natural psychological resistance to change. This whole area is dealt with more fully later in the book.

Skills and personality requirements

Undoubtedly, a great deal of the success of O. & M. depends on the personality, character, skills and knowledge of the person performing it.

Although a person may have the right character, knowledge and experience, he may be altogether unsuitable in his type of personality, which is a very important matter! He must be pleasant and tactful, he must be able to inspire confidence and, above all, he must be sincere. He must not appear to be superior, and yet he must have an air of authority by which his worth will be measured. He must be acceptable to the lowest level of workers and yet be believed by the top managers to whom he reports. He must be shrewd; able to assess the unstated; persuasive and able to sell his ideas.

In character, he must be determined to seek out all that needs to be found out. But at the same time he must have a balanced outlook and be able to see things in perspective. He must, of course, be devoted to his job, and honest in his opinions, and be bold enough to state them.

In skills, he must not only have a good knowledge of all O. & M. techniques, but also of all office management affairs, and he must be extremely methodical in approach to his job.

In all, an O. & M. officer must be something of an accountant, a salesman, a detective, a tactician and a technician, and he often has to act as a mediator. Despite his expertise, he must have sufficient humility to recognise when his theories are at fault. In fact, since he should always be learning new ideas, humility is a basic virtue, for he must never think that he knows it all. Methods and machines are changing almost daily, and he must have a mind receptive to new ideas, although also the courage to assess their true worth.

Where O. & M. has extended into management activities and perhaps is termed Management Services (*see* next Chapter), then the O. & M. officer must also be something of a management consultant, mathematician, and computer expert.

In all areas, the O. & M. man needs a critical but constructive mind. Qualities of curiosity, keen observation, sound judgment, and common sense are very important. He also needs imagination, initiative, and above all, enthusiasm for his O. & M. duties.

To be a good O. & M. man, in short, requires a wide range of disciplines and talents, and it could be said he should be paid a much higher salary than is often offered to him!

History of O. & M.

Some date O. & M. to even before the First World War, but the setting up of the Treasury O. & M. in 1941 seems to have been the first time official blessing was given to what was previously only a movement.

In 1951, the O. & M. Division (now the Management Services Unit) of the London Boroughs was established, to serve local authorities all over London.

Of course, there were awakenings in many places in the years before this date: the B.B.C. established its Central Establishments Department in 1947. This was set up to assess staffing requirements, but an interesting sidelight on office efficiency was demonstrated, *i.e.* that it is not possible to assess staffing numbers or gradings without assessing the work and the methods employed. In effect, this was the B.B.C.'s O. & M. department.

Specialist or not?

George Bernard Shaw once stated something to the effect that anyone who was a complete specialist must be an idiot! To some extent, this must be true, because a complete specialist in office efficiency would be unable to cope with modern office problems unless he knew something of the principles of management, of the techniques of work study, and so on.

With the growth of O. & M., and its spread into many other disciplines (*see* next Chapter), a problem with large concerns is whether to have technique-oriented divisions (dealing with work study, operational research, and so on), or whether to have a general O. & M. department, where the staff are problem-oriented, and use whatever technique is required.

With the technique-oriented approach, there is likely to be a bending of the problems to suit the technique chosen and, as with all specialisations, there might be a narrowness of vision. Also, of course, it may be expensive of staffing; at least one large concern known to the author has a staff of over seventy in its operational research department who have to devise problems, if there are insufficient to keep them occupied.

On the other hand, the generalist approach of the problem-oriented organisation means that whatever the problem requires will be prescribed. But it can be argued that the science employed in modern management has become so advanced and complex that it is not possible for a general O. & M. expert to know all that is necessary for dealing with (say) computer programming or an operational research problem.

No doubt a great deal will depend on the size of the concern and its consequent volume of work, but in the two large O. & M. departments of the Treasury and the London Boroughs Management Services, they now have separate divisions with their experts in the different techniques. As with medicine, healing the patient depends very much on proper diagnosis, and if the general practitioner finds a case beyond his capabilities, then it should be referred to a specialist.

Chapter 3 Management Services

Since the 1950s, when computers were first used for commercial purposes, O. & M. has had to move with the times. Perhaps the electronic computer has been the biggest stimulus.)

The computer is generally big and expensive, and business concerns wanting to make full use of it have given it a centralised location and used it for data processing for all departments. The advent of a computer always demands a fresh management look at the whole scene of administration. O. & M. could not thereafter be concerned with just a particular office system, or the use of various office machines, it has had to concern itself more with the running of the whole concern.

Various mathematical and statistical techniques gradually evolved, which helped top management in its decision-making (often assisted by the computer), and this also contributed to a wider application of O. & M. As O. & M. departments concerned themselves more and more with these techniques, it was obvious it needed some new more all-embracing title, and during the 1960s, the term Management Services became more popular. The term includes O. & M., but is wider since it implies the need to deal with management problems, and to use much more sophisticated techniques.

Work measurement

As the size of business units became larger and the numbers of clerical staff also greatly increased, there developed a need to assess work performance. As a result, some of the techniques of work study were borrowed, work measurement and work standards were introduced, and scientific measurements were made of all kinds of work. The use of the technique has grown to such an extent that many organisations are now using sophisticated schemes of incentive payments for office workers (*see* Chapter 35). Premium Payments Bonus systems were also introduced, taken from the work study field, and the trend was no doubt accelerated by the ever-increasing use of machines in the office.

Operational research

Mathematics and statistics invaded the office and it was discovered that Operational Research (O.R.) and critical path diagrams could be used in planning and control of work. O.R. controls help solve problems of stock levels, routing of transport, best use of machines, and so on. Furthermore, these scientific devices give better planning and control over the manual side of the business, so that production planning, investment in new machines, and even economic ordering quantities in the buying department, could all be decided mathematically.

In a way, these new mathematical tools gave the office greater importance, and in some cases increased office staff, with a corresponding decrease in manual staff.

O.R. techniques in general did not replace the old office methods, but only added to their application, made them more precise, and certainly added to the burden of the O. & M. man.

Management accounting

At the same time, accounting practice (which has always been the backbone of office work) developed and took on the wider term of management accounting. Budgetary control and costing techniques grew ever more complicated and, of course, required more office staff to operate them.

Then accountants discovered that they were required to do more than just report on the historical financial background of the concern. They were expected to assist in management forecasting and planning, and techniques such as Discounted Cash Flow were introduced to help in the assessment of capital expenditure.

New thinking and new formulae were introduced for the replacement of assets, for the payment of dividends, for the calculation of working capital, and so on. Sometimes, even the basic divisions of traditional accounting looked like being forgotten, as it became increasingly difficult to assess what was capital and what was revenue, and how capital and profit should be measured.

Then of greater importance still to management, because it is very much concerned with the basic policies, there arose in the Civil Service the use of P.P.B. (Programming, Planning, Budgeting systems), which in a way is an exercise of cost/benefit analysis on the grand scale. Although basically concerned with the better use of money, management accounting must impinge on the systems and methods used in controlling expenditure.

Specialisation

It is amazing how specialisation has increased in the last decade or so. We now have P.D.M. (Physical Distribution Management), which deals with all the aspects related to the transport of goods. We have specialised journals, dealing, for example, with nothing but offset lithography and its related arts. There have even been whole exhibitions devoted to the display and furtherance of micro-photography, which has now been extended to the computer field.

There have always been specialists in personnel matters and it would seem sometimes now as if personnel aspects are considered totally apart from the work performed or the methods used.

There is little doubt that improved communications have been a big factor in increasing office efficiency, and in some concerns there is now a communications officer who is a specialist in office communications.

A branch of work study concerned with the physical working environment has also grown into a specialisation called "ergonomics," and there is now even a University Chair in the subject, so it is undoubtedly of growing importance.

Management by objectives

Then, akin to personnel's "merit rating," but combining it with a kind of budgetary-control technique over individual effort, there arose M.B.O. This again introduced scientific methods. Individual objectives are laid down, but in consultation with the personnel involved, and at regular interviews achievements are compared with those forecast previously. This involved more records, more work on the personnel side, and yet is concerned with the work, and how it is performed, as well as with standards of staffing.

Barclays Bank have, in particular, publicised its successful use, and when M.B.O. has been practised, it has certainly improved efficiency from a costing point of view. Thus at one bank, a manager was told of his volume of work (represented by "sales" statistics, which is not necessarily an accurate measure of work), and his corresponding overhead charges (represented by his number of clerks), and had been asked how he could reduce them, as they were much higher than in any other branch.

Management development

It is little use having new systems and new methods, if the staff who operate them cannot understand them, so there has also grown up an emphasis on the overall training of all staff at all levels of management. The emphasis here is not only on training staff to play their full part in the current developments, but in preparing them for management changes in the future.

It is recognised that better management requires proper training, so the emphasis has been laid on management development. Training is often thought of as being suitable for the working levels but, with all the new modern techniques, it is realised that it is also top management which needs training, so executive development is as important as job training for staff at working levels.

Productivity

Productivity is indivisible, for it consists of interrelated and closely-matching factors. Increases in productivity can be achieved by the appropriate use of one or other of the above-mentioned disciplines, but while organisation is important and the methods and systems used are also important, it is obvious that much more is involved than just O. & M.

A difficulty is that it is not easy to define "productivity," and if it is taken to be the ratio of the output to the input resources in any venture, then the management accountant will tend to express it in monetary terms when inflation tends to make such terms rather meaningless. An alternative suggested is to take resources and years, so that 100 per cent efficiency could be described as the achievement of the prescribed objectives with the absolute minimum of resources at any one time.

It is the objective of management services to increase productivity, using O. & M., work study, O.R., E.D.P., and various other techniques. It seeks *systematically* to improve all the various aspects of management with which it is concerned.

The whole management services complex is concerned with giving advice to management on how to reduce its input resources, while maintaining or increasing its output. In fact "Productivity Services" has been suggested as an alternative name to "Management Services."

Conclusion

O. & M. and Management Services can be said to be a specialist subject because it has become so vast and so complicated, that it takes a lifetime of learning and experience to be really knowledgeable about it. On the other hand, it could be argued that it has become so diffuse that it is no longer a specialist affair. It involves a knowledge of computers, operational research, statistics and mathematics, work study, management accounting and it could be said that it is beyond the capacity of one person completely to understand all these disciplines.

This is borne out if we consider the organisation of the London Boroughs Management Services Committee, which now has departments dealing with O. & M. and O.R.; Work Study; and Computers.

The Government's Civil Service Management Services (General) Division is now divided (in addition to the Computer Divisions) into:

1. M.B.O. Liaison or Training.
2. Efficiency Committee and Management Consultants.
3. Accounting, Audit, Costing, and Accountable Management.
4. Work Measurement (Typing and Secretarial).
5. Work Study, Office Systems, Transport, Mechanical Handling and Stores.
6. Micro-copying, Reprographic systems.
7. Information retrieval, Libraries, Drawing Office, Forms and Algorithms.
8. Working Environment and Communications.

Management Services thus can be said to include anything which contributes to the productivity and efficiency of management. It is realised today that office efficiency is not enough, and that management efficiency is the real objective.

Although it is an all-embracing subject, its various tools need to be used with care, and for the proper purpose. Where O.R. could assist a large enterprise, simple O. & M. techniques might be of greater benefit to a small concern; where a computer survey might be useful to a large local authority, a report on the latest electronic accounting machines might be sufficient for a small one. To be of greatest benefit to management, the right emphasis must be laid on using the right tools for the right purpose.

Chapter 4 Management

If Management Services provides a service to management, it is thus necessary to know about the content of "management." What is management, and how does the office contribute to it? Why cannot office efficiency itself produce good management? Why is management so important that it deserves special study, and why is it so difficult?

Management is most important, and must be studied because (taking the analogy of a clock) it is the mainspring of an enterprise, whereas office management can be likened to the hairspring and the escape mechanism. In other words, if the mainspring is faulty, no matter how perfect the escape mechanism, the clock will not go. Equally, there might be a very good mainspring, but its functioning depends on having a good hairspring.

Anyone who has visited numerous business concerns which seem to be thriving, will be appalled at the lack of office efficiency, but the management must be sound for the business to exist at all.

Another reason why management is so important, is because, in the course of assessing office efficiency, it often becomes apparent that the main cause of trouble is either bad organisation of the whole enterprise, or bad policies. Most of the published investigations of the well-known management consultants usually contain recommendations about both of these areas, usually recommending a greater degree of decentralisation and the setting-up of a policy-making body (perhaps for corporate planning) where probably none existed before. The managing body also usually concerns itself too much with control.

What is management?

The *Concise Oxford Dictionary* (5th Edition) includes in its definition of management "treachery" and "deceitful connivance," and while this may seem a little facetious, it shows that it is not easy to give a simple precise definition. A modern management writer, Peter Drucker, has stated that management is managing (or controlling) a business, managing managers, managing workers, and managing work.

Some people have stated that management is really the driving force within each concern, representing the personal element in the life of a business.

Others, again, have stated that management is the "organisation, control, and co-ordination of personnel and processing to produce optimum results."

In recent years, Professor Revans has stated that the manager "decides what to do, and the technologist provides the tools and the machines to do it. The manager poses the questions, and the technologist answers them."

Again, it has been stated that management means making the most efficient use of the four Ms—*M*en, *M*oney, *M*aterials, and *M*achines.

As is usual, all nutshell definitions have in them a germ of truth, and the whole truth lies somewhere between all of them, but as good a definition as any is "the science or art of reaching a given end with the utmost economy of means" (Allcutt).

Science or art?

It will be noticed in this last definition, that management is defined as a science *or* art, and it is more than academic inquiry to ascertain which term really does apply. In so far as it is an art, then like all other arts its practice relies on the personality, skills, and personal attitudes of managers. Frederick Hooper, another management writer (previously Managing Director of Schweppes), would have us believe that managers are born and not made.

But on the other hand, in so far as management is a science, it is a body of knowledge which can be learned (by anyone with a scientific mind), and is not dependent on personal attributes.

The answer, surely, is that it is both an art *and* a science. While the personal qualities of managers will have a great bearing on their success as managers, they need to have a knowledge of management principles and practice (even though they are unaware of their formal existence).

There is little doubt that with the growth of Operational Research, management accounting techniques, Critical Path Analysis, and work study techniques, management is becoming more scientific every day. This is not to say that there will never be room for the hunch or intuition. No matter how scientifically management problems are tackled, there are always the imponderables, and there are always unpredictable factors (*e.g.*, in sales forecasting)—even the weather can upset the most scientific of forecasts!

Content of management

If the definitions of management mentioned above are studied, certain elements will be seen to recur, which can be traced back to the father of management theory, H. Fayol. He described management as consisting of:

1. Forecasting and planning.
2. Organisation.
3. Command and authority.
4. Control.
5. Co-ordination.

To these might be added some modern elements which have received considerable attention in recent years:

6. Policy-making and decision-making.
7. Communication.
8. Motivation.

Several American writers have written whole books on (6) and (7), and the human relations school (or behavioural scientists) have given prominence to (8).

These are the elements which are discussed in Part Three of this book, and whatever elaborations modern writers may produce, these basic elements remain the same.

Relationship with office management

Office management has been defined as performing the functions of communication and record (communication means giving and receiving information), as well as its analysis and arrangement in a style suitable to management.

If any office work is examined, it will be seen to come under one or other of the above-mentioned elements of management. Even the writing of letters comes under (7); the keeping of accounting records under (4); the work of a board of directors under (4), (5), and (6); and the operation of a computer is usually in connection with (1), (4), (6), and (7).

In O. & M. and Management Services, the great importance of management is that it makes policy in many directions (or, of course, may fail to make policies when it should), which affect the whole administration of an enterprise.

For example, if customers complain, should goods sold to them be exchanged or cash be refunded?—this is a policy decision. Should customers be allowed ten days or thirty days credit?—a policy decision. Should £1,000 or £100,000 be spent on office machines in a year?—a policy decision. All of these will have profound influence on the staffing and efficiency of the office.

Management decisions about the degree of control over credit, over staffing, over paperwork, over factory production, and even over maintenance of office machines, will all have great bearing on the records and staffing an office needs.

Furthermore, unless the right decisions are made and the right policies formulated, the office work created is often almost a waste of time.

In short, office efficiency cannot be disassociated from management efficiency. Again, it is like the mainspring and the hairspring in a clock. One is more important than the other (hence the trend from O. & M. to Management Services), but both play their part in the efficient working of the whole concern.

Future trends

From the indications of the last few years, both general management and office management are going to become more scientific.

Undoubtedly, more machines will be used in the office, and office work will become more routine and mechanical. We are only at the beginning of the electronic age, and filing, communication, etc. will become more and more sophisticated. Machines have proliferated, and older machines have given way to more compact, more efficient machines.

Management, particularly of the larger enterprise, will become more a matter of numbers and be decided by mathematicians, and the tendency in business, in local government and in government bodies, is for the size of the operating unit ever to increase.

The larger the size of an enterprise, the more will the scientific approach be used, and the more will the future Management Services expert have to know about.

A word of warning should be sounded, however. Some of these new management techniques are so facile (in the right hands), that the manager should be beware of being placed totally in the hands of the specialist. It is an oft-repeated remark that "specialists should be on tap and not on top." The difficulty is (and this has happened with computers), that the subject-matter of the new scientific tool becomes so complicated that it is difficult to understand it, least of all communicate with the specialists, who often devise their own esoteric jargon.

What is the answer then, and what attitude should be taken? The answer lies in the tenet that a manager (and the M.S. officer) should know enough about the techniques to be able to ask the right questions, and the manager should always remember that such aids should be advisory to, and should not supplant, management. This applies to accounting techniques as well, and much of the paperwork and record-keeping required by accountants should be questioned concerning its validity and purpose. Even ledgers have been found to be superfluous in many large concerns today.

Then, again, many of the techniques of O.R., P.D.M., D.C.F., etc., rely on certain measurable premises. These are not always reliable, even though they are precise and expressed in measurable form.

Thus O.R. (*see* Chapter 28), can assist in stock control, but the premises on which it is based, such as annual usage, lead-time for delivery, cost of handling, cost of storing, can all alter inside a few months, and the figures derived from them may need constant re-calculation.

This is not to deny the value of using these techniques, but they should be viewed with caution, and as an expert in Market Research has stated, the findings of M.R. provide management with a navigational aid to sales forecasting, *i.e.* a tool which helps in making decisions about marketing, but by no means replaces the use of intuition, experience, and common sense.

Again, and this is one of the problems of management, in large O.R. departments staff are often told that their findings are not acceptable, and that they should recalculate so as to provide proof for the decisions that are wanted! In such cases, it is apparent that for political and pressure group motives, the scientific tools are not only being misused, but completely ignored. An enterprise like this could save many thousands of pounds by eliminating their O.R. experts.

The same applies with office management—to compare the overhead costs of one branch with that of another doing identical work may not be realistic without a proper scientific assessment of staffing, relative efficiency, records and methods used.

What seems to be scientific, is often a brushing aside of the non-scientific, and there are always "experts" who want to reduce everything to a science. They seem to be entranced by their techniques, regardless of the fundamentals of management behind facts and figures they tabulate.

Part Two: Office Efficiency

Chapter 5 Purposes

Introduction

In this section of the book, it is proposed to examine each of the constituents of office efficiency. The first, and probably the most important, is "purpose." In other words, what is the system for, and what are the results expected from the work performed?

Of course, no office system ever has one purpose, although it may have one main purpose, such as submitting sales invoices to customers. But there are questions of time, of security, of cost, of notification to other departments, and so on. So the concern should really be with "purposes," and it is as well to recognise which are the most important ones, so that others, which may not be attainable, are viewed as less important.

Importance

Assessment of the purposes of a system is vital, for many reasons. First, unless they are achieved, the whole office may be wasting its time. The furniture, machines, and not least, the staffing might be better employed in the factory if they are not achieving the main purposes aimed at. Thus, if a stock-control section has as its main purpose the ability to ascertain the quantity in stock of any item at any time, and it fails to do so, then it is all just a waste of effort.

Secondly, the purposes will have a bearing on what machines should be installed. Thus for ten copies of an invoice, spirit duplicating might be better than if only three copies are required, when no-carbon methods might be used.

Thirdly, it helps put in perspective what the system and the staff are trying to achieve, and it not only gives the staff a sense of purpose, but indicates exactly what kind of system is required.

Fourthly, if the purposes are correctly stated, then it can help prevent errors and can help deter fraud.

Fifthly, it gives the O. & M. man the guidelines as to whether the

23

work being performed is really necessary (often a difficult task). Every step in a system should contribute to its purposes.

Lastly, by stating the purposes, they can be compared with overall management objectives, as well as management's general policies.

"Put it in writing"

One of the first jobs of an O. & M. assignment should be to ascertain the purposes of a system, and to put them in writing. This is then the working code, the checklist to bear in mind when examining the work being performed.

Management does not always realise that there can be many purposes to a system, and least of all do they commit them to writing. Nor do they realise that different purposes can sometimes be conflicting. Thus, to reduce the administrative costs to a minimum and to prevent fraud may be in conflict, for the prevention of fraud may incur expense of control records and staffing which the business is not prepared to face.

Control information may be required in other directions, but some businessmen cannot see that if it is essential it costs money to achieve. A company director once asked the author how to analyse his sales, and when acquainted with the possible methods, he was aghast at the possible extra expense involved.

So a golden rule is, put the purposes of an office system in writing, and differentiate between those which are essential, and those which are advisable, and those which seem desirable. Here, the O. & M. man must divine, by consultation with managers, what the purposes are at present, and whether they are sufficient, or too many or not worthwhile. This is a question of policy, and harks back to what was said in the last chapter on the relationship of O. & M. to management.

There is the apocryphal story of the managing director who requested statistics on how many single girls aged between 18 and 21 were employed, and what length of service each had. When told that the administrative cost of obtaining the information would be x thousands of pounds, the managing director said "Forget it."

Specifics

It is impossible to lay down general purposes for all systems in all concerns, because circumstances vary according to availability of staff, to whether there is a seasonal trade, to the philosophy of top management, to the geographical spread of the customers, the type of trade, and above all to the size of the enterprise.

To take the delivery of goods to customers, one business may think a few days' delay as good, whereas a firm selling important drugs may want a one-hour service.

Similarly, a business selling computers may want to keep its sales invoices indefinitely, whereas a company selling articles costing 10p each may only keep them six months. The purpose of keeping records in a hotel business is altogether a different thing from keeping hospital records.

While it might be possible to have more common purposes in businesses of the same size, selling the same products, etc., there are always areas of policy which are matters of judgment rather than of efficiency.

General purposes

However, ignoring the specifics, there are always some general purposes which can be incorporated into every system for a business of any size. These could include the following:

1. to achieve the purposes at the lowest cost possible;
2. to achieve them in the specified time or shortest possible time (thus, to produce sales statistics as soon as possible after the sales period has ended);
3. to prevent the making of errors, or at any rate to be able to correct them before they have dire consequences;
4. to deter the staff from committing theft or fraud (it is almost impossible to prevent them, but it can be made as difficult as possible);
5. to incur the lowest cost; while the lowest cost is required, it is not usually desired at the expense of a high labour turnover, as the introduction of incentive bonus schemes may cause;
6. to create the minimum amount of paperwork;
7. to use the most appropriate machines, consistent with the management's ability to afford their purchase or rental.

Example: wages system

With these general principles in mind, the specific purposes of a wages system might be:

1. To calculate precisely the amount of wages due to each employee on the pay-roll.
2. To be able to pay out such wages on Friday morning for the working week ending Wednesday (this is a matter of management policy, for some firms pay a standard week and then make

adjustments on the following week's pay for a working week ending Friday. Some pay fortnightly, some pay to the nearest 50p, and so on).

3. To record the differences between gross and net pay, and to have an independent check to see that all deductions are in fact applied to their appropriate sources.
4. To issue statements of pay with the wages, so that any mistakes can be notified and corrected promptly.
5. To ensure that all adjustments in the standard pay-roll are properly notified and taken notice of, in good time before the pay-roll preparation. Many a poor employee who has just started work, has discovered that his name had not been included on the pay-roll for his first week. Similarly, all holidays and sickness must be notified within the proper period of time.
6. To prevent fraud and theft; this is mentioned as a general purpose above, but it is of particular importance with a wages system, and not only prevention of crime committed by employees, but precautions against pay-roll theft must also be taken.
7. In a large business, it is essential also, that there should be some method of identification to ensure that wages are in fact paid to the right people.
8. Then, there may be specific requirements to the business, such as the automatic charging to jobs or processes for the purposes of costing. If this can be performed at the same time as the preparation of the pay-roll, then it may be the most efficient thing to do.

Example: sales invoicing

Every business has the task of invoicing its customers, and again, the system will depend on whether all the sales are for cash (fairly simple matter here, with the use of cash registers or autographic machines), or on credit terms or on hire-purchase terms.

However, there are some general purposes of sales invoicing:

1. That before an invoice is prepared it is checked that the goods are in stock or are obtainable (if not immediately obtainable, then some method of deferring invoice preparation until they are in hand).
2. That even if the goods ordered are in hand, the order has been checked with the credit control section. Sales are not desired at the expense of bad debts.

3. That the terminology used by the customer on his order is translated into the Company's official catalogue numbers or terminology, so that it facilitates its progress and avoids mistakes.
4. To ensure that current prices (or those quoted) are charged on the invoices.
5. To ensure that the right names and addresses are used for receiving the accounts (often different from delivery addresses).
6. To ensure that extensions are accurate, and that the correct trade discount is allowed.
7. That invoices are not sent out until the goods are delivered (many firms send invoices with the goods).
8. If invoices are not sent with the goods, that they are sent as soon as possible after delivery.
9. That while the invoices are being prepared, as many other documents bearing the same information be prepared at the same time (Delivery Note, Advice Note, etc.).
10. That other departments concerned are notified immediately of the order, such as Stores, Transport, Accounts, Sales Representative, and so on.
11. Specific purposes may then include that sales invoices should (if possible) be automatically charged in the stock records, in costing records, and so on.
12. That the office copy of the sales invoice is stored properly and is kept for the appropriate length of time.

Example: purchasing

Again, the purposes of a purchasing system will depend greatly on the policy of top management. Thus, will purchases be "spot purchases," made by quotation, or by contract, or will all three be used according to the type of goods being purchased?

It is still possible, however, to lay down some general purposes:

1. No purchases should be made unless a properly authorised indent is received from specified officials.
2. To buy the most suitable commodities, and at the lowest price (this will depend on the buying policy as mentioned above).
3. When a supplier has been decided on, to send him an official order form—in all cases. Even urgent orders placed over the telephone must be confirmed with official orders.
4. Order forms must always contain supplier's catalogue numbers or descriptions, to avoid mistakes.
5. All order forms must contain quoted prices and terms of payment.

6. A copy of the order form must be retained in the order book, and another copy placed in the progress files—the same day.

7. Progressing is an important aspect of purchasing, and copy orders should be filed in date order, so that slow suppliers can be hurried.

8. In this connection, purchasing departments of large concerns often maintain a suppliers' rating system, so that orders are placed only with reliable firms.

9. Copies of all orders placed must be passed immediately to the Stores Department, so that they can check the goods when delivered.

10. To ensure that copy orders are also passed to an Invoice Section for the purpose of checking purchase invoices when received.

11. To deter fraud, all orders should be signed only by an authorised official (although in large purchasing departments, the order clerks themselves are so authorised).

12. That stock orders are notified to the Stock Control section, so that they are informed of goods ordered.

13. That specific goods required by different departments are ordered unless very expensive, or in conflict with company policy (there may be bulk buying of one type of goods for the whole concern). While the Purchasing Office should have the final word on goods ordered, there may be special circumstances which justify the using department having the last word. This is an example of how authority should be properly allocated in the company organisation, and in accordance with the company requirements.

Conclusion

Thus the purposes of office systems can be general, but there are always some which must be specific to the concern. These purposes could be multiplied for systems of filing, of duplicating, for accounting, for budgetary control, and so on, but only the main ones for wages, sales-invoicing and purchasing have been included, being the most common.

CASE STUDY

Purpose

1. FACTS

British Rail operates a car ferry from Holyhead to Dun Laoghaire in Ireland, and with over 50,000 bookings in a short summer season, it does not justify any expensive machine system of booking.

There are 150 available car spaces on each ferry, and booking has to be made for both forward and return journeys. Often complications occur through last-minute cancellations.

2. PURPOSES

A clerical system was required to deal with the bookings made on the car ferries, which was:

(a) simple;
(b) inexpensive;
(c) essentially flexible (because of cancellations);
(d) capable of giving statistical evidence at any time of bookings made.

3. SOLUTION

The O. & M. Division of London Midland Region put the following into operation:

(a) Plastic cards are pre-embossed with 1—150 car space bookings for both the forward and return journeys, and, for example, 50/3 indicates ferry journey number 50, car space number 3.

(b) These cards are housed in pigeon holes, being easily visible to the booking clerk, and if a card or cards remain, then there is booking space left.

(c) Immediately a booking is made, the plastic-embossed card is placed in a small addressing machine which prints the detail on both sides of a manilla folder which contains all the correspondence relating to a booking.

(d) When the card has been used, it is placed in a lower pigeon hole representing bookings made.

(e) At any time, by glancing along the upper racks of cards, it can be seen immediately if there are any free car spaces available on ferries for any day.

4. RESULTS

(a) The system, having now been in use for several years, is an unqualified success.

(b) It achieves all the purposes desired—simplicity, cheapness, etc.

(c) It avoids duplication of bookings, and gives "at a glance" assessment of the booking situation.

[*Business Systems and Equipment* November 1967

CHECK LIST

1. Have we spelled out the purposes of the system being investigated?
2. Are the purposes (previously aimed at) the right ones?
3. What should they be?
4. Have we linked the purposes with management policies?
5. Are some purposes advisable, but too costly?
6. If the right purposes are aimed at, are they at lower cost?
7. Are they in fact achieved?
8. What do we mean by "control information"?
9. Are the controls actually used?
10. Have we agreed the office purposes with top management?
11. Should we persuade them of other desirable purposes?
12. Have we ensured the necessity of the purposes?
13. Can the different purposes be achieved simultaneously?
14. Do the staff really know the purposes of their work?
15. Are the purposes of the office in line with management objectives?
16. If the purposes are to be changed, how to achieve them?
17. Does top management know the purposes required?
18. Do they realise the cost of achieving them?
19. Have we stressed the different purposes of different systems, even in the same office?
20. Do the theoretically desirable purposes conflict in practice?

Chapter 6 Personnel

Introduction

Some writers on office management barely mention personnel matters, while others ignore it altogether. Because a personnel officer is appointed in large concerns as a specialist in personnel affairs, it is thought that such matters can be excluded from O. & M. In fact, it is probably the most important factor in office efficiency, for no matter how superior the systems and paperwork, no matter how expensive and sophisticated the machines, if poor staffing is employed there will be inefficiency.

Although for academic reasons, personnel, organisation, systems, etc. are examined separately, they are all interrelated, and personnel policies will affect the organisation, the working of systems, the use of paperwork, and so on. Anyone who has worked in an otherwise efficient office will readily testify to the effect of bad supervision on the work performed.

Not least, of course, is the effect on the whole morale of the business, which may be very closely related to the personnel policies followed. The Managing Director of Marks and Spencer Limited states that "no section of any business is more vital than the personnel side." Although his Company spend £3–£4 million on welfare services annually, they do not have the high absenteeism rate of other large business concerns.

Staff numbers

An important question these days, is how to control the ever-increasing number of clerical staff. The answer is not simple by any means, although a full O. & M. inquiry might be useful.

Staff numbers cannot be merely related to the volume of work, as is popularly supposed, for a great deal depends on how the work is performed, in other words, what methods and systems are employed.

To go back to the "volume of work"—does this mean in relationship to increased sales, or customers, or just that new work requirements arise without any real increase in the business?

Where office work is measurable, and where work standards have been set up, then a simple calculation can indicate the number of staff required, and if more are required than indicated, then it would seem that there is something wrong with the recruitment of staff (*see* Chapter 35).

When the work is not measurable, then it is extremely difficult, and only by some technique such as Activity Sampling, can it be ascertained whether staff are fully employed. An indication of shortage of staff might be the amount of overtime that is regularly worked—but if it is paid for at enhanced rates, it might not! Good supervisors, who report on staff application to work can be of great assistance, but even here, supervisors are not always fully aware of jobs "stretched out," or a very capable supervisor might assess a certain volume as sufficient for one person, whereas two people of *average* ability might be needed.

Then, again, there is the aspect of staff grading, a few well-paid, really capable staff often produce much more than twice the number of inexperienced staff of lower capability. Numbers of staff in themselves might be meaningless, and even total salary costs might be misleading if a preponderance of older staff was employed.

Job evaluation

In a recent B.I.M. survey, it was reported that only 56 per cent of firms used any scheme of job evaluation and job grading. But this cannot be accepted without reservation, because in smaller firms, even if (as is usual) they have different rates of pay for shorthand typists, copy typists, filing clerks, etc. then they have a form of job grading, however elementary it may be. When an enterprise grows in size, with hundreds or perhaps thousands of employees, job grading must be used, otherwise a multiplication of job titles will evolve, coupled with a multiplicity of rates of pay.

The basis of job evaluation is the job specification, and how staff can ever be successfully recruited without a job specification is really astonishing. This is not to say that job evaluation is easy, for clerical work has a number of aspects which may be difficult to quantify, such as telephone calls, dealing with work problems, and, furthermore, a clerical job is usually of mixed content. But it should always be attempted, and there are several methods: job factoring, the grading process, and the pointing method.

Probably the last is the most popular and the most scientific. In essence, it involves drawing up a job description, and then awarding points under different headings for the job, so that the job can earn a total number of points, which decides the grading and the relevant scale of pay.

The usual qualities assessed when awarding them to a job are:

1. Education required.
2. Experience required.
3. Initiative required.
4. Supervision (both given and received).
5. Responsibility.

Although job grading is an attempt scientifically to assess the work content of a job, it is to some extent subjective, and it is not always easy to assess accurately. Thus, what is meant by the education required to do a job? What would be the standards? For a job of accounts clerk, what would be the comparison between a public school education, and a primary school education with subsequent R.S.A. Stage III in book-keeping?

Also, supposing a certain length of experience is viewed as necessary for a particular job, might not one person have learned more in two years' experience, than another in ten years?

Whatever qualities are included, the total of all the qualities should be sufficient to cover all the jobs, and since there is wide divergence in the work of different concerns, there can be no standard list of qualities. The list must be drawn up with relevance to the different jobs in the concern.

The Institute of Administrative Management recommended six job grades which have been very closely followed in the U.K., but the number of grades included will depend on the size of the organisation and the diversification of work. In the local authority world, there are Administrative and Professional Grades 1–10. Even in the Civil Service, different names are given to different job grades, which in principle is still job grading.

In short, clerical job grading is not easy, but in the interests of orderly staffing structure, it is essential. But the work content of clerical jobs is apt to change with the times, and to be fair, jobs should be revalued periodically. It is usually the job of the O. & M. department to institute job evaluation and to carry out reassessment as required.

If job descriptions are too precise, it may inhibit the performance of duties not specifically included, but this does not mean that job evaluation should not be attempted.

Staff recruitment

It has been said that the essence of good personnel management, is to attract good staff, make the best use of them when employed, and make sure they do not leave.

The first part, recruiting good staff, can be achieved much more scientifically than is often realised. Too many employers still rely solely on the interview, which has many defects: it is limited in time, rather artificial, and to a great extent subjective on both sides. The techniques which can be used to improve the efficiency of recruitment of staff are:

1. Have a job specification to start with.
2. Have a specification of the qualities required.
3. Printed application forms, which ensure that vital information is supplied, and which makes comparisons easier.
4. Use of various tests: I.Q., aptitude, psychological, etc. Probably, the most useful test where skills are concerned, is the occupational test, which is a work test, testing exactly the qualities required to do the job.
5. Properly planned and prepared interviews.
6. Use of a quality rating at the interview.*
7. Taking up references.

It is important that applicants should be informed about all the duties of the post, and many a high labour turnover is the result of a job being described too lavishly at the interview. While an organisation wants to employ good quality staff who will be capable of promotion, perhaps even to management level, it should not over-recruit so that over-qualified staff are employed for routine jobs. This is a major problem of recruitment, particularly where increasing mechanisation of office work is occurring.

Promotion

For a more scientific system of promotion, some form of merit rating should be used, a regular periodic assessment of how a person is doing his job. The basic qualities assessed are usually:

1. Quantity of work.
2. Quality of work.
3. Reliability (particularly supervision required).
4. Loyalty (can be interpreted in different ways).

Many other qualities such as time-keeping, initiative, etc., and even sickness and absenteeism may also be included.

This is an attempt to assess the capabilities of staff scientifically, but, again, it is rather subjective, and often it is found that supervisors need training before they can complete their merit ratings satisfactorily.

* See example in the author's *Office Management*, Macdonald and Evans, 1974.

One of the problems with promotion is that it does not depend only on how a person is performing his job, but how well he might do the higher job for which he is being considered. To assist this hypothetical venture, written examinations, qualifications, and personal interviews are also used in addition to the merit rating. The higher a management job, the more will the emphasis be on character and personality, and despite the striving of psychologists, no perfect scientific assessment of these has yet been evolved.

Much depends on the management policy of promotion from within as opposed to appointment from outside. If there is not a regular policy of internal promotion, then staff morale is sure to fall and an over-high labour turnover will develop. Both will adversely affect efficiency.

Training

Training of staff is very important, because however good the staff are when recruited, unless properly trained, they can be a constant source of inefficiency.

A good training programme ensures that the right amount of training is provided (too much can lead to high labour turnover, if staff cannot be promptly promoted); that the right methods of training are used; and that the training is controlled and evaluated to assess its efficiency.

As to who should be trained, it is more a matter of management policy, but the company must look at its future vacancies and its existing staff, and then decide how many should be trained and in what kinds of skills.

Different types of training are:

1. Induction training.
2. Job training.
3. Supervisory training.
4. Management training.

Many firms give attention to (1) and (4), but overlook the importance of (2) and (3). Bad training of any kind means the subsequent use of bad habits, lack of knowledge of the total system, of the organisation, and of course to overall inefficiency.

Job training may be provided in very large concerns like banks, at central training centres, but more often it is left to the supervisor, who being too busy (and lacking ability) reverts to "sitting next to Nellie" as a form of training. If job training is left to supervision, then obviously a knowledge of training should be included in the supervisor's training course.

Some simple rules for ordinary clerical training are:

1. First study the job to establish clearly what is going to be taught.
2. Explain to the worker in a way that will impress
   (a) the purpose of the work,
   (b) relationship to other work,
   (c) relative importance of details of the job, and
   (d) the manner in which it is done.
3. Have the undivided attention of the worker, and remove all things extraneous to the job being shown.
4. Tell the worker how it is going to benefit *him*.
5. Start with the known things and lead to the unknown.
6. Explain the simple things before the complicated ones.
7. Keep to the point—leave out irrelevant detail.
8. Have the best arrangement of work and workplace.
9. Demonstrate way of performing tasks, using the best methods.
10. Leave habits of speed to later on.
11. Emphasise points where accuracy is essential.
12. Let the worker try his hand at the job.
13. Comment on performance and do the job again if necessary.
14. Do not attempt to give too much information at one time (a common mistake).
15. Follow up at regular intervals to see that the job is being done in the correct manner, that the worker likes the work, and that he knows why the work is performed.

Supervisory training

After the Second World War T.W.I. (Training Within Industry) courses were developed by the Department of Employment. These consisted of thirty hours of instruction divided into six sessions of five hours, or one week of six hours a day. The technique used is one of discussions rather than formal lectures, and the content can be briefly stated as:

1. Leadership (staff problems and interviewing).
2. Training (how to job train).
3. Work methods.

The Institute of Administrative Management also has an Office Supervisor's Certificate which currently requires four written examination papers and a project.

While the T.W.I. course is valuable because it stimulates discussion and therefore thinking, and the I.A.M. Certificate is good because it tests knowledge, undoubtedly what is also needed is some practical training as well. Thus, those with the necessary personal qualities should be given the opportunity of acting as deputies to supervisors on holiday, and assisting supervisors in certain areas of work, so that it can be seen what is involved.

Office supervision is very important and yet appears to receive little attention from management. In practice there is a great deal of bad office supervision; but it is important because it is the last link in the chain of management stretching downwards from the managing body, and to the worker, the supervisor is the representative of management (very often the only member of management with whom contact is made).

Management training

Most large business concerns give attention to some form of management training, even if it is only encouraging staff to study and prepare themselves for one of the professional examinations, perhaps coupled with an in-service management training rota moving from one department to another.

Training of future managers is also very important because the whole future success of the business and its management policies may depend on them. The management trainee system is not always ideal, because trainees are often viewed as supernumerary to establishment and some odd job is found to keep them busy. To learn about a job properly, it is suggested, requires the fixing of some responsibility for the job, and a long-term scheme is therefore better than a short one involving only spending a few weeks in each department.

Placement of staff

Staff might be recruited for particular jobs, but in the interests of the concern (as well as the individual) they should gravitate to the kind of job they are best suited for. To this end, it is not only advisable to assess ability in doing the job recruited for (*see* Promotion *above*), but also to assess what other job they might be suited to perform if the opportunity presents itself.

Thus, a person doing a routine clerical job might have personal attributes which suit him for dealing with the public, and unknown to himself, be most suitable for sales training. It is therefore advisable to have in the merit rating some assessment of personal and academic qualities not at present being used, and to ask what the person might be more suitable for.

It should be the aim of personnel work not only to recruit the best staff, but to make the best use of them when employed, and ensure they do not leave!

Labour turnover

Labour turnover is important because it reflects the stability of staff, and a high labour turnover means some failure in recruitment, promotion, salary scales, supervision, or even in organisation or morale. Apart from the costs of constantly recruiting new staff, there is the cost of training them (no matter how experienced they might be), as well as the hidden costs of lowered efficiency while inexperienced staff are learning their jobs.

Labour turnover will however vary with the sex of staff (if, as is usual, a high proportion of women are employed, it can be expected to be high); with the age of staff (the higher the age, the lower the turnover); with the kind of work (the more routine, the higher the turnover); and with the location of the enterprise (are there other opportunities in the area?)

Staff are always leaving to retire, to get married, have babies, and so on, which is hardly a reflection on the personnel policies of the concern, so a refined formula which can be used is:

$$\text{L.T.O.} = \frac{100(R-U)}{W}$$

Where R = replacements (not merely staff leaving or joining).
U = unavoidable replacements (*see above*).
W = average number of full-time staff.

This then gives a percentage L.T.O., which on inquiry will invariably be found to be higher in some departments than others. All the aspects of personnel need to be assessed in trying to improve L.T.O. It must be borne in mind that even with good salaries, good conditions and holidays, etc., there may still be a high L.T.O. if there is bad morale, probably due to bad leadership or bad management policies in other areas.

If L.T.O. is in fact high for the industry or business concerned, the usual technique for discovering the reasons is to have an Attitude Survey. This is simply a questionnaire asked of all existing workers, or of leavers only. The questionnaire is anonymous, and questions are asked on all the relevant areas of pay, promotion, work, supervision, management and so on, so that an analysis of the questionnaires then reveals the reasons for the high L.T.O.

Conclusion

The above aspects of personnel probably have most bearing on office efficiency, but there are many other unstated areas which may be just as important, depending on local circumstances. Thus, the salary scales, the welfare benefits, the conditions of service, and so on, may also be very important, but these can be referred to elsewhere.

CASE STUDY

Personnel

HENDON GROUP HOSPITAL MANAGEMENT COMMITTEE

1. PROBLEMS

(a) Increasing difficulty in recruiting staff, and high labour turnover.

(b) Different method of recruiting throughout the Group, with duplication of recruiting campaigns.

(c) Rising personnel costs and time-consuming activity (without comparable returns).

(d) Geographical spread of the hospitals—on the outskirts of London, surrounded by wealthy residential area.

(e) Catchment area served by three different local authorities.

2. APPROACH

It was thought that to appoint merely a Recruitment Officer would not in itself make for reduced labour turnover, nor improve conditions. On the other hand, a full-time Personnel Department would aid:

(a) recruitment of staff;

(b) induction;

(c) job training;

(d) retention of staff;

(e) a sustained effort to retain them.

3. ACTION

(a) A voluntary member of the Management Committee carried out an attitude survey of all leavers, to discover the reasons for staff leaving, from which it was apparent that there was a need for better supervision and for some management training.

(b) Since it was unlikely that more staff or finance would be available, it was mainly a question of making better use of the staff employed.

(c) A fortnight's training course was arranged for all members of staff, even of professionally qualified ones, e.g. radiographers, laboratory technicians, etc.

(d) To establish a full-time Personnel Department, the advice and resources of the King's Fund Administrative Staff College was used as a sounding board for testing reaction to the new ideas.

4. PERSONNEL DEPARTMENT

By redeployment within the organisation, the following posts were then created:

(a) Personnel Officer;
(b) Assistant Personnel Officer;
(c) Recruitment Officer;
(d) Clerical Officer;
(e) and Secretarial Staff (one whole- and one part-timer).

Stages in the development of the Department and projects undertaken were:

(a) Statistical statements of staff, labour turnover, etc. were prepared (over 2,000 employed in the Group).

(b) Regular attitude surveys were made of all staff leaving.

(c) Centralised recruitment of staff (previously, there was poor interviewing and documentation)—interview by the Personnel Department and then by the Departmental Manager.

(d) Induction and training courses: a two-day off-the-job training scheme was introduced, even for domestics—then on-the-job training by the supervisor. Planned management training for all administrative staff was also instituted. The extension of training schemes was found to aid recruitment of staff and better quality applicants were appointed.

(e) Visiting of employees while sick or in hospital.

(f) Staff accommodation improvement—a staff hostel was planned.

(*g*) Job analysis and job descriptions prepared for every post in the Group.

(*h*) Plans to launch a suggestion scheme (J.C.C. already in existence).

5. RESULTS

This new functional approach cutting across long-established methods in the hospitals needed meticulous planning, and the exercise of considerable tact in its application.

Provided there is full consultation with line management, such a Personnel Department can improve recruitment, improve the quality of candidates and improve training; above all, it is claimed to have improved staff morale.

[*The Hospital* December 1968

CHECK LIST

1. Are we clear about the relative authorities of O. & M. and the Personnel Department?
2. Who should perform job evaluation, and why?
3. Can O. & M. help in staff recruitment, even if only in forms design?
4. Is there a more efficient method of recruitment?
5. What is the most efficient method of promotion?
6. What kinds of training are provided?
7. Do we make the best use of staff when we have recruited them?
8. Do we measure labour turnover?
9. Have we carried out an attitude survey?
10. Have we got job specifications for all staff?
11. Do we regularly assess work content and regrade?
12. Are the staffing numbers appropriate to the volume of work?
13. Would a lesser number of more senior staff be more efficient?
14. What is the optimum cost of staffing?
15. Do we have job grading related to salary scales?
16. Is there merit rating to assess ability?
17. Do we have career development?
18. Is the morale of staff as high as practicable?
19. Is there good supervision?
20. Do we use any form of testing of new recruits to assess suitability?

Chapter 7 Organisation

Introduction

"Organisation" is a very much misused word. The contribution of organisation to management theory is still being researched, and extensions of theory are being added almost daily (particularly in America).

In this chapter, it is proposed to look only at office organisation, and not at its wider application to the whole enterprise, which is examined more closely in Chapter 14.

The mechanistic or formal theory of organisation is that it is concerned with:

"The division of activities, the allocation of duties, authority and responsibilities."

The "division of activities" means how the work is divided into sections, the work of the different sections, and their size. "Responsibilities" are areas of work for which one is accountable; "authority" is the prescribed or legal right to make decisions and to take action; and "duties" are the detailed work requirements arising from the responsibilities. Variations will be found in the meanings of these terms, thus in some management books "accountability" is treated as separate from "responsibility," which of course can arise, although usually they are the same. The definitions given above will be used throughout this book.

Importance of organisation

The larger the office, the more important will organisation become, because it is hard to achieve the ideal organisation. However, it should be noted that there is no one ideal organisation, but only the organisation best suited to a particular office.

Organisation is important because it is concerned with the "span of control" (*see below*), with the allocation of responsibilities, and with the delegation of authority, as well as the fixing of tasks.

42

With bad organisation:

1. Sections may be too big (or too small) for effec
2. Responsibilities may not be defined (or badly d... there are floating areas of responsibility, which may no. allocated at all.
3. Staff are afraid of making decisions, because they are unaware of their precise authority.
4. Work is boring (leading to high L.T.O.), because there is too much specialisation.
5. Delays in work occur because there is too much specialisation.
6. Staff are made responsible for performing certain work without being given sufficient authority to settle problems, which make them dispirited.
7. There is an inequitable distribution of work, either by quantity or type.
8. Workers are responsible to more than one superior, creating conflicting loyalties.

The definition of organisation quoted above is the formal or mechanistic one, and it is true that however good the formal organisation happens to be, it will not in itself make for efficient organisation. In fact, one of the principles of good organisation is that it should be flexible, and should change with changing requirements.

A great deal also depends on the human relationships of the staff concerned, and in fact the human factors can be as important as the formal factors in making for overall efficiency. But, however willing staff may be, unless there is good formal organisation to start with, it will become "organised chaos."

Span of control

How many staff should be responsible to one supervisor? More than one firm has discovered its mistake after putting a supervisor in charge of (say) thirty clerks, and have found they needed to appoint several supervisors in charge of (say) six clerks each.

There can be no standard span of control, but it can be said that it should be appropriate to the circumstances. The factors determining the span of control will be:

1. the quality (and age) of subordinates;
2. the quality of the supervision;
3. the variety of the work (the greater the variety, the smaller the span of control should be);
4. the nature of the work (the more mechanised and self-contained

the job, the less is it likely to require much supervision, therefore a greater span of control is possible);

5. the experience of existing staff (and L.T.O.)—they are likely to require less supervision with increasing length of experience.

In practice, work is grouped according to its content and a supervisor is put in charge, often regardless of the best span of control for effective supervision.

Technique of organisation

In organising (or reorganising) an office, the technique should be as follows:

1. Study the objectives and purposes of the office.
2. Decide on systems and methods appropriate to attain the end results.
3. Assess the total volume of work and the proportions of different kinds of work.
4. Decide on the method of grouping (either homogeneous or heterogeneous—*see below*).
5. Decide on the degree of specialisation to be employed in the allocation of work.
6. Decide on the span of control, *i.e.* the size of groupings, and how many supervisors.
7. Take account of human considerations (*see below*).
8. Then allocate responsibilities, authority and duties, in accordance with the principles of good organisation.
9. Draw up an organisation chart and job specifications for all the jobs.

Homogeneous and heterogeneous groupings

Homogeneous grouping means placing all workers together who are concerned with the same kind of work activity, regardless of the section (*e.g.*, as in a typing pool or duplicating section).

Heterogeneous grouping means placing workers in groups strictly according to the function of the work, but regardless of the kind of work activity (such a group might consist of clerks, typists, filing clerks, etc.).

The advantages of homogeneous grouping are that it facilitates the better use of machines, reduces the effect of work fluctuation, makes better use of specialisation, facilitates training, and makes it easier to compare the work of different members of staff.

The advantages of heterogeneous grouping are that it makes it easier to exchange staffs, assists the creation of a team spirit, makes it easier to fix responsibility, makes it easier when installing new systems or methods, and gives greater interest and variety to the workers. The last point is quite an important one in these days of high specialisation.

The best method of grouping will of course depend on the work, on the size of the office, and on what is likely to be most efficient and create the least human problems.

Principles of organisation

Because of the diversity in style of organisation, some writers deny the existence of universal principles of organisation. The following are, however, suggested as being of general validity:

1. Every person should be immediately responsible to one person only, and not to several supervisors. This does not mean that work cannot be performed subject to the direction of several seniors, but that there should be only one superior able to give orders, to whom the subordinate is ultimately responsible.
2. Authority should be granted to match responsibility. If this is not done, it often leads to a decline of initiative in the subordinate.
3. The span of control should be appropriate to the circumstances, so that it is neither too wide nor too narrow.
4. The best use should be made of specialisation.
5. In a very large office, there might be chief clerks, section leaders, supervisors, and so on, but the number of levels of management should be kept as low as possible. Too many levels lead to bureaucracy, and to distortion or loss of communication.
6. There should be the right degree of centralisation (*see below*).
7. There should be an equitable distribution of work, both in the type of work and in its quantity.
8. Maximum use should be made of the abilities of the staff in the distribution of duties and responsibilities.
9. Even if only in outline, there should be some definition of duties, authority and responsibility. If this is not done, it may lead to "empire-building" and to "poaching."

Human factors

Many modern writers on management stress the need to look at the human factors in organisation, and they are certainly just as important as the formal factors.

Human factors include such things as grouping of males and females. Probably an admixture is best, but one woman will not usually be very happy if included in a large group of men, or vice-versa.

Age is also important; thus a young person placed in a group of older persons will not find it easy to understand their ways, nor vice-versa.

Should a man be placed in charge of women, or a woman in charge of men? A great deal depends on the man or woman concerned, but generally speaking, a woman in charge of other women is likely to be more understanding of subordinate females, and yet harder with her own sex than a man would be—that is why a woman is usually appointed.

Then, there are the informal groupings in organisation by reason of marital status, race, religion, etc., and if management can ensure that the formal groupings coincide with the informal groupings, more work is likely to be performed then if it is ignored. Friends can spend too much time in gossiping, but co-operation is likely to be better, and surely gossiping depends on having enough work to do, as well as on the quality of supervision, and the placing of desks? The problem is to maintain an equilibrium between the morale boosting of informal organisation and the demands of efficiency.

Specialisation

The bigger the concern, the more likely is specialisation to be used on a wide scale—it is so easy to divide up the work in such small parcels that each person has one particular job activity and nothing else—and it is so administratively tidy and easy. But it should be recognised that there are advantages and disadvantages to specialisation.

The advantages include the creation of experts, the encouragement of greater productivity, easier training, the easier fixing of responsibility, and it may even facilitate the recruitment of staff for one narrow aspect of work.

But, on the other hand, workers tend to have a very limited knowledge of the total work, specialisation militates against co-ordination, and can lead to delays and bottlenecks in work. Probably the biggest disadvantage is the reduction of work to a boring routine, with a consequent loss of morale and higher L.T.O.

The answer is, of course, to make the best use of specialisation, while recognising its disadvantages. There seems now to be a movement away from over-specialisation, for in recent years Philips Ltd., the international electronics group, introduced what is called "work structuring" in their factory, whereby instead of employing girls to specialise in assembling valves, wiring, etc., groups of employees are organised to make a whole television set, thus giving each girl a variety of jobs. It is claimed that productivity has not suffered, while L.T.O. has been reduced. For such a scheme of organisation there will obviously be problems of training, of quality control, and so on, but the gains in human benefits must be prodigious, although it is likely that running costs would be higher.

Delegation

The foundation of all organisation is delegation, for the managing body delegates some of its authority and responsibility to departmental managers, who in turn delegate some to supervisors, and so on—down to the workers, who cannot delegate to anybody.

Usually, the responsibilities and duties delegated are at the discretion of the delegator, so that one supervisor might delegate nearly everything, leaving himself with little to do, while another might be afraid of delegating and try to do everything himself.

Although an enterprise may decide on the span of control and how the work is divided, etc. it often leaves details of delegation to the local supervisors, who have had little (if any) training in delegation theory.

The important principles here are that authority can be delegated, but not responsibility, because the superior is responsible for what is done by the subordinate; and because of this, it is necessary to exercise a measure of control on the work of subordinates. In practice, responsibility is probably shared between the delegator and the delegatee, the proportion varying with the level of management and the inexperience of the subordinate.

No subordinate likes to be closely supervised, with a supervisor "breathing down his neck," and this is an example of too much control. In a court case, it was reported that an office girl ordered a hundred years' supply of typewriter carbon paper, which seems to be evidence of lack of control. It can be said to be part of the art of management to exercise control without appearing to do so. Appropriate methods should be used, and as tactfully as possible!

Centralisation

Is it better to have a central typing department, central filing department, central duplicating department, and so on, than to have individual office services? Here, again, it depends on the individual circumstances of the concern, on its size, and on the efficiency with which a centralised service is provided.

1. ADVANTAGES OF CENTRALISED OFFICE SERVICES

    1. Most economic use of skilled staff.
    2. Maximum use can be made of expensive machines.
    3. Better and systematic training of staff.
    4. Reduces machine noise for clerks in other offices.
    5. Better working conditions suitable to the job.
    6. Better supervision.
    7. Better opportunity to compare the work of different staff.
    8. Encouragement of specialisation.

2. DISADVANTAGES

    1. Loss of personal contact with other staff (human factor).
    2. Possible loss of work interest.
    3. Work may vary in quality, according to the staff concerned.
    4. Possible delays in getting work done (time taken in transferring
       to and from the central department).
    5. A typing pool may encourage gossiping.
    6. Unfamiliarity of typists, filing clerks, etc., with technical or
       special departmental terms and requirements.

This is not to say that the choice is necessarily between one single
centralised service or an individual service in each office. A compromise
can be effected whereby:

3. EXAMPLE: TYPING

    1. Two or three typing pools can service specialised areas of the
       business, such as legal, accounting, etc.
    2. Typists in a typing pool can work on a personal basis for differ-
       ent members of staff, but still be in the typing pool to help other
       typists with their work-load.
    3. Even private secretaries can be accommodated in a typing pool;
       this provides a secretarial service to the business, and not just
       typing.

4. EXAMPLE: FILING

    1. While each department retains its current records, a central filing
       department can take care of all dead records, thus saving space
       and accumulation of records in the departments.
    2. Records (apart from those which are private and confidential,
       like staff records, or which do not concern other departments,
       like sales invoices) can be centralised.

5. EXAMPLE: REPROGRAPHY

1. With the growing complexity of photocopying equipment, it might be advisable to centralise photocopying, but to decentralise duplicating;
2. or to supply each department that needs it with a thermal photocopier for convenience of making quick copies, while centralising electrostatic and/or transfer diffusion processes;
3. or to decentralise all photocopying and duplicating, and to centralise the offset-litho work.

6. EXAMPLE: CALCULATING

1. It is almost impossible to centralise *all* calculations, but if a large volume of calculations is involved in work in different departments, it might be better to have a central calculating department with full-time trained operators, than to install expensive calculating machines in different departments.
2. A programmed electronic calculator might be centralised (because of its expense), on which standard programmed calculations can be performed for different departments, while leaving them to use more conventional calculating machines for their daily needs.

It can be seen that centralisation is an important aspect of organisation, but all that can be stated as a general principle of organisation is that the right degree of centralisation should be chosen, that which is most conducive to maximum efficiency. Only a study of the work, its requirements, its volume, and of the existing premises and communication services will indicate which is the best solution.

CASE STUDY

Organisation

LOCKHEED

1. BACKGROUND

Lockheed Missile and Space Co., of California, U.S., has a mechanised accounting system, but manual clearing and document matching system: there are 150,000 purchase invoices a year, involving 200,000 receipts of material and relevant invoices.

2. SYSTEM IN USE

(*a*) Purchase order files maintained alphabetically.

(*b*) Each invoicing clerk responsible for files corresponding to certain letters of the alphabet.

(*c*) Orthodox matching of invoice with official order and with goods received notes.

(*d*) When cleared, invoices stored in vertical filing cabinets, in folders, which are cleared periodically for payment.

(*e*) Part items overdue for payment are followed up by telephone and letter.

3. PROBLEMS

(*a*) The system evolved when the department was smaller, but was unsuitable to the expanded business.

(*b*) New and inexperienced personnel.

(*c*) Mismatching of paperwork.

(*d*) Need for expediting delivery often caused material to by-pass proper receiving records.

(*e*) Decentralisation of operations caused decentralisation of materials received.

(*f*) Great disparity between volume of invoices cleared by different clerks due to old invoice "queries."

(*g*) Some staff spent a great deal of time on the queries and held up "clean" documents, while others kept queries for a long time and dealt with current work.

(*h*) Invoices, orders and G.R. Notes became difficult to find.

(*i*) Documents held in desk drawers, and delay in quality testing held up passing of invoices.

(*j*) Cash discounts often lost by delays in invoice clearing.

(*k*) Increasing complaints from customers regarding non-payment.

4. DIFFERENT POSSIBLE METHODS OF ORGANISATION

(*a*) Assignment of responsibility for certain suppliers' accounts (as at present).

(*b*) Assignment for a certain series (*e.g.*, by contract) of purchase orders—regardless of supplier.

(*c*) Assignment of purchase orders by serial number in blocks of numbers—regardless of supplier.

5. O. & M. SOLUTION

(*a*) Files were converted from alphabetical to numerical sequence (Terminal Digit system), and invoice checking assigned by number block regardless of supplier.

(*b*) Staff were reorganised, so that some were assigned to file orders and G.R. Notes, and others to matching them with suppliers' invoices.

(*c*) A central control then allocated the invoices to the processing clerks.

(*d*) New equipment: orders and G.R.N.s filed in open tub files (instead of wallets in cabinets).

(*e*) Operating procedure: as invoices are received and matched with orders, they are separated into two groups: cash discount, and net invoices. Each processor passes discount items immediately and initiates payment within the discount time.

(*f*) Invoices which cannot be cleared are also put forward for payment and are charged to a transit account called In-transit Payment, or held over for future processing with net invoices. Follow-up is maintained by each individual processor.

Results

The revised system was a vast improvement. Production increased by over 100 per cent, and the backlog of unpaid invoices decreased, but

(*a*) there was increased labour turnover, although training time was reduced considerably; and

(*b*) there was delay in getting G.R. Notes on time—and it appeared that some quality testing could not be speeded up, that it might be better to pay first and verify later.

6. FURTHER CHANGES

(*a*) A "flash" receiving memo system was developed—a flash memo being made as soon as material was received.

(*b*) Some vendors with a high rejection rate were placed on a "matched document" basis. All invoices were then cleared on flash receiving memos—except specified suppliers on matched document basis.

This increased production and reduced the number of unpaid items.

7. OTHER MODIFICATIONS

For two years, further improvements and modifications were made, but the basic policy remained of "pay now, check later."

(*a*) Invoices for *services* are now paid before obtaining checking— just on an approved signature, and sent for checking after payment.

(*b*) Experience showed that with discrepant documentation, more than 50 per cent is due to faulty orders or G.R. Notes.

(*c*) The Supervisor can now authorise payments within monetary limits (no losses to date through this action).

(*d*) The most time-saving device, however, relates to other divisions of the company, and by treating their invoices as internal and not so formal as external ones—one member of staff was saved.

8. DIFFICULTIES

These were still experienced.

(*a*) Invoices on hand but unpaid were difficult to locate.

(*b*) Absenteeism caused a backlog of unpaid invoices.

(*c*) The number of overdue items varied depending on processor's time and productivity for follow-up.

(*d*) It was difficult to determine individual productivity.

9. FINAL FURTHER CHANGES

Since the last reorganisation and review of procedures, 250,000 invoices a year were cleared worth $40 million, and the final solution was as follows.

Central control of files

(*a*) A single central control of files of invoices for clearing (to remove burden of decision-making from junior employees, and allow better control).

(*b*) This involved gathering together of all uncleared invoices in one file.

(*c*) Invoices were then divided into five categories:

(*i*) Those with cash discounts.

(*ii*) Net invoices due for immediate attention.

(*iii*) Those due—the next week.

(*iv*) Net invoices due for clearing in that and subsequent weeks.

(*v*) Invoices previously paid in transit, but still waiting to be cleared.

(*d*) Central filing also controlled invoices where material had been returned to suppliers.

(*e*) Each day, discount invoices were cleared first, and those which could not be cleared were passed to the Supervisor to determine whether to pay.

(*f*) Invoices not cleared because of discrepancy in order or G.R.N. —passed to Supervisor for follow-up action.

10. RESULTS

(*a*) The number of overdue invoices was reduced by 50 per cent and invoices unpaid for over 30 days disappeared altogether.

(*b*) Invoice processors no longer responsible for maintaining and follow-up on overdue items—their responsibility is limited to processing documents received each day.

(*c*) The absence of any processor causes little inconvenience because the work load is spread among fewer employees.

(*d*) Backlog receives constant surveillance by the Supervisor to preclude long overdue items and lost discounts.

(*e*) Unpaid invoices are available at all times and easily accessible.

(*f*) Greater production with few complaints from customers.

(*g*) Reduced costs, and smoother working in the office.

CHECK LIST

1. What authority is delegated?
2. Have we delegated to the right persons?
3. Is the authority clear to the delegatee?
4. What forms of control are exercised over the delegated work?
5. Is there the right span of control of different sections?
6. Is it best to have homogeneous or heterogeneous grouping of staff?
7. Have we taken account of human factors?
8. Are we making the best use of specialisation?
9. Have we centralised the right services?

10. Can we make a compromise with full centralisation?
11. Are responsibilities clearly allocated?
12. Is the work shared equitably?
13. Are we making the best use of the staff abilities?
14. Have we got an organisation chart?
15. Have we got job specifications?
16. Have we the organisation most suitable to our circumstances?
17. Do we ensure that organisation is a flexible, dynamic thing?
18. Who makes decisions (are they too centralised)?
19. Do the lower levels of staff have too many superiors giving them instructions?
20. Does our organisation give maximum control and efficient decision-making?

Chapter 8 **Office systems**

Introduction

The term O. & M. is not liked by all practitioners, because if taken literally, it can be misleading. Thus "methods" is only a part of office systems, and it is systems that O. & M. is very much concerned with.

It is suggested that "method" is *how* a particular job is performed, and is therefore a part of the larger concept of "system." Thus, in a sales invoicing system, the method used might be by spirit duplicator, addressing machine, punched-card machines, accounting machine or computer.

System is a very much misused word, often being confused with "organisation," and it is suggested that "system" is:

"a standard sequence of operations, and is concerned with *how* they are performed (method), and with *when* and *where* they are performed. A system is closely connected with (and can often be revealed by) the forms used."

[An operation is the smallest step taken in performing the work required by the system.]

Thus, to expand, a system is a *standard* sequence of events, *i.e.* the sequence usually laid down and used on all occasions, and it includes methods of doing things (*i.e.* probably the use of machines), and it is concerned with whether an operation should be performed in this or that office, as well as when it is performed. A system is not concerned with *who* performs the operations, because this depends on the allocation of duties, which is organisation.

O. & M. practitioners usually refer to "procedures," which are really sub-systems, or particular lines of activities forming part of the total system. Thus, dealing with the inwards mail in an accountant's department would be part of the total system for dealing with the accounting. But since the word "system" is in universal use, and since a procedure might be the total system, the word "system" is preserved in this chapter.

Importance of systems

It can be seen that a system is based on the work performed, and is therefore related to organisation, which is also based on the work, as well as concerned with machines, being the methods used. It is closely connected also with personnel aspects, because often a particular system is chosen so that existing staff can be used, without needing to bring in a whole new set of specialist staff from outside.

Since system is so closely related to forms, it is therefore also related to the amount of paperwork, and of course the overhead expenses.

A bad system (*e.g.*, of filing classification) may be so complicated that in itself it encourages mistakes, so that it can be said to be related to the quality of work performed.

A good system incorporates internal checks which make it difficult for fraud to be perpetrated, so it is related to security. Equally, it can be said to be related to control of the activities concerned.

If a system is very informal, *i.e.* without proper official forms, it may not be implemented, because it is not clear what has to be done, and even if it is done, may not be performed properly. It is therefore very much an aspect of overall efficiency.

If a system is simple, it can make it easy to learn, and therefore makes it easier to train staff, and therefore related to the training aspect of personnel, as well as to recruitment.

If the methods chosen are slow, it can happen that work is delayed and bottlenecks occur, so it is related to the despatch of work.

Principles

In designing a new system, or when improving an existing system, it is useful to have some principles of good systems in mind, and it is suggested that the following are the most important principles:

1. Ensure that the *purposes* of the system are achieved (this means prior investigation and crystallisation of such purposes).
2. Have a good *flow of work*, without causing bottlenecks. This is relevant to the speed of performance of different operations, and ensuring the best sequence of operations.
3. *Avoid duplication* of work and of records. Thus, can basic data recorded in several offices be prepared in a master form and be duplicated or photocopied for other departments?
4. *Keep movement* of staff *to a minimum*. Thus, whether a particular operation should be performed in this office or the other, must take into account the movement involved.

5. *Avoid unnecessary writing.* Thus, the exceptions which require information should not govern the information requirements for the routine cases.

6. Make the *best use of specialisation.* Although really an aspect of organisation, it involves, for example, whether a particular machine can be used, which may require specialisation.

7. *Keep* the amount of *paperwork to the minimum.* The best system has the least number of forms.

8. To this end, *use* the principle of *management by exception (see below).*

9. Make as *few exceptions to the rule* as possible. Because a system is a standard way of doing things, deviations from the system, if allowed too often, will mean destruction of the system.

10. *Avoid unnecessary checking.* Thus, if purchase invoices over £100 only are checked, in a large concern, it has been demonstrated that this will save nearly 80 per cent of the checking labour. The degree and the extent of checking must be appropriate to the task (*see* Chapter 36 on Quality Control).

11. Make the *best use of machines.* This means not to use them just because they are there, but only to the extent that they can add to total efficiency.

12. To *seek simplicity,* because complicated systems usually lead to mistakes. Thus, a twelve-figure coding of stores is inviting mistakes to occur.

13. Ensure that there are *built-in controls* in the system. An example is the use of control accounts attached to the sales and purchases ledgers.

14. Make it *difficult for fraud and theft.* Numbering sales invoices, and then checking the serial numbers when posting to the ledgers, is a good example.

It may well be, in practice, that some of these principles conflict, so that avoiding duplication of work may involve greater movement of staff, and so on, but there must be a scientific assessment of clerical costs included in both cases, to assist the decision on the best compromise.

The "exception principle"

Much needless recording and checking can be avoided by using the "exception principle," which simply means the setting up of standards, and recording the exceptions to the standards for control purposes. Or, in other words, recording all the negatives in a series, instead of all the positives.

Thus, for credit-control purposes, instead of requiring a list of all debts outstanding at the end of the month, set up a standard of (say) more than £20 owing for more than two months; the list will be shorter, and will save clerical work.

Designing an office system

When planning a new office system, whether it be for sales invoicing, purchasing, wages, or any other aspect of administration, the steps will probably include the following:

1. Decide on the purposes of the system. Basically, this will usually include the provision of information, and the keeping of records which give the information.
2. Decide where the information is coming from and how it is communicated; the chart of sources of information might be useful here (*see* Chapter 32).
3. Decide on what form will be required for the communication and recording of information (incidence of forms design, number of copies, etc.).
4. Concentrate, then, on the operations involved. The basic clerical operations are:

   > Writing (including machine writing).
   > Copying (duplicating, photocopying, etc.).
   > Calculating.
   > Comparing (and checking).
   > Sorting (or collating).
   > Filing and indexing.
   > Communicating (orally or in writing).

5. Bearing in mind the principles of systems listed above, decide on the best method of performing the basic operations. These will probably include the best machine method.
6. Decide on when and where the operations should be performed.
7. Then chart the system in a procedure record, and depict the system on a procedure chart, and invite criticism from managers with a knowledge of what is required.
8. It is then a good idea to have a trial run with duplicated forms *before* printed stationery is ordered, because what seems feasible in theory is not always practical.

It will be seen that a system involves forms, machines, staff to perform the operations, and the office where the different operations are performed. Therefore, it is useful with a complicated system to have schedules or charts showing:

1. statement of purposes;
2. forms (and titles) designating their purposes;
3. schedules of machines and equipment involved;
4. staffing involved (grading and numbers);
5. a chart of office layout showing where the different operations are to be performed.

Improving an office system

Improving an office system can be said to be a main activity of O. & M. staff, and the steps involved are very much the same as mentioned above for the design of a new system.

There are, however, some notable differences, as will be apparent from the following:

1. Decide (in consultation with management) on the purposes of the existing system and whether in fact they are being achieved. Then ask whether there should be other purposes included (such as prevention of fraud), or are some of the old purposes out of date?
2. Investigate the existing system, and chart all the operations involved.
3. Then assess what are the faults which need improvement, and list them.
4. Collect a set of forms used in the system, and perhaps write on them briefly their function in the system and who uses them. Assess the forms for their need, their function in the system, and their design (forms design is dealt with in Chapter 25).
5. Then examine the procedure chart and decide what operations are essential, bearing in mind the *purposes*, *cost*, and *control*, and then eliminate the unnecessary operations.
6. Concentrate on the essential operations and assess the methods used; here the experience and knowledge of the O. & M. expert should indicate the best methods which should be chosen, bearing in mind existing staffing, management's policy on staffing (they do not usually want to dismiss long-service staff).
7. Having decided on the new system, with new methods, and possibly a new sequence of operations, new places where they have to be performed, and possibly new forms, compile schedules of staffing, machines, work-flow and forms, as well as a new procedure chart, and submit to top management for approval.
8. Write a report recommending all the changes of system, setting out clearly and succinctly the changes involved, and showing, at

the end, a summary of the improvement made, and cost comparisons.

	Old System	New System	Savings	
			%	Actual
Staffing (*p.a.*)	10,000	5,000	50	5,000
Machines	1,000	750	25	250
Stationery	2,000	1,000	50	1,000
	£13,000	£6,750	48%	£6,250

9. *Implementation.* An outside management consultant may well stop at (8) in submitting his report to management, but an O. & M. officer may have a much more onerous task: carrying out his recommendations and seeing how they work. For this, he will need utmost co-operation from line managers (hence the need to gain their co-operation all the time), for a changeover programme may be involved, to cover such things as:

(*a*) Introduction of new forms.
(*b*) Installation of new methods.
(*c*) Training of staff in both forms and methods.
(*d*) Staggered dates for introducing some parts of the new system, particularly if it impinges on other departments.
(*e*) Agreement on a period of parallel running with the old system, before it is abandoned in favour of the new.

There are some who think it better when improving an existing system, to ignore the old system completely as though designing a new system. The main advantage of this approach (and it is useful with computer installation), is that one is not blinded by existing practices and existing forms which have been used for years, and because of their apparent importance seem to be essential, but which close examination will reveal not to be so.

It is, however, very easy to throw out the "baby with the bath water," and often there are hidden reasons for the existence of certain forms and methods used. Such reasons are not immediately apparent, and if too radical an approach is adopted, it may well cause hostility from the very beginning. This is not to say that a completely new system and new forms might not be recommended on occasion, where the old methods are completely out of date and out of keeping with requirements. But an over-enthusiastic O. & M. man can be a distinct liability, for the way to hell is paved with good intentions!

Practical points

If a system involves a number of staff (as it usually does), then it is not sufficient just to give each of them a copy of a procedure chart and tell them to read it. The author has known a clerk to be given a twenty-page report on a new system, and told to take it home and study it! Even if they understood it all, it is doubtful if they would remember it, and so it is a good idea to discuss personally with each member of staff, the extent to which *his work* is likely to be affected by a new system, as well as giving a broad view of the system as a whole.

It is a good idea to then issue new Job Descriptions to each member of staff involved, setting out their new duties and responsibilities in detail.

If possible, staff should be allowed to comment openly, and make suggestions for improvement (before the O. & M. report is submitted). Participation means involvement, and a degree of commitment which is necessary to the success of any new idea.

If management has doubts about the practicability of a proposed new system, it might be a good idea to hold a meeting of staff involved, at which proposals can be outlined and comments invited. Such a meeting must be properly prepared, using visual aids such as overhead projectors, distributions of copies of forms, and so on.

Office manuals

It is sometimes asked whether it is a good idea to have an office manual setting out details of the office system. Such a manual usually has a written outline of each system, with specimen forms, and details of the organisation and job titles of staff performing different operations.

1. ADVANTAGES

Such a manual aids supervision and assists training. It stabilises systems and forms, as well as helping in the organisation of the office. It minimises misunderstanding of instructions, and provides a reference for all employees. It aids in the use of substitute personnel and increases the flexibility of their use. It is also useful when it comes to improving or changing the system.

2. DISADVANTAGES

Office manuals may be expensive of time to produce, and they may be difficult to keep up to date. Many employees prefer to ask questions than to refer to a book. It may introduce rigidity in the methods used, and limit flexibility.

On balance, therefore, it might be said that office manuals are good provided (a) there is time available to prepare them, and keep them up to date, (b) provided they are in loose-leaf form so that they can be easily amended, and (c) they are not misused in the course of training, and do not take the place of oral explanations.

An office manual which gets out of date is ignored and becomes a cause of cynical merriment, although when introducing new computer systems for the first time, they are invaluable.

Systems and forms

Forms control and forms design are dealt with elsewhere in the book, but some investigators view the forms used as the system. Forms are important, for they often form the backbone of a system, but in the techniques used in planning a new system (*see above*), purposes should come first, then methods, and then forms, in that order.

In practice, when a system has been established a long time, management is loathe to change it for fear of wasting stocks of expensive forms in hand, and they therefore will not often contemplate a change of system until a new basic form needs re-ordering and re-designing. This may be short-sighted because even if sacks of forms are wasted (and reports have mentioned such a happening), it may well mean that the labour costs saved by a new system using different forms, more than pays for the cost of forms wasted.

Method, forms, machines, and staffing all enter into the concept of system, as illustrated in the following case study.

CASE STUDY

Office system

1. BACKGROUND INFORMATION

The A.A. pays for 500,000 breakdowns each year (10,000 a week) to 10,000 different garages, on behalf of its members.

2. OLD SYSTEM

As accounts are received from the garages, they are sorted alphabetically, and details (cost, with Member's name and address and number) are typed on large forms, with interleaved carbons, 40 lines to a page. Each form is in quadruplicate: 1 to Accounts Dept., 2 used for payment to garages, 3 to Membership Dept., 4 retained in file of the Breakdown Dept.

Every month, the sheets are sorted and collated for each garage, passed to a girl with an add/listing machine who totals the amount for each garage. Then, another girl draws a cheque for the total, tears off appropriate sections of each page (the second copies are divided by horizontal perforations) and after fastening a compliments slip passes them for cheque signing.

Machines and staff: 17 typists, using typewriters with 18 in. carriages to accommodate the large forms.

3. DIFFICULTIES

(a) Expense of large forms (with expensive perforations) and carbons.

(b) Volume of work increasing, and no room for extra staff.

(c) A desire, if possible, to reduce cost, since the A.A. is responsible to its members for the use of their subscriptions.

(d) Incidence of errors in sorting charge slips.

(e) New and more efficient machinery required, but without changing long-service staff.

(f) Pages with 40-line capacity, but with sometimes only a few items on them.

4. NEW SYSTEM

The forms were redesigned and reduced to half the previous size (much of previous information was superfluous); 40-line capacity retained but now arranged in two columns of 20; carbon paper abolished in favour of N.C.R. The smaller forms meant that one can be used for each garage—eliminating the previous sorting of perforated sections.

The form is also headed with "compliments," thus avoiding the work and expense of attaching compliments slips.

The entries on the forms are made by using an R.U.F. "3 in 1" machine (electric typewriters linked to a solenoid box on an electric adding machine).

This meant that existing typing staff could be used, that while entering the items, the adding machines automatically adds them up; and that the typewriters and adding machines can be used separately for other purposes.

The machines were specially adapted by the manufacturers so that automatic carriage return was to the half-way position when entering the second column on the form.

The same girl now enters the "breakdowns," adds them up, and all that is necessary is for cheques to be drawn and attached.

5. RESULTS

(a) Cost of stationery has been reduced.

(b) Less work means greater output (particularly from the form simplification).

(c) Typing staff has been reduced by 50 per cent (9 instead of 17 typists).

(d) Output has increased from 480 a day to upwards of 700.

(e) Less errors than previously.

(f) Same staff retained, and no specially-trained operators required.

(g) The versatility of the machines means that they need never stand idle.

NOTE: The A.A. has further up-dated its system since this case history was published.

CHECK LIST

1. Are we sure of the purposes of the system being investigated?
2. Are they the right purposes?

3. Are they in fact achieved?
4. At what cost?
5. Have we checked the system with basic principles?
6. Do we use the exception principle?
7. Do we have regard to controls in the system?
8. Does management policy impinge on the system?
9. Have we discussed proposed changes with management?
10. Would it be a good idea to call a meeting of staff to have their comments?
11. Have we got specimens of all forms in use, and do we know how each is used?
12. Have we examined the incidence of forms design in the system?
13. Are the best methods (and machines) used?
14. Is there unnecessary checking?
15. To what extent do we have to implement the new system?
16. Have we earned full co-operation of the line managers?
17. Have we properly prepared the staff (and managers) for the new system?
18. What are the faults of the old system?
19. Can we improve the methods, the forms, or office layout?
20. Should we adopt an office manual for the new system?

Chapter 9 **Environment**

The term environment refers to the total surroundings in which office work is performed. It therefore includes:

1. Acquiring new office buildings.
2. Arrangement of departments.
3. The open office.
4. Office landscaping.
5. Office layout.
6. Physical conditions
7. Office furniture.

All of these are important, because they are all connected with the efficiency with which work is performed (particularly absence of distraction); with health and comfort of the worker; with morale and labour turnover; and with the overall appearance of the office. Although separately stated, they are of course interrelated, thus office landscaping includes air-conditioning, carpeting, layout, and so on.

In most books on O. & M., layout is given prominence, probably because it forms part of the total system, *i.e.* the sequence in which operations are performed. But a good layout can be negated by bad choice of furniture, by bad decoration, etc., so that lay-out is much more than just "flow of work."

Acquiring new premises

Many factors have to be considered, and the main ones are:

1. SITING

Business requires to be within easy reach of Post Offices, banks, and transport. Staff have to be able to travel to it easily, and since many employees own cars, convenient road access is important.

Under the *Town and Country Planning Act* 1947, local authorities have a duty of planning in their areas, and it is not always a question of where it is wished to have an office building, so much as where it can be erected with full planning permission.

2. FINANCE

Financial costs will depend a great deal on whether a building is bought (or erected) freehold, or purchased leasehold, but the main items of cost to investigate are:

1. capital outlay;
2. conversion costs (if an old building);
3. maintenance and running costs (possibly increased running costs);
4. communication costs (possibly increased).

3. SUITABILITY

Here, perhaps, "size" is most important, and is usually measured in so many thousand square feet. Reference to the number of staff to be housed, as well as equipment must be compared with the standards laid down in the *Offices, Shops and Railway Premises Act* 1963 (*see below*). An often overlooked factor is the need to leave room for future expansion, which is more easily done in a freehold building than in a leasehold one, where sub-letting is also more possible, without wasting the use of floor-space. If buying an old building, attention should be given to the proportion desired in large and small rooms, because if it is not suitable, quite expensive conversions may have to be made.

4. PHYSICAL REQUIREMENTS

These include such things as windows (an old building with small windows is likely to increase costs of lighting), and the provision of ventilation (perhaps air-conditioning), heating, and lift services.

Arrangement of departments

Although often confused with office layout, this aspect is concerned with how the different offices are arranged inside a building. It is quite important, because if badly performed, it means unnecessary movement of staff, unnecessary telephones, lack of co-ordination, unnecessary noise distraction, visitors losing their way in the building, and so on.

It requires scientific study, particularly of the volume of movement of paper and of people between offices, but the following are the general factors for consideration:

1. Departments that work together should be contiguous, but merely "working together" would not be sufficient reason unless accompanied by a need for staff movement and transfer of papers between them.
2. Departments with heavy traffic from outside should be close to the reception area (*e.g.*, buying, personnel, etc.).
3. Important operating departments should be near to the executive suite (if there is one); this probably includes the Marketing Manager in a business.
4. Mail, messenger, and other central services should be sited centrally, within closest reach of the departments they serve (bearing in mind the incidence of stairs and lifts in a multi-storey building).
5. Conference rooms (especially the board-room) should be sited at the rear of the building, to enjoy quiet conditions.
6. Offices using heavy machines should be on the ground floor.
7. Arrange rooms so that departments likely to expand can do so, without causing too much disturbance (*e.g.*, siting a records room next to the Sales Department).
8. Private offices should be only allocated to those who really need privacy.
9. Toilets and cloakrooms should be within easy reach of the bulk of staff who have to use them (this seems an obvious point, but it is amazing how badly designed some buildings are).
10. Drawing offices should be at the top of the building to obtain maximum light.
11. There should be room for records to be stored in the departments that accumulate them.
12. Kitchens should either be on the ground floor (to facilitate delivery of goods), and provided proper ventilation prevents smells of cooking rising to upper floors, or at the top of the building, provided an excellent goods lift is provided.
13. Above all (and this is a common fault), there should be overall room for expansion in the years to come.

As with layout of individual offices, many of these factors may conflict in practice, and some compromise may have to be decided on, but as with office layout, the flow of work is the most important factor.

The open office

There has been a growing trend towards large open offices, and the advantages are mainly on the employer's side, giving above all saving in floorspace (as much as 25 per cent can be taken up by corridors and party walls), but also better supervision, better communication, cheaper heating and lighting, and better use of machines. Some employees also like the chance of greater social contact.

But, on the other hand, it may not look businesslike, communal noise may be a problem, distraction, and loss of staff morale may detract from the value of open offices. This is apart from a common difficulty (without air-conditioning), of having ventilation and heating suitable to everybody.

Office landscaping

"Bürolandschaft" came from Germany, and is quite a considerable development on "open plan," for instead of just putting desks in straight rows in a large office, it aims at giving psychological satisfaction to staff working in large areas, by providing:

1. flexible asymmetric layout (*see* Fig. 1 on p. 70);
2. fully carpeted floors;
3. carefully designed acoustics;
4. air-conditioning;
5. new system-furniture;
6. modern décor;
7. all laid out in a way that defines sections or departments—usually divided by plant troughs or screens (the manager of Walls Ltd. of Gloucester said "what we are doing is introducing a new culture").

In other words, landscaping is a total concept aimed at making the office workers feel that they are important, and by providing a good all-round pleasant environment.

One of the biggest hurdles to overcome is the resentment of different levels of management, who, losing their private rooms, feel a loss of status. The answer to this is either to make their sections of the office extra attractive so that they will want to work there, or by the use of partitioning. Partitioning, however, may interfere with the provision of lighting and with good ventilation, as well as spoiling communication and the team spirit engendered in an open office.

Office layout

A revised office layout may be required where:

1. a new building is being considered;

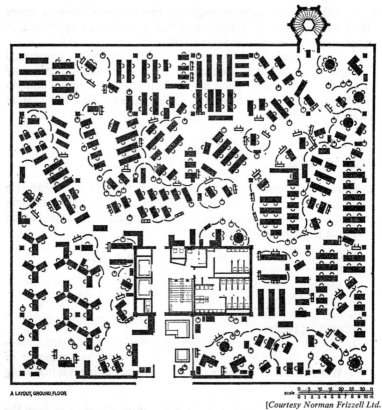

A LAYOUT, GROUND, FLOOR

scale

[*Courtesy Norman Frizzell Ltd.*

FIG. 1.—This outstanding example of a landscaped office won first prize in the
I.A.M. Office of the Year competition in 1973.

    2. an office has to be moved from one part of the building to
another;

    3. where changes occur within the office, *e.g.* where:

        (*a*) there is an increase or decrease in personnel;
        (*b*) work flow is altered by new procedures;
        (*c*) additional work space is needed;
        (*d*) delays occur in work flow;
        (*e*) employees complain about the layout;
        (*f*) new equipment is bought or replaced;
        (*g*) there is too much gossiping.

There is little doubt that the office layout should be planned for
productivity in the same way as in the factory, and it is important
because it affects:

1. flow of work;
2. use of machines and equipment;
3. internal communication;
4. supervision;
5. best use of floor-space;
6. best use of daylight;
7. morale of office workers.

But rarely is it possible to have the perfect layout, and generally the final layout decided on is a compromise between the following principles.

1. PRINCIPLES OF LAYOUT

1. Layout should be in harmony with the *flow of work*, so as to avoid or reduce movement of people and paper.
2. Each clerk should be allowed sufficient floor-space to perform his job properly (*i.e.*, without files piling up on the floor, etc.).
3. Each clerk should be allowed a minimum of 40 sq. ft. (if ceiling height is 10 ft. or more)—*see* the *Offices, Shops and Railway Premises Act* 1963.
4. Office machines and equipment (particularly files) should be placed close to the people who use them, and there should be ample floor-space for referring to them.
5. The number and location of aisles should be sufficient to allow ease of access to desks.
6. Tall cupboards and other impediments to vision and movement should be placed against the wall, and not in the middle of the floor-space.
7. Consideration of natural lighting means that clerks working on machines, etc., who need most light, should be placed close to the windows. For writing purposes, light should preferably fall over the left shoulder (for right-handed workers).
8. A human consideration is that women usually prefer to be close to radiators, and men near the windows.
9. Noisy machines should be segregated from other workers if possible.
10. Office layout should be balanced and pleasing in appearance.

2. TECHNIQUES OF LAYOUT

1. Secure a drawing of all available area (usually $\frac{1}{4}$ in.:1 ft.).
2. Determine areas of main traffic movement (mark on plan the doors, lifts, etc.).
3. Gain complete overall picture of work to be done in the area (involves flow of work, office organisation, etc.).

4. Make list of all existing equipment and furniture occupying floor-space, with sizes.
5. Identify basic groups in the office (organisation chart).
6. Consult briefly with the heads of each basic group, to give chance for suggestions for improvement in furniture, size, etc.
7. Make templates (using same scale as plan) of all physical units on the revised list.
8. Arrange them on plan in accordance with the principles of layout (*see above*).
9. Check on travelling distances of people and paper in accordance with flow of work (use of procedure charts).
10. Arrange templates on plan and mark with telephone points, heating, etc.
11. Re-check with heads of sections and head of department, and submit to top management.

Layout is not an easy aspect, because although movement of work and personnel can be scientifically measured by using a "string diagram" (*see below*), the final solution often means an uneasy compromise between what is most efficient on the one hand, and what is least detrimental to staff morale on the other. The use of a common telephone, and the degree of reference to files, may interfere with the use of machines or even the flow of work (*see* Fig. 2).

The answer is to assess, perhaps by a sampling technique, the movement of staff and the activities of staff, so that a choice can be made which more nearly satisfies all criteria. Very rarely is it possible to have the ideal layout which satisfies all the principles mentioned above, but the best solution has to be found, which gives the most advantages with the fewest inconveniences and inefficiencies.

Physical conditions

The main provisions of the *Offices, Shops and Railway Premises Act 1963* are well known; the measurable standards are most important:

1. Offices must be *cleaned* at least once a week.
2. To prevent *overcrowding*, a minimum of 400 ft³ of space per person, ignoring ceiling height over 10 ft. (this is calculated by comparing the number of workers with the total cubic capacity of an office).
3. Minimum *temperature* of 16°C. (60·8°F.), after one hour from the commencement of business. A thermometer must be conspicuously displayed on each floor.

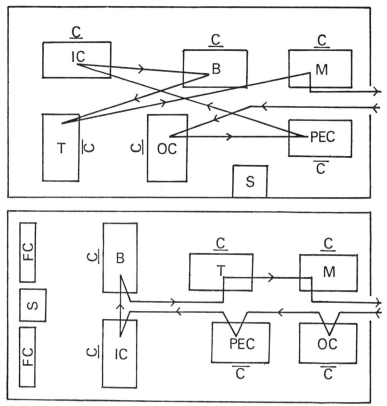

FIG. 2.—Showing how the movement of documents and staffing can be improved, by studying the flow of work.

4. *Sanitary conveniences* must be provided, at least one for each sex if more than five employees, and then in the following ratios:

1–15	employees	1 water closet
16–30		2
31–50		3
51–75		4
76–100		5

plus 1 additional w.c. for every 25 staff employed over 100.

5. *Wash basins* must also be provided in the same ratios (approximately 5 for the first 100 and 4 per subsequent 100 employees).

6. A *first-aid box* must be provided for each 150 employees, and where more than 150 staff are employed, at least one person must be trained in first-aid.

7. Where more than 20 staff are employed, then a *Fire Certificate* on means of escape must be obtained from the local fire authority.

Office furniture

1. PURPOSE

When buying office furniture, the first question to ask is "What is its purpose?". Furniture can be classified into:

1. *Executive furniture:* made more to impress the visitor than anything, but such furniture is often required to accommodate small committee meetings, and the ability to sit at it properly with knees underneath the top of the desk should be remembered. Such furniture can be very expensive, and appearance is not the only factor to be considered.
2. *Special-purpose furniture:* outstanding examples are the special typist and calculating machine operator desks, with wells to accommodate the machines at the right height for the operators.
3. *Built-in furniture:* such as shelves and cupboards built into recesses in the wall. Where large volumes of records are to be accommodated, this can be the cheapest method.
4. *General clerical furniture* is probably the most important, and often given the least attention.

The general factors to be considered when buying furniture are:

(*a*) Design (*see below*).

(*b*) Capital outlay: the cheapest not necessarily being the most economical, and the dearest not necessarily the best value.

(*c*) Durability: metal furniture will probably last longer, but is rather expensive, while the modern laminated plastic-topped furniture is scratch-proof and long-lasting.

(*d*) Saving in space: some furniture is specially designed to save floor-space (systems or modular furniture).

(*e*) Fire-risk: again, metal furniture is a better fire-risk than wooden.

(*f*) Weight: if furniture has to be moved around, as it often does in a large office, then light-weight equipment is preferable.

(*g*) Hygiene: how easy is it to clean, and the floor underneath?

(*h*) Appearance: it should not only be functional, but also pleasing to the eye.

(*i*) Comfort of the office worker: this means less distraction.

(*j*) Safety: some furniture has plate glass on the top, which may not be safe.

(*k*) Finish: if there is too high a gloss, it can cause glare and distraction.

(*l*) Saving in labour: some furniture has built-in file units and cupboards, which can save movement and walking about by the clerks. But close assessment has to be made as to whether such furniture is really justified.

2. DESIGN OF FURNITURE

Probably the most important factor after the use to be made of the furniture is its design. In fact a whole science of "ergonomics" has developed which is concerned mainly with the design of furniture so that it is suitable to the working environment.

The first point to consider is the *chair*:

1. The right height from the ground, so that its occupant has his thighs fully supported and his feet flat on the ground. Human beings do not come in standard sizes, so ideally all chairs should be adjustable in height, to suit the length of leg of the occupant. Such adjustable chairs are mostly only provided for typists and telephone operators, but they should really be provided for everybody.
2. The size of the seat should be sufficient (*see* B.S.S. listed in Appendix I), in width and depth, and the most comfortable shape for long periods of sitting is the saddle seat. The front of the seat should be rounded, so that it does not press on the nerves running at the back of the legs.
3. The back of the chair should be shaped so that it gives not only support to the small of the back, but also to the lumbar regions.
4. Arms to a chair are not necessary, and castors should never be fitted unless the occupant has to constantly turn around from his desk to refer to side files.

The ideal chair that can be adjusted to suit all persons, and at a reasonable price, has yet to be invented.

The next point to consider is the *desk*:

1. Having established the height of the chair, the height of the desk should be appropriate so that it is not too high, neither is the clerk slumped over the desk. The right height will give the right posture at the desk.
2. The size of the top should be relevant to the work to be performed on it.
3. The modern style is to provide light-weight desks, with perhaps one drawer, but if the work requires constant reference to files, then file drawers might be included.
4. For women, a draught panel (sometimes called a "modesty" screen) might be provided for the front of the desk.
5. Ideally, to give the clerk correct posture, the desk top should be sloping slightly forward.
6. An important feature might be saving in floor-space.

7. For typists, and others using machines, the work-top should generally be several inches below that of an ordinary desk. The test here, is that when the machine is used, the arms should be horizontal when the fingers are on the machine.

CASE STUDY

Layout

DEPT. OF HEALTH AND SOCIAL SECURITY

1. OBJECT

To achieve the best layout most suited to the flow of work, after two offices were merged together. Although the systems and work flow were known by O. & M. staff, it was desired to check on what was thought to be most desirable.

2. COURSE OF ACTION

Every member of staff was given two questionnaires:

(*a*) listing all the work units, and testing their need to be close to the others;

(*b*) listing all locations and files of records in use.

Opposite each unit and file on the records, were vertical columns headed:

(*a*) essential you should be near;
(*b*) important, but not essential;
(*c*) helpful and convenient to be near;
(*d*) convenient but not necessary to be near;
(*e*) not at all important to be near.

The questionnaires were issued, checked and returned within three days, after which it was possible to summarise and value the relationships. (*d*) and (*e*) were ignored in this summarising, and the value of three times for (*a*) and twice for (*b*) and one for (*c*) were inserted on the plan. Thus, the greater the number of contacts between two stations, the greater the need for proximity.

3. COMMENTS

1. This is a simple time-saving method of assessing the relative importance of work contact in layout. The resultant figures could be easily set out in a table, and the total of (a), (b), and (c) in terms of 3, 2, and 1 could be added, to give the best relationship.
2. Such a technique could be used where perhaps full systems detail is not available, or where time is limited for improving layout.
3. Layout on this principle alone is of course only concerned with flow of work, which while it is the most important factor is not the only one.

CHECK LIST

1. Have we got management's backing for an open office?
2. What are the possible disadvantages?
3. Would office landscaping be worth the cost?
4. Have we got the best office layout?
5. Have we taken account of all the things which cause distraction?
6. Have we given attention to the legal requirements?
7. In choosing furniture, have we first examined its precise purpose?
8. What furniture is most functional and economical in floor-space?
9. What policy are we adopting regarding siting of noisy machines?
10. Can quieter machines be used?
11. Have we examined the flow of work?
12. Have we considered health factors?
13. Would desks with built-in files save staff movement?
14. Do we prefer to have work put away in a cupboard?
15. Is equipment sited close to people who have most use of it?
16. Have we taken account of human factors in layout?
17. Have we examined telephone use of different workers?
18. Have we looked at ease of supervision in the layout?
19. Do we need private offices (for other than prestige reasons)?
20. Have we studied the interaction of different aspects, e.g., lighting, on glossy furniture, noise for staff requiring concentration, and so on?

Chapter 10 Machines and equipment

"One machine can do the work of fifty ordinary men. No machines can do the work of one extraordinary man" (Hubbard 1859–1915).

Although the industrial revolution dates from the eighteenth and nineteenth century, the mechanisation of the office really belongs to the twentieth century, and as machines have become paramount in the factory, so they have become of increasing importance in the office.

It is difficult to generalise about office machines, because their diversity extends from a small stapling machine to a computer costing several hundred thousand pounds. While some machines have been bought just to be in the fashion, others (the result of persuasion of salesmen) have subsequently been relegated to the cellar after the salesman's spell has worn off.

Many offices have the wrong kind of machines, and even if they have the right kind, they are often not fully used (because their different applications are not always known), and very often they are in the wrong places.

As an example of the misuse of machines (and staff), a report on the management of the Associated Portland Cement Company stated that only twelve of the 260 managerial staff dictated letters and reports, while the others used longhand. The girls' shorthand therefore deteriorated with every month they stayed with the company, which led to a high L.T.O.

Buying a new machine

1. QUESTIONS TO ASK

The main questions to ask when buying any machine are:

1. What are the work requirements? This will decide the type and size of machine to be bought (very often a better method of work will obviate the use of a machine altogether).
2. Is there a suitable machine on the market? Manufacturers will always claim they have the ideal machine for your application,

but this is a matter of judgment where experience and an impartial assessment is needed.

3. Is the work satisfactory at present, and if not, what advantages might be expected from using a machine?

4. What are the possible disadvantages?

5. What was the cost of the work previously, and what will it be with a machine?

6. Not only capital outlay, but what are the running costs likely to be?

7. Consider not only these costs, but also any auxiliary expenses which might be involved, such as special filing equipment, special office accommodation, stationery, etc.

8. Consider not only the machine, but can an operator be obtained (if special operation is required), and at what cost?

9. Can the machine be used for other purposes?

10. Do savings in one office mean probable increases in expense in another office?

11. What will happen if the machine breaks down, etc., what maintenance service is provided, and at what cost?

2. ADVANTAGES

1. To save labour; but this must mean a saving on the pay-roll, or by releasing staff for other work.

2. To save time; some jobs must be completed by a certain time, and a machine may be worth its purchase price just for this reason.

3. To promote accuracy, such as usually occurs with an accounting machine (provided an experienced operator is employed).

4. To perform work faster; some machines relieve monotony, compared with hand-written methods.

5. To provide work of better appearance (*e.g.*, machine-typed invoices).

6. To avoid fraud (such as a cheque-writing machine).

7. To reduce fatigue of office workers (*e.g.*, electric typewriters).

8. To provide management with more information and faster (*e.g.*, as with a computer).

9. If a machine saves in staffing, it will also save in office space and overheads generally.

3. DISADVANTAGES

1. Machines cannot do work requiring great intelligence.

2. Obsolescence of some machines is very heavy.

3. Expense of special stationery and printing.
4. Cost of training staff and difficulty of recruiting them (*e.g.*, computer personnel).
5. Some machines lack mobility, whereas when work is done by hand, workers can be transferred from one office to another.
6. Noise in the office, causing distraction of other workers.
7. Capital outlay (although almost anything can be rented these days).
8. Machine breakdown, and delays in work while waiting for repairs.
9. Lack of flexibility, whereby office systems become tied to the machine application.

Basic office machines

It is not proposed here to deal with all office machines, and the reader is referred to *Office Management* (Macdonald and Evans, 1974) for detailed exposition, but basic office machines and equipment are:

1. *Typewriters:* standard, electric, automatic, and variable-type machines.
2. *Shorthand machine:* Palantype, which is claimed to be easier to learn than shorthand, and can be used for long periods without tiring.
3. *Continuous stationery:* roll, interfold, and fanfold, and methods of copying can be one-time carbon, carbon backing, N.C.R., and anchored carbon devices.
4. *Dictating:* can be individual machines or central dictating systems using magnetic or inscribed media of recording. Central dictating can be multi-bank or tandem.
5. *Duplicating:* spirit, stencil, offset-lithography, or typeset lithography.
6. *Photocopying:* reflex, transfer diffusion, dyeline, thermal, electrostatic, and dual-spectrum are the main methods.
7. *Addressing:* embossed metal plates, embossed plastic plates, spirit and stencil addressing machines are available.
8. *Adding:* machines are made for addition and subtraction, which can be add/listing, with tally roll, or without.
9. *Calculating:* machines are made for multiplication and division, and while key-driven and rotary types are still in use, the modern developments have been printing calculators, programmable electronic calculators, and electronic printing calculators.

10. *Accounting:* while simple electro-mechanical machines are still available, they are rapidly being overtaken by V.R.C.s (Visible Record Computers), which are reducing in price, so that they are almost as cheap to buy (and many times faster) than the old electro-mechanical models.
11. *Punched cards:* not used so much today (*i.e.*, just punched-card machines) as in previous years, for many large punched-card installations have been converted to the use of computers, and then use different means of input.
12. *Writing boards (or three-in-one system):* a method of posting for the smaller business, not requiring specially trained operators.
13. *Hand analysis:* marginal punched cards, slotted cards, feature cards, and peg boards are all types of equipment to assist easy analysis of multiple data.
14. *Computers:* these are dealt with later in the book (Chapters 30–34).
15. *Filing machines and equipment (see* Chapter 11).
16. *Microfilm machines and equipment:* here, there is the great virtue of saving office space, as well as giving fast data retrieval, and these machines are being increasingly used in computer installations.
17. *Telephone systems:* both internal and external (*see* Chapter 18).
18. *Facsimile telegraphy and teleprinters and telex (see* Chapter 18).
19. *Post-room machines:* franking, folding, letter sealing, etc.
20. *Sundry others:* cheque-writing machines, document shredders, etc.

Some writers on O. & M. prefer to classify machines under headings of machines used for writing, copying, calculating, etc., but such classification can be harmful, because every day some new uses are found for machines originally intended for other purposes. Manufacturers also adapt their machines to new uses, so that an electrostatic copier is being recommended now as a duplicator. For convenience and speed it is better than a duplicator, but it is doubtful whether it is as cheap.

A *typewriter* can be used for producing many copies of a document (up to twenty on an electric machine), provided air-mail paper and fly-weight carbons are used. Automatic typewriters are also used for invoicing purposes.

Everyone knows that *continuous stationery* is used very widely for producing several copies of orders or invoices, but how many know that it can be used for the production of a combined statement of pay and pay envelopes (as at Vauxhall Motors Limited)?

Dictating machines are widely known for the dictation of routine correspondence, but such machines are useful for recording goods to be ordered each day from stock records, and even for the dictation of salesmen's reports while motoring around their sales areas.

Offset lithography is basically a printing machine, but the production of paper and plastic plates is so cheap, that it is being used more and more for duplicating and even for the production of sales invoices.

There is no end to the uses of *photocopying machines*—in the Accounts Department for production of monthly statements from sales ledgers, in the Registrar's Department for copying marriage and death certificates, in the sales department for providing sales representatives with up-to-date lists of customers, and even in the Wages Department for production of the pay-roll.

Addressing machines have certainly gone a long way from the original purpose of reproducing names and addresses. With embossed plastic plates, they can be used for credit control, and even as input for electronic data processing.

Calculating machines will now perform a series of formula calculations instead of one-off calculations for occasional use.

Accounting machines can be used for production of sales invoices, posting of ledgers (and will perform analysis while doing it), as well as punched tape, etc., for data processing by a computer.

Marginal punched cards and other methods of analysis are being used in connection with market research and for stock-control purposes.

Microfilm is not merely used to save office space, but is now increasingly being used as a medium of data storage and retrieval, as well as a medium for sales invoicing.

Telephone systems are used (Datel) as a medium for computer input, as well as for credit control.

This is only a selection of uses, and there will doubtless be further extended use of all machines in the future. The O. & M. practitioner needs to have a knowledge of all machines, and to know which one is applicable in different circumstances.

Control of machines

Machines are often centrally installed for the use of several departments, and (like a communal garden for a block of flats, where no one person cultivates it) it is best to fix responsibility for specific machines. Not only does this fix responsibility for their operation, but ensures that the machines are cleaned and receive maintenance when needed. It should also be clear to whom the staff in charge of machine should report.

However, the staff in charge of running machines are usually junior to the staff wishing to make use of them, and an O. & M. officer should endeavour to obtain agreement to rules for the usage of machines. Thus, for example, a stencil might be created when a spirit master would be more economical, and it is a simple matter to issue a duplicated leaflet stating something along the following lines:

1. *Spirit duplicator* must only be used where 10–100 copies are required, or where more than one colour is required.
2. *Stencil duplicator* must only be used when 100–1,000 copies are required and/or work of better quality than spirit.
3. *Offset litho* paper plates should be used when 1,000 + copies are required, and where the master can be made photographically.

This is only a specimen, and its application would have to be varied according to local circumstances (*e.g.*, if there is an electronic stencil cutter).

Of importance here is the use of photocopying machines, which should, other things being equal, only be used for, say, up to five copies.

In the day-to-day running of machines, the O. & M. department can also give instruction cards (many machines delivered these days have no instruction manuals—or they get lost) on the need for switching off the pressure control on duplicators; on the need for adjustment of the thickness feed; on the need to stab the keys of calculating (not electronic) machines, and so on.

In one big typing pool when an automatic typewriter was installed, it was found that a great deal of the work performed on it was not justifiable, and so all requests for its use had to be channelled through the supervisor, who was trained in assessing its applications.

Maintenance

Should one sign a maintenance contract or pay for individual calls? The more complicated a machine, the more likely is it to be worthwhile signing a maintenance contract. Machines have a habit of going wrong at a most crucial time.

1. ADVANTAGES OF MAINTENANCE CONTRACT

1. May be cheaper, perhaps only parts to pay for.
2. May produce better service.
3. Skilled mechanics have proper spare-parts.
4. New machines often require a "breaking in" period before they run properly.
5. Better to have a maintenance call than prevent serious machine faults developing.

2. DISADVANTAGES

1. May be expensive if a large number of machines involved.
2. Sometimes better service can be obtained from local firms (*e.g.*, with typewriters) instead of waiting for the routine mechanic call.
3. Cleaning and oiling should be performed by the operators, and this saves on what is often only a cursory clean and inspection.
4. Inexperienced mechanics often cause more trouble—discovered after they have left.

Of course, a great deal depends on the age of the machine, and the older the machine, the more likely is it to need regular maintenance and perhaps more important it is to have a maintenance contract.

Instead of machines

In this mechanical age, it seems that a machine is often introduced before a full examination has been made of its suitability, and in certain cases there is little doubt that machines create work and increase staffing numbers. Here, then, are a few ideas which can obviate the use of a machine:

1. Instead of typing letters or internal memos, write them on a three-in-one form, one copy to keep and two to send, one of which is returned—using N.C.R. paper.
2. Instead of using calculating machines, and especially where the calculations are fairly standard, use specially devised ready-reckoner tables.
3. For analysis, use a peg-board or slotted cards.
4. For posting, and even for wages and ledger posting, use a three-in-one writing board.
5. Why not have forms pre-punched, to avoid the constant use of a hand punch, when filing papers?
6. Above all, make sure that the best possible hand methods are available before installing a machine; an improved jig can often improve a clerical operation, *e.g.*, a special circular rack when sorting out returned cheques, and so on.

Cost/benefit analysis

Although it can be one of several advantages to be gained from using a machine, invariably it is hoped that it will save money. But in carrying out a cost/benefit survey, it is not always necessary that a machine need to be used continuously to make it worthwhile.

Thus, if a folding machine costing, say, £200, saves two hours a day of a clerk, it may easily pay for itself in the course of the first year.

All factors of expense must be taken into account, not merely the cost of the machine, but its maintenance, its floor-space, its operation, and any special stationery requirements. In assessing the benefits, not only saving in staff time, but indirect savings should also be assessed, such as better credit control where speedier sales ledger posting is facilitated.

In management accounting, the three methods used for assessing the financial viability of a machine are:

1. The *pay-back* method: in how many years will its savings pay for its purchase?
2. The *percentage income method*: by comparing its cost savings with its capital outlay.
3. *Discounted Cash Flow:* this involves the use of tables and comparing the relative income of different machines, discounting the future income in terms of current interest that could be earned with the capital by investing it elsewhere.

The method used will vary with the cost of the particular machine, and it must be remembered that this is the accountant's approach. While it is a factor to be considered when buying machines, often a machine which seems not worthwhile financially, may more than pay for itself in indirect advantages which are almost impossible to cost precisely.

CASE STUDY

Machine productivity

DEPT. OF HEALTH AND SOCIAL SECURITY

1. OBJECT

An addressing machine department with two machines and an embosser was staffed by three operators. The unit was not keeping pace with demands (despite overtime), work was falling in arrear, and O. & M. was requested to establish the possible need of another machine and another operator.

2. PROBLEM

The unit had not been established very long, so there were no reliable work records over a period, nor means of measuring whether output had fallen.

3. O. & M. OBJECTIVES

1. To find out what use was being made of the machines.
2. The extent of the arrears, and the incidence of overtime.
3. To assess reliable estimates of total demand on the unit.
4. Whether the existing machines could meet this demand.
5. To assess the time required to carry out ancillary tasks of tabbing plates for automatic selection and of embossing.
6. The reasons for arrears of work.

4. COURSE OF ACTION

Over a period of seventeen weeks, the operators maintained self-recording diaries of all the work produced, showing volume of work and time taken. From this information, a bar chart was prepared showing the work performed each week, the arrears outstanding at the end of each week, and the overtime worked.

5. RESULTS

1. The existing machines were quite capable of meeting the work demand with little overtime and without excessive arrears of work.
2. For most of the time, the machines were not working to capacity.
3. The second addressing machine was so little used, that rather than a third machine being necessary, it was doubtful whether the second machine was really required.

6. ACTION TAKEN

1. After timing work on the machine, the operators agreed the standards of operating speed.
2. Allowances were made for the time lost owing to repairs, maintenance and breakdowns (based on mechanic's time-sheets). Stoppages were assessed by actual observation.
3. From the total work demand, the total annual machine hours were assessed to be 1,105 or 4·4 hours a day.

4. Arrangements were made for the second machine to be removed.
5. Having assessed the machine time and made a good allowance for embossing and tabbing (arrived at by actual recording), it was apparent that two operators would be sufficient.
6. One of the causes of delay and arrears was the lack of effective procedures for ordering stationery to be addressed and indicating its priority.
7. By using a proper requisition procedure, with dates required for the work, degrees of priority could be established and work planned in advance—rather than just a record of requests for work and on which dates.

Arrears of work and overtime were drastically reduced, one machine and one operator was saved as a result of the inquiry.

[*O. & M.* November 1966

CHECK LIST

1. Have we found the best manual method before considering a machine?
2. What advantages are there to be derived from using a machine?
3. What are the possible disadvantages?
4. Is there a machine on the market really suitable to the purpose?
5. What are the purposes of the work?
6. Have we considered the costs before and after using a machine?
7. Have we considered all elements of cost, including stationery?
8. Will noise be a problem?
9. Would the machine have most use if it was centralised?
10. Is the machine envisaged simple to operate, even by a junior?
11. Is it better to have a maintenance contract or "as required" basis?
12. Have we given full instructions on the proper use of the machine?
13. Is there sufficient control on the proper use of a machine?
14. Have we performed a cost/benefit study on the machine envisaged?
15. Will the machine form a bottleneck in the work?
16. Shall we need to train two operators, even if there is only work for one?
17. Have we checked on office space, special furniture, and electric points?
18. What effect will a machine have on the systems and forms design?
19. What effect will a machine have on the kinds of staffing and numbers?
20. Will a machine really increase efficiency, and how?

Chapter 11 Records and filing

The basic function of the office lies in the recording, arranging and disseminating of information, and usually this takes place on office forms. A simple, effective filing system is very often the keystone of office efficiency, and it is certain that nothing can more easily cause chaos than a bad records and filing system.

Records control

Business records have a habit of accumulating and then getting out of control. To improve such control, there should be:

1. Avoidance of unnecessary filing, *e.g.*, by marking some as "T" for temporary, so that after one month such papers can be destroyed. Often files are glutted with unnecessary unimportant papers which could have been thrown away.
2. Certainty that current papers are filed up to date. There should be a regular system of reporting (say every Monday morning) and the transfer of staff to ensure filing is up to date.
3. A retention programme, so that it is known what is kept and for how long.
4. Certainty that the most suitable filing equipment is provided, especially bearing in mind economy of floor-space.
5. Revision of all filing practices and systems of classification, say, once a year.
6. Exploration of the use of microfilming, instead of expensive floor-space for storing thousands of documents.
7. Designation of responsibility for filing and care of files.
8. Clear rules about what should be transferred to archival filing (if any), and records of what is kept and where.
9. A handbook of operations and procedures on classification, retention periods, archival filing, instructions for destruction, etc.
10. A great deal of the success of any filing system depends on recruiting the right staff who are "filing-minded," and then ensuring their proper training.

Essentials of good filing systems

1. Compactness: filing cabinets should occupy a minimum of floor-space.
2. Accessibility: the type of equipment installed must facilitate the easy reference of those who have to use them.
3. Simplicity: the filing classification should be as simple as possible.
4. Economy: there is a limit to the amount of money spent on equipment.
5. Elasticity: the equipment adopted, and the space allocated, must allow for expansion forecast for the future.
6. Location: records should be located so that they can be referred to with the minimum possible delay (this does not always mean instant reference).
7. Cross-reference: especially for subject and geographical classification, cross-references must be inserted so that documents can be found under different headings.
8. Retention: dead material must be capable of being discarded without too much disturbance (*e.g.*, as with Terminal Digit classification).
9. Out-guides: where papers or files are important, and there is not too much reference to them, then a system of out-guides to indicate where the missing documents or files can be found is invaluable.
10. Classification: to have the most suitable system of classification, without bulky miscellaneous files.

Systems of classification

The ability to locate a document or file when required may depend very much on having the right system of classification. This will depend on:

1. Size of the filing system (the larger it is, the more likely is it to be numerical).
2. Convenience of reference (only inquiry will reveal this).
3. Management control (*e.g.*, sales records in sales area order).
4. Ease of getting rid of dead material.
5. Whether the information on the records is intended for data processing on a computer (preference for numerical).
6. Expertise of filing staff.
7. Need for a separate index (it might be with numerical, but this

depends whether a numerical reference is automatically provided, *e.g.*, National Insurance No., etc., for filing purposes).

8. Whether more than one classification is required of the same documents for different purposes? (*e.g.*, alphabetically for customers, as well as subject).

The most usual systems of classification are:

1. ALPHABETICAL (with variant of vowel filing by first vowel in the name for small systems)

This is fairly simple to understand, although it is surprising how many things can be intelligently filed under different headings (*e.g.*, I.C.I. or Imperial Chemical Industries); in large systems there is congestion under common names, and it is difficult to forecast space requirements for different letters of the alphabet.

It does, however, mean that there can be miscellaneous files for the "one-off" letters, so it is still widely used for correspondence, order and invoice filing.

From an O. & M. point of view, it is advisable to provide a filing guide, and to restrict the opening of new files without permission.

2. NUMERICAL

1. Decimal numeric (Dewey Decimal, as in the libraries), which can be combined with subject filing, say in the Buying Department, when 1.1 might be Furniture/Chairs, 1.2 Furniture/Desks, and so on.
2. Soundex Vowel system, aimed at translating different phonetic sounds of names into numbers.
3. Terminal Digit filing, where documents or files are arranged in order of the first digits, so that 19314 precedes 19214, and 19114, and so on. The great advantage of this system (used by Lloyds Register and many hospitals) is that the same guide cards and cabinet labels can be used *ad infinitum*, and that it is easy to weed out dead files when drawers are full.

Numerical classification gives greater accuracy than alphabetical; the file numbers can be quoted as references on letters; it has unlimited expansion; and although an index may be required, it can be used for other purposes. An outstanding advantage is the ability to use numerical classification with a computer, *e.g.*, as with stores classification.

On the other hand, reference to an index has to be considered, as well as the floor-space it requires; and transposition of figures is a common mistake with numerical classification. Where a numerical classification is used, particularly if it is (say) a twelve-figure stores classification, then it is advisable to prepare a filing guide leaflet setting out clearly the style of classification, and giving examples in use.

3. GEOGRAPHICAL

1. In sales areas designated according to the company's sales distribution.
2. Simply Home and Overseas.
3. By name of town or county.

This has the convenience of grouping all customers in a specific area, *e.g.*, for giving instructions to sales representatives, and is a means of direct filing without the need of an index.

But there is room for error where knowledge of geography is weak, and often an index is required (*e.g.*, for designation of places in different sales areas).

4. CHRONOLOGICAL

Where files or papers are placed strictly in date order, which may be an advantage when clearing out dead material, or when turning up orders, etc. But if the date of a letter or date of an order is not known, it may be a disadvantage.

Its most popular use is in a follow-up file, where a clerk checks on whether replies have been received to letters sent out.

5. SUBJECT

Subject classification is found most useful in such departments as buying and the Company Secretary's office.

It has the advantage of making it easy to find an item provided its subject is known (which it usually is), but difficulties may occur where an item might be filed quite intelligently under two or three headings, and where a letter, say, has two or more subjects in its contents.

6. COMBINATION OF PREVIOUS METHODS

This is probably the most widespread classification of all. Alpha-numerical systems are very common, where, for example, a sales ledger may be divided into Accounts A1, A2, A3, etc., giving the degree of direct reference of alphabetical, while retaining some of the expandibility of the numerical method.

The Foreign Office uses an alphabetically coded department, combined with a geographical, and numerically coded subject. Thus FC/15318/36, refers to "F" department, "C" stands for China, 153 is a subject heading, 18 is a sub-heading, while No. 36 refers to the letter number in the file.

Central filing

Depending on the volume and the importance, records can be classified into (a) current, (b) inactive, and (c) archival, and it is a matter of policy whether individual offices keep (a) and (b) and just a central archive is provided for (c). In some small- and medium-sized concerns, all records (apart from personnel, sales, and accounting) are filed centrally, and individual offices do not maintain their own filing systems at all. Or, as a compromise, (a) might be kept in individual offices, and (b) and (c) kept in a central filing department.

The advantages and disadvantages of central filing will depend on the policy followed, but, generally speaking, there will be better control of records with central filing; it can ensure uniform procedures; it will be easier to fix responsibility; and it may eliminate separate office copies of documents. On the other hand, it may mean delay in files being made available; it may be harder to find lost papers; there will be lack of knowledge of filing by office juniors; and there will probably be more mistakes than when filing is done locally.

When there is a central filing department, whether for all records or just archival ones, it is as well to have a set of rules for its control.

1. No person shall remove files other than the authorised Filing Clerk(s).
2. Whenever files are removed, a Tracer Card must be used, inserting the name of person, department, and date. This information must be ruled through when the file is returned.
3. At the end of each month, a check must be made on all Tracer Cards and a report on those outstanding for more than a week submitted to the Company Secretary.
4. When a telephone call is received for a file, it must be taken as soon as possible to the Department requiring it.
5. All letters must have written on them the name of the appropriate file.
6. No letters must be filed unless accompanied by a carbon copy of a reply, OR the letter is marked N/R for "No Reply," and initialled by the sending department.

7. All correspondence and other records to be filed from the previous day must be sent to the C.F.D. first thing each morning.
8. No individual letters to be removed from files by any office.
9. At the end of each year, all current files must be removed to the Transfer Boxes provided in Room 29; all such boxes to be numbered, and marked with contents and dates. This must be performed by the end of January of the following year.
10. No new files to be opened without the permission of the Supervisor of the C.F.D.

Records retention

When records are becoming voluminous and when filing cabinets are over-full, then action needs to be taken, which can be:

1. Weeding out—to get rid of paper which can be destroyed.
2. Transfer of older records to reserve storage (*see above*).
3. Destroying the older records in accordance with a laid-down retention programme.
4. Microfilming the old records, and then destroying them.

A retention programme is important, because it ensures the regular destruction of old records, which saves office space, and filing equipment. Without a proper retention programme, it is likely that records that should be kept will be destroyed, and, what is more common, the accumulation of worthless records which should have been destroyed long ago.

Apart from official records (such as share registers, and tax records, etc.) it is doubtful whether any universal retention periods can be laid down for the same type of records in all concerns. Retention periods must be laid down by each concern for all its records, bearing in mind the following:

1. How much office space is available, and at what cost? Even if floor-space is expensive, if it cannot be sub-let or used for other purposes, then there is no point in saving it, but usually office space is at a premium.
2. What is the volume of the individual records? Thus, if six years' sales invoices require a million cubic feet, then the six years' limit might be revised.
3. What are the legal requirements? With the exception of certain prescribed categories (*see below*), action cannot be taken on a simple contract after six years, and on a speciality contract after twelve years. This does not mean that all papers concerned with

simple contracts need to be kept six years, but only if it is likely that they will need to be produced in a court action.

4. What is the frequency of reference? If it is found in practice that it is never necessary to refer back further than two years, then that might be the retention period for a particular record.

5. Type of industry or trade will have a bearing on the retention periods. Thus, if computers costing £200,000 each are sold, the sales invoices are much more important than those when selling articles for only a few pence each.

Legal requirements

The law requires certain records to be kept.

1. The tax inspector can re-open accounts for up to six years back, and even further if fraud is suspected.

2. The *Companies Act* 1948 does not prescribe any definite retention periods, but if a company goes into liquidation, it is an offence if proper books of account have not been kept during the two years preceding liquidation (the same applies to bankruptcy of an individual trader or partnership).

3. Records concerning V.A.T. should also be retained for at least two years.

A retention programme should then be prepared under headings something like the following:

Retention Period	*Records*
1 YEAR	Paid dividend warrants
2 YEARS	Petty cash vouchers
	Cheque counterfoils
	Bank paying-in books
	Purchase invoices
	Sales invoices and credit notes
	Order books
6 YEARS	Bank statements
INDEFINITELY	Books of account
	Share register, and share transfers
	Minute books

Some indication of the need for a retention programme is evidenced by the appointment of an O. & M. officer in a pharmaceutical concern; he removed six tons of paper in the first week of his appointment.

Indexing

As mentioned above, some methods of classification will need an index, besides which offices have telephone indexes, credit indexes, customer and supplier indexes, and so on. A general-purpose index for staff reference can be a very useful thing, but it is time-wasting and inefficient if it is not reliable, and there must be:

1. responsibility designated for keeping it up to date;
2. some simple system for notifying changes;
3. the most appropriate equipment provided for accommodating the index (bearing office space in mind);
4. if frequently used, it must give speed of reference.

Without exploring all their pros and cons (although each has its own specific uses), the following are the commonest forms of index obtainable:

1. *Book index:* either bound, or loose-leaf, with thumb guide.
2. *Loose or vertical card index:* cheap, but more effective than a book, provided the cards do not get mislaid.
3. *Strip index:* more suitable for one-line pieces of information such as names and addresses, telephone numbers, etc.
4. *Visible card index:* the most expensive, but more than just an index. Useful for personnel, stock, price records, etc. and gives the great facility of signalling to indicate actions taken or required to be taken.
5. *Visible book index:* a cheap form of 4, and can be used for the same purposes, but not so durable or so speedy in reference or in inserting or deleting records.
6. *Rotary index:* the most modern development, giving greatest speed of reference. For large concerns, motorised versions are in use.

Filing equipment

It is not necessary to describe the variations in detail, but the following types of equipment are available:

1. Box files (useful for temporary storage).
2. Lever arch files (cheapest and most universal).
3. Transfer boxes (metal and cardboard).
4. Suspension filing (keeps files tidier, but accommodates fewer).
5. Lateral filing (saves as much as 50 per cent of floor-space).
6. Motorised filing: (where filing trays are suspended round a drum which can be brought to view at the press of a button).

Microfilming

1. PURPOSE

The increasing popularity of microfilming probably originated from two causes: (a) the increasing cost of office space, and (b) the fact that 40 per cent of office records can be thrown away. The problem is—which ones to get rid of?

While it may not be efficient to microfilm worthless documents, it might be cheaper than the labour cost of winnowing by hand.

While space-saving is the main advantage of microfilming, it also gives speedy reference, avoids misfiling, and overcomes the nagging doubt about whether this or that record should be retained—microfilm the lot, and then throw them away!

It should always be borne in mind that where the law requires certain contracts to be in writing, then they should be retained in that form and not microfilmed. Even where there is no legal requirement, it is advisable to complete a certificate to prove the authenticity of the film record. Such a certificate should be signed by an official of the company after the documents have been microfilmed, but before they are destroyed. It should be typed on headed paper of the organisation, and should then be microfilmed and become part of the records on the microfilm. The microfilm, accompanied by such a certificate would then, it is thought, be acceptable in a court of law, should the documents need to be produced as evidence.

After microfilming, the images should be examined and compared with the originals; some may be illegible or omitted altogether. Then fresh microfilm must be prepared from those originals, and the additional film attached to the original roll. A fresh certificate should then be signed to cover the additions.

Figure 3 shows the form of certificate recommended by the I.C.S.A.

2. MICROFILM INSTALLATION

It is not necessary to install expensive microfilm equipment, for there are specialist concerns who will (at low rental) store archival records and will make reference to them and supply information from them as required from time to time.

However, to make the decision on whether to microfilm or not, regard must be paid to the following factors:

1. cost of office space taken by accumulated records (as much as 97 per cent floor-space can be saved);

EXCEL PRODUCE CO. LTD.

**12 Old Broad St,
E.C.1.**

CERTIFICATE OF INTENT

This is to certify that the microfilmed records that appear on this roll are accurate and true records of ....
These records have been photographed in the ordinary course of business to be preserved in this roll exactly as in the originals. These records are microfilmed with the specific intention of .... (*name of firm or organisation*) to destroy the original records and to retain in their stead permanent microfilm images in order to save space, time labour and cost of filing equipment. I also certify that the original documents recorded on this roll of microfilm will be destroyed only after the accuracy and content of the documents and their film images has been assured by an inspection of the film.

          Name of organisation ....

          Signed ....

          Date ....

    This is to certify that the additional microfilm images on this roll of microfilm are accurate and true images of the documents that were missed or found unreadable on inspection of the original roll of microfilm to which they are now attached.

          Name of organisation ....

          Signed ....

          Date ....

FIG. 3.—Recommended certificate to accompany business microfilms.

2. cost of buying extra filing cabinets and other filing equipment;
3. cost of microfilming equipment, film and processing;
4. comparative costs of staffing both before and after microfilming.

It is difficult to make a precise cost/benefit analysis beforehand, because many of the advantages are incapable of cost assessment (*e.g.*, speed of reference), and because the volume of reference may change.

Also among the disadvantages may be the hidden costs of removal of all pins and staples and the pre-sorting of records before microfilming, as well as re-filming when the images are illegible.

However, in making a decision to microfilm, the following methods should be considered:

1. to install camera, reader and processing unit;
2. to install camera, reader, and send films away for processing (fairly cheap);
3. to get microfilming done by a specialist outside contractor, and install readers only.

Also, in making a choice of equipment, there are six types of microfilm equipment available:

1. *roll film*, in widths of 16mm and 35mm; the latter is usually used for plans, and the former for ordinary office records;
2. *microfiche*, where several dozen frames are accommodated on an oblong strip of film, which can be housed in envelopes with visible index strips typed on them;
3. *microfiche* stored in transparent *jackets*;
4. *aperture cards*, 35mm microfilms mounted in ordinary data-processing punched cards;
5. rolls of film contained in quick-loading *cassettes*;
6. special microfilm techniques such as electrostatic beam microfilming for *computer output* (*see* Chapter 30 on Computers).

It is not always simply a choice between these six, because some companies prefer to have 3 stored in customers' folders, and 1 as a duplicate record stored in the company safe. Again, where a large volume of records is stored (particularly plans), and when there is frequent reference, 4 is preferred. One and a half million print-outs from aperture cards were used in the preparation of drawings for the Concorde project in recent years. The use of cassettes obviously facilitates speedy reference where the film is constantly referred to as a part of everyday use in office systems.

Finally, in the choice of equipment, it has to be considered whether reference to the microfilm by a reader will be sufficient, or whether prints may be required of the images, in which case, a machine capable of printing out as well as photocopying will have to be purchased.

CASE STUDY

Filing

LLOYDS

1. PROBLEM

A very common problem of a great increase in the volume of records, which consisted of record cards and reference books. There was danger of overflow, and the vital irreplaceable record cards were also in danger of becoming damaged beyond use.

Another everyday problem was that several people needed access to the same records, which created a multi-reference problem, as well as a space problem.

2. O. & M. RECOMMENDATIONS

1. All records were initially divided into "live" and "dead" categories—live records being those to which written information was being added, and dead when no additions were expected.
2. All dead records have been put on to 16mm microfilm (a total of 250,000 cards and 200,000 pages of a Confidential Index).
3. When records become "dead," they are amassed in a motorised file until there are sufficient to justify an economic microfilming operation (about 3,000 a year were expected).
4. Since only occasional microfilming will be required, the services of an outside microfilm consultant were used.
5. The films are stored in microfilm cartridges, and a clerk has a reader/printer mounted on a specially built desk, in the drawers of which she can refer to fifty years' of microfilmed records—all contained in one drawer. The clerk is fitted with ear-phones, so that she can answer telephone calls with both hands free for reference purposes.
6. The "live" records were then divided into those where simultaneous access was required by up to four people at a time, and those where only one person at a time needed reference.
7. Simultaneous access was provided by the use of a five-tier carousel file, which has a capacity of 7,500 index cards, 5 in. × 3 in.
8. To allow for expansion, a spare capacity of 20 per cent allows for future growth. The carousel unit is strategically placed within arm's length of each of the four main users.

9. The motorised file provides for the storage of the rest of the live records, which are mainly records of ships still in service. The unit has removable trays, which can easily be taken out when reference is required to a whole batch of records.

3. BENEFITS

(a) Reference speed from microfilm cartridges is at least as fast as reference to actual cards.

(b) But, unlike a card, misfiling of the records is impossible.

(c) Staff no longer have to handle heavy and dirty records, books, etc.

(d) Staff do far less walking about the office, and the majority of the work can be carried out from a seated position.

(e) The saving in floor-space is estimated to be about 80 per cent.

(f) Fifty years of records are now held in one desk drawer.

(g) There is sufficient expansion space for more than 150 years.

4. COSTS

Cost of equipment was in the region of £2,000, and updating on microfilm is expected to be less than £100 per annum.

[*Business Systems and Equipment* February 1973

CHECK LIST

1. Have we got full control over our stored records?
2. Have we got a retention programme?
3. What is the best system of classification for these records?
4. Have we compared labour costs with equipment costs?
5. Is speed of reference really essential?
6. Have we got the best equipment?
7. Would it be better to have some central filing?
8. Should it be of inactive or archival records, or both?
9. What kinds of index do we need?
10. Have we considered the use of motorised files?
11. Would microfilming save space, and how much?
12. Would its cost be offset by indirect savings?
13. What is the best method of microfilm installation?
14. Would roll film, cassette, microfiche, or aperture cards be best?
15. Have we considered Terminal Digit filing?
16. Do we fix responsibility for filing?
17. Have we got a regular report system on the state of the filing?
18. Are our record filing systems efficient, if not, why?
19. Do we use cross-references (or if we do, are they necessary)?
20. Do we use tracer cards to locate missing papers or files?

Part Three: Elements of Management

Chapter 12 Management Efficiency

Introduction

As previously stated, the aim of management is *to achieve the objectives of the concern in the most economical way.* So, in the first instance, management efficiency is to know what the objectives are, so that it can be ascertained whether and to what extent they are being achieved. Secondly comes the big question of whether they are being achieved in the most economical way.

Objectives refer to the long-term aims of the proprietors and managers of a concern. It can be said in the absence of laid-down objectives that there are always implied objectives, such as (*a*) wishing to continue in existence, (*b*) to make as much profit as possible (in a business), and (*c*) to continue to expand (also in business, and unfortunately also in some public enterprises). Objectives may be decided on and even publicised, thus "Securicor" have published some of their objectives as being:

1. To be among the most respected companies in the British Commonwealth.
2. To practise new and better methods of commerce.
3. To put principle before expediency and make sure our word is our bond.
4. While not deviating from what is practical, to enrol the idealism of youth.
5. To ignore class or race; to judge only by merit; to work in comradeship.
6. To divide more fairly the fruits of investment and work by means of the Mutual Company.
7. To combine what is best in public service, *e.g.*, devotion to duty, with what is best in private enterprise, *e.g.*, adaptability.
8. To express in the tangible terms of guarding and watching Man's regard for his neighbour and wish to serve him.

These are rather philosophical, and more precise objectives for a company might be:

"The company should aim to become a rapidly-growing *publicly owned*, medium-sized company designing and assembling high-quality electric and electrical instruments *and industrial control systems in two factories* marketing primarily in France (80 per cent) through *its own sales force* with limited export sales through agents and *relying for technical improvement largely on American licences.*"

But it can be seen that policies may qualify and in fact spell out objectives which have not been defined. Thus, the Chairman of one well-known chain-store has stated that if their profits on sales exceeded 10 per cent, they would feel they had an obligation to reduce prices to customers. So the implication is that more profit could be made, but the business wished to expand and perhaps get a greater volume of profit, but not an increased percentage compared to sales.

Similarly, if objective (c) mentioned above is examined, while it can be said that this is an implied objective of most concerns, there are some proprietors who, when the business grows to a certain size, prefer to sell out to another concern and would prefer to have cash in the bank and work as a manager in a much bigger concern than run a large business of their own.

Policies

Even if the objectives are clear, there are usually a variety of policies, or courses of action which can be followed, in achieving them. Thus, a business can expand its home sales, enter into exporting, diversify its products, enter into licensing agreements, and so on.

An objective is broad in scope and with regard to personnel an objective may be to give employee satisfaction, but the policies followed may vary considerably from giving pensions at fifty, to giving employees shares in a co-partnership scheme, by having a recognised policy of internal promotion, or by giving regular wage and salary increases in accordance with the cost of living.

The decisions on broad policy, in whatever aspect of management is concerned, will be the job of top management. It is not the job of management services to make policy, but if it can prove that, for example, a bad recruitment policy has increased labour turnover, then it is the job of management services to recommend a change in policy.

So much of management in the past has been a matter of guesswork and intuition, that the modern scientific aids of operational research, work study, standard costing, and so on, should be used to give proof, when it is needed, of the need to change policy.

This is not to say that all management policy decisions can be arrived at by scientific methods, because there is, and always will be, an area of judgment, and to this extent, policies decided by top management must be accepted and implemented.

In pursuing different policies, there will be clashes of interest, thus to give shareholders greater dividends might be at the expense of wage increases to employees. It is the job of management in its policies to resolve all such differences.

Management efficiency

Now to achieving objectives *in the most economical way*. In business, the conventional efficiency ratios are:

1. net profit (before tax) as a percentage of capital employed, and
2. net profit (before tax) per employee.

But it is doubtful if the ratio (1) say, of a capital-intensive concern like a motor manufacturer could be compared with a labour-intensive firm like a chain-store. Then, again, the ratio depends on the interpretation of "capital employed," is it just the value of fixed assets, or is it the total capital minus working capital?

However, suppose the ratio (1) is higher than all other similar industries, does it mean that such a business is necessarily the most efficient? The answer is that it may seem to be most efficient compared with its rivals, but it is not necessarily most efficient in the use of its resources (*i.e.*, discounting all other factors such as valuation of assets, etc.). Real efficiency can be said to be not only judging what is produced from the available resources, but by comparing with what is possible, *i.e.*, *the potential.*

Similarly, ratio (2), profit per employee, can be as high as £2,000 in an oil company, and less than a tenth of that in a labour-intensive concern like a grocery retailer.

Productivity

One way of measuring efficiency is by assessing productivity, but the term "productivity" is used in many different ways, depending on whether it is used by an accountant, an engineer, a politician, an economist, or a trade-union leader.

The simple test of company "output" with "input," or "sales" with "resources" is one measure of total productivity, without necessarily achieving maximum profitability.

Thus, if OUTPUT (Sales)   100
INPUT
   Capital 10
   Labour 10
   Other   70
           —
                              90

SURPLUS   10 (Profit)

Input (90) as a percentage of Output (100) equals 90 per cent which is very high, and profitability is also high (10 per cent) compared with Capital (10) equals 100 per cent.

But supposing the business buys more machinery and the figures then become (with bigger sales):

OUTPUT (Sales)   120
INPUT
   Capital 15
   Labour 5
   Others 90
           —
                        110

SURPLUS   10 (Profit)

Thus Input (110) as a percentage of Output (120) equals 92 per cent (*i.e.*, higher than previously), but profitability (10) compared with Capital (15) has fallen to 66 per cent. Thus *productivity* may not be synonymous with *profitability*.

Equally, it will be noticed from the above-mentioned example that if labour productivity is examined, it has increased from $\frac{10}{100} = 10$ per cent to $\frac{5}{120} = 24$ per cent, *i.e.*, it has more than doubled, but profitability has still been reduced. It is apparent that a higher labour productivity, in itself, does not mean higher profitability.

It will be noticed that in the second example the cost of labour has been halved, which of course does not necessarily happen, although newer, more modern machinery usually does result in reduced labour costs.

Such measurements of productivity have been developed by management accountants, but it is apparent when one looks at the different valuations of assets (particularly property) that it is far from precise.

Economists, on the other hand, convert all inputs into terms of labour time and express materials and services in what is called labour-time methods of measurement.

A modern alternative approach is "productive costing" conceived by Professor Harold Martin, which is based on the *maximum practical capacity*, *i.e.*, on the feasible capacity to produce, not on the ability to sell. Yet it can be seen straightaway that maximum production is useless if the goods are not sold. This theory assesses the value added to the throughput materials by converting them into saleable or usable products (*i.e.*, sales value less materials).

An example of this approach shows:
Motor Vehicle Industry:

Current added value	£2,106
Potential A.V.	£3,042
Increase	44 per cent

Thus, it can be seen that instead of finding additional manpower, management should seek ways of utilising its existing labour more efficiently. As the result of work study, it is revealed that as much as 40 per cent of an operator's time (apart from normal relaxation) is taken up by non-productive duties.

To give a further example, as a result of research at Birmingham into the use of 25-ton power presses, it was found that only 14 per cent of the jobs had a tonnage requirement of over 15 tons.

The real yardstick of value added to throughput material by production equipment and labour should be the value that *would* have been added by using the optimum size, *i.e.*, the correct machine for the job, working at the optimum machine speeds.

Rationalisation

The term "rationalisation" refers to the use of principles of reason, yet it is amazing how managements fail to rationalise their marketing, their production, their R. and D., and so on.

Thus, it has been found that a shirt manufacturer earned 60 per cent of his revenue from less than 25 per cent of his trading accounts, and that 25 per cent of his trading accounts produced less than 2 per cent of his revenue, in fact, 30 per cent of his trading accounts were unprofitable. This is the management accounting approach, and while it is obvious what needs to be done to rationalise the position, in practice, it is not always so simple, because a small customer may one day be a big customer, and a great deal of business is based on goodwill.

But, to take another example from the marketing area, salesmen often carry too big a load and cannot adequately cover the territory allocated, nor at the right intervals. In nearly every case investigated, Sales Audits Ltd. (consultants) found a need for re-allocating territories and re-planning routes.

Again, it is a question of how the existing revenue compares with expenses, and what it would be with better coverage and service to customers. There is often a reluctance to change, or reluctance to take the risk of change.

The need for rationalisation of product variety is really amazing in British industry. Thus, in one large iron and steel company, 1,500 varieties of steel specification were produced (apart from individual sizes and dimensions), whereas less than 10 per cent of these were needed to meet the technical requirements of the businesses. It has also been found in the electric industry that less than 20 per cent of the products contributed over 80 per cent of the added value.

In short, rationalisation not only increases efficiency, it also reduces stock-holdings (thus releasing capital) and greatly reduces costs.

Non-profit-making concerns

A large proportion of this country's productive capacity is in the social services, such as local government, civil service, hospitals, and so on. What is the test of management efficiency which can be applied to such enterprises?

As with business concerns, it is still whether it is achieving its objectives, and in the most economical way. A development of some note here, is the technique of "Planning Programming Budgeting," which is a way of spelling out the objectives into major programmes. Thus for a police service (*O. & M. Journal* November 1970) these were laid down as:

1. *Operational:* Ground cover.
   Crime investigation and control.
   Traffic control.
   Additional services.
2. *Support:* Management.
   Training.
   Support services.
3. *Overhead:* Pensions.
   Accommodation.

These areas are then broken down into other convenient groups, so that costings could be identified in terms of sections of responsibility. Computer information on detailed costs is then considered monthly, so that police management can make accurate decisions about resource allocation.

Thus, the technique is about (*a*) setting objectives, (*b*) giving better control, (*c*) helping decision-making for the future, and (*d*) assessing efficient use of resources.

Of course, the cost of running the service as set out above has to be compared with the objectives of the police force, which were stated by the Royal Commission on Police in 1962, as being:

1. Duty to maintain law and order and to protect persons and property.
2. To prevent crime.
3. To detect criminals and to play a part in the early stages of the judicial process.
4. To decide whether or not to prosecute.
5. To conduct prosecution for less serious offences.
6. To control road traffic and advise on traffic questions.
7. To conduct inquiries into applications by persons wishing British nationality.
8. To befriend anyone who needs help and advise with minor or major emergencies.

Non-profit-making efficiency

The use of P.P.B. is a step in the right direction, but in itself, it will not make for efficiency, for an enterprise might achieve its objectives at lowest cost, but have a high labour turnover, be rent by internal rivalries, and so on.

Of interest here is the following case study on the visit of management consultants to an Australian hospital, where, in addition to reducing costs, they succeeded in reducing labour turnover, improving morale, reducing interdepartmental friction, as well as reducing the stock of linen, and improving the efficiency of service departments such as laundry and catering.

CASE STUDY

Management efficiency

SYDNEY HOSPITAL

1. OBJECTS

To improve standards of patient care.
To provide more interesting work for staff.
To improve value obtained for money spent.

2. BACKGROUND

Sydney Hospital is Australia's oldest hospital, dating back to 1881.
It is a public teaching hospital, depending on Government subsidies.
It has 507 beds, of which only 459 are in use (staff shortages).

3. PROBLEMS

To devise a measure for an intangible result—"patient care," was not easy.
Staff shortages, particularly nursing, with high labour turnover.
Additional nursing services required by new specialist medical units—but with too few nursing staff.

4. METHODOLOGY

Instead of the usual investigations, followed by a glossy report, the management consultants held group discussions over several months, a major purpose of which was to encourage participation.

The first phase of a management development programme was to create a new awareness in people about their jobs; to agree the purposes of their work; to get them to differentiate between what was important in their jobs; and to see the need for setting standards of accomplishment.

The second phase was concerned with practical work: developing a measure of patient care; designing management controls for ward management.

5. RECOMMENDATIONS

1. Abolition of the centralised Matron's office, and making the Matron's post into Director of Nursing Services, and introducing a new decentralised nursing administrative structure.
2. Dividing the nursing service into three departments: Service (wards), Education, and Personnel, each headed by a Principal Nursing Officer.
3. A patient care check list (devised by the Sisters in their discussion sessions) was introduced.
4. Instituting regular weekly action meetings between the P.N.O. (Services) and her four senior nursing officers, who in turn held regular meetings with their charge sisters. The meetings are brief, but all decisions are recorded on an action statement. The purpose of such meetings was to decide *who* is to do *what*, and *when*.

5. The collection of control data, and institution of management controls, with subsequent interpretation of results and decision-making.

6. RESULTS

1. All managers now know more about their jobs.
2. A better service to the community, with 30 per cent more patients receiving treatment.
3. The cost of treating each patient is less than it was previously.
4. All staff now realise that management is not a solo performance, but an interdependent one, and all administrative staff are a part of management.
5. Better morale and better co-ordination, welding the diverse divisions and departments of the hospital into an integrated management entity.
6. Huge financial benefits.
7. Reduced labour turnover, and better job interest.

NOTE: This efficiency improvement project is seen to include Objectives, Organisation, Co-ordination, Control, Motivation, and staff participation.

[*The Hospital* July 1971

CHECK LIST

1. Have we established objectives of the enterprise?
2. Have we checked on labour productivity?
3. Have we checked on machine productivity?
4. Why not compare present with potential use of resources?
5. Have we checked on organisation and its effectiveness?
6. Have we assessed policies (either laid-down or implied) in the light of the objectives?
7. Have we assessed the impact of policies on one another, *e.g.*, sales and production, personnel, and shareholders?
8. Have we assessed financial policies, and whether they are integrated with general management policies?
9. Assessed the nature, extent, and frequency of controls?
10. Assessed measures of co-ordination inside the concern?
11. Are the right periods and the right subjects chosen in future forecasting and planning?
12. Does the overall organisation contribute to maximum efficiency?
13. To what extent can operations be rationalised?
14. Is there a good financial control system in being?
15. Is automation used to its fullest extent (materials handling does not have to be high cost)?

16. Has group technology been considered in the factory layout?
17. Has value analysis been attempted?
18. Are good methods of communication used, and are they effective?
19. Is there a proper policy and system for replacement of assets?
20. Could P.P.B. be used?

Chapter *13* Forecasting and planning

Forecasting and planning are separate activities, and yet they are inextricably bound together. No planning should be attempted without proper forecasting, and forecasting itself is not enough. The difference between the two words, is that "forecasting" is simply looking into the future, whereas "planning" is *the making of decisions on what should be done, where, how, and when it should be done.*

There is often some confusion between "policies" and "plans," and in fact the two are often identical. But a policy is an established way of doing things, or an internal law, whereas plans are the decisions made— often in accordance with the policies. Equally, policies are not always deliberately contrived, they often evolve in the course of making plans.

Office administration can assist very greatly in the forecasting of events, but in so far as plans involve policies, then it is more a matter of judgment.

Small and medium-sized concerns often find it difficult to indulge in anything but short-term planning, but the bigger an enterprise becomes, the more important planning becomes.

Importance

Planning is important for many reasons, not least being the psychological effect on staff, even if the plans are not accurate. But in addition it helps to classify the end results, or objectives, and to concentrate attention on what each section of the enterprise has to do in order to achieve the plans.

As mentioned above, it may even cause the adoption of policies which were not even thought of previously, and it helps anticipate problems and should help avert crises.

Plans are also important to an enterprise because they establish quantitative goals and thereby set up standards, which is the first step in establishing control.

So, planning is connected with policies, with communication, with co-ordination, with control, and with organisation. It should be noted that the ability to communicate plans to salesmen and others in the company whose co-operation is essential, is often more important than the brilliance of the plans—so that planning is related to morale, and a feeling that we are getting somewhere!

The normal sequence of events is therefore something like the following:

OBJECTIVES
↓
POLICIES
↓
PLANS
↓
STANDARDS
↓
WORKING RULES

Long-range planning

In the marketing field, a growing science of "econometrics" endeavours to plan scientifically, and when a car manufacturer has to plan at least three years ahead before production actually starts, it can be seen why L.R.P. is important to some industries.

L.R.P. has been defined as planning in excess of twelve months, and while I.B.M. plans for seven years ahead, and I.C.I. for ten years the large number of smaller concerns are happy if they can plan for twelve months ahead.

A great deal depends not only on size, but on the type of industry, thus even in a large firm with an international reputation, it was stated that its short-term forecasting had to be adjusted by as much as 25 per cent when an unexpected large foreign order was received. On the other hand, a medium-sized bakery finds that daily adjustments to its forecasts are necessary according to variations in the weather.

In the larger concern, no matter how difficult it is, there must be some element of L.R.P., because its major decisions (such as capital expenditure) are so important and so far-reaching. Thus, Pilkington decided as a long-term project to invest in R. and D. on "Armourclad" glass as a building material, and coupled with Management by Objectives, shows that the General Manager of Pilkington is convinced of the value of forward planning.

This emphasis on R. and D. is an essential part of planning, because with every product there is a definite life-cycle, and new products must always be planned to take the place of the old ones which are dying out.

Difficulties

In this connection, one of the difficulties of planning is that although the life-cycle of a product may be planned as in Fig. 4(*a*), as the result of new packaging, re-pricing, or change in the market, its real life-cycle might be more in accordance with Fig. 4(*b*).

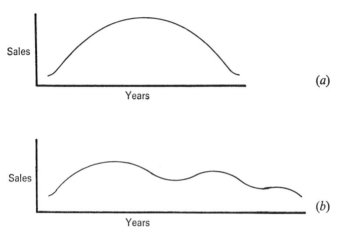

FIG. 4.—Showing how a normal product's life cycle may be (*a*) planned and (*b*) revised.

It is very difficult to plan precisely because even in a monopolistic concern there are so many factors which can upset the plans.

1. Technological change, by which a product becomes out of date, or can be produced at a tenth of the price.
2. Change in fashion, *i.e.*, fashion in the manner of usage, whether it be in eating habits, design of cars, or even the mode of living (*e.g.*, Do It Yourself has grown to a tremendous extent, thus changing the requirements in sizes of tins of paint).
3. The weather (the most unpredictable of all) can affect building, fruit bottling, frozen foods, as well as the sale of clothing and shoes.
4. Government restrictions may be increased or relaxed. Hire purchase is a good example here, which has for instance greatly affected the sale of motor bikes, and television sets.
5. Political events, such as entering the Common Market, can have a vast impact on the running of businesses.

This is apart from the fact that over-precise planning can dampen the initiative of staff, and that planning itself takes a great deal of time and can be expensive. In the section of the book dealing with Operational Research, it is stressed that however scientific a project, its accuracy depends on the accuracy of the premises used, and these are often nothing much more than "guesstimates."

Areas of planning

In recent years, emphasis has been given to the concept of corporate planning, which of course means the planning of all sides of an enterprise simultaneously, and is not anything very new. But it is nevertheless important, because in many concerns, planning is either restricted to this or that aspect, or different aspects are planned in isolation from one another.

Management has been said to be concerned with the four Ms: Men, Money, Materials, and Machines, and if to this is added Marketing, then it gives an indication of the areas of management which should be planned.

An accountant would probably place "money" or financial planning first (and in some concerns, this *is* the only planning aspect), but while it is important, it is probably not the most important.

1. In business, planning of the *marketing* side of the business should always have priority, because it is the life blood of the business, and as in budgetary control (*see below*), everything else depends on sales revenue.

    Marketing of course is a much wider term that just "sales," and includes transport, advertising, warehousing, packaging, and in fact everything involved in selling and transferring the product to the consumer.

2. Planning of *materials* means not only raw materials and their supply (or replacement), but also (this is half-way between production and sales) the R. and D. necessary for the development of new products.

3. Planning of *men*, or manpower planning as it is called today, means the careful forecasting of future requirements in terms of numbers and skills, and taking into account the labour turnover and retirements, what recruitment and promotions and training are necessary.

4. Planning of *machines* is essential (although often ignored) for it refers to a policy of planned replacement of machines, as well as to their planned maintenance.

    The corollary of this is, of course, that *production* must be jointly planned with marketing, for it is little use planning increased sales if the goods are not forthcoming.

5. Planning of *money*, or financial planning, is dealt with more fully below, but it is obviously related to all the above aspects of strategic planning. But it should be recognised that however restrictive money appears in the planning of other aspects, they are distinct, and very often the planning of more capital, for example, is a secondary consideration to the basic planning, *i.e.*, of what to do with it afterwards.

In all these areas of planning, the office can provide information, and it is here where "information services," *e.g.*, provided by a computer, can give the basic figures on which planning can be attempted.

Financial planning

The cornerstone of management accounting is budgetary control, which will be referred to later in the chapter dealing with management control, but here it is proposed to examine its planning aspect.

The essence of budgetary control is the planning of:

1. Sales budget;
2. Output budget;
3. Material budget;
4. Labour budget;
5. Expenses budget;
6. Capital budget;

and the *subsequent comparison* of actual events with these budgeted figures.

However, as an aspect of planning, how are these figures obtained? To take the most important first, the sales budget is supplied by the Marketing Manager, on information supplied by sales representatives. They are likely to submit (*a*) budgets that are too low, so that their actual sales appear to be brilliant, or (*b*) the Marketing Manager may impose tight (or high) budgets so as to increase sales by offering incentives.

With both of these approaches, it is doubtful if true planning is attempted, and it is therefore worth noting that in really large businesses, three sets of figures are often prepared, from the Marketing Manager, from the Market Research Division, and from the Company Economist, and the real planned sales figures will be found to be somewhere in between all three. The sales budget from inside the Sales Department is likely to be biased, the figure from Market Research is likely to be coloured by the nature of the research, and the economist's figures are likely to ignore the market state or the impact of competition and the Company policies.

It has been suggested (see *The Accountant*, May 1968) that in many firms it would be advisable to set sales targets contained in budgets separate from the actual planned (or expected) sales.

Financial planning apart from budgetary control also includes what additional capital will be required (*a*) for fixed assets, and (*b*) for working capital. In addition, an overall plan will indicate what profits will accrue (sometimes referred to as profit planning), and how much will be distributed to shareholders and how much retained. Again, one of the difficulties of planning is to make allowances for Government changes in profits tax, depreciation allowances, and so on (if possible!).

The aspects of corporate planning in a large business having a Planning Committee are shown in Fig. 5.

FIG. 5.—Co-ordination required from different departments in order to establish Corporate Planning.

Principles of planning

Some common principles of planning might be:

1. Plan for the right length of time.
2. In the right amount of detail—usually the further ahead the less the detail.
3. All possible courses of action must be considered before plans are finalised.
4. Planning must be based on facts as far as possible, more than on opinions.
5. Planning must be performed by the right persons (this is a matter of organisation) but usually top management plans strategy, middle management plans tactics, and lower levels plan operational policies.
6. Planning should be co-ordinated, and the effect of one plan should be considered in the light of its effect on another planned aspect of the concern.

7. Plans should always incorporate standards to give control.
8. The making of plans in itself is not enough, they should be communicated to all concerned with them.
9. Because planning can never be 100 per cent accurate, a degree of flexibility should always be included.
10. Plans must be feasible, and not too ambitious, nor too timorous.

It must be remembered, even in the smallest business, that there must be some planning, even if it is only to ensure that there is sufficient money in the bank to pay the wages at the end of the week. It is all a question of degree.

Technique of planning

Top management plans strategy, objectives and policies, middle management plans tactics and facilities, while supervisors plan working activities. Thus planning is carried on at all levels of management, becoming narrower and more precise at the lower levels.

But some common stages can be observed in whatever type of planning is involved:

1. a clear statement of objectives (in the case of supervisors, it may be the purposes of the work);
2. appraisal of the present position;
3. a survey of the different courses of action available, with the possible advantages and disadvantages of each (it has been said that if there are no alternative courses of action, then there can be no planning);
4. collection and analysis of data (this is the office function, and where computers can be useful in larger concerns);
5. making decisions on the course of action to be taken (including measurable standards at the same time);
6. take steps necessary to implement the plan.

Planning in the office

Although planning is an aspect of general management, which will occupy more time of top executives, it is also an aspect of office supervision, and an office supervisor should plan:

1. office systems;
2. continuous flow of work;

3. division of work among personnel (organisation);
4. layout of office furniture and equipment;
5. replacement and maintenance of office machines;
6. controls over quantity and quality of work;
7. time-scheduling, where work has to be performed to a timetable;
8. records and reporting systems to give control;
9. training and interchange of staff to cover absences.

Unfortunately, there is often insufficient delegation of authority for supervisors to perform such planning, and middle management rarely has the time, so that many aspects of such office planning are overlooked.

CASE STUDY

Planning

THE BATA ORGANISATION

1. Unique in many ways, the Bata Organisation has spread into 65 different countries and employs more than 50,000 people; the smallest unit has 10, and the largest 15,000.
2. Their products—shoes—are the subject of fashion whim and furthermore market conditions vary from one territory to another.
3. There are in fact 58 independent Bata companies, each of which has its own board of directors and each is largely self-financed.
4. Planning is achieved by two "service" companies, one in Canada and one in the U.K., which have advisory functions only. Their function is to advise on technical and commercial research, forecasting and personnel development.
5. From its local knowledge, each operating company draws up a five-year plan, known throughout the organisation as "Pathfinder;" it is based on experience, local Government regulations, business statistics, and market conditions.
6. Each "Pathfinder" plan is reviewed annually, and it

> (*a*) sets specific company targets;
> (*b*) provides a yardstick by which progress can be measured; and

(c) places a restraint on over-ambitious short-term projects (this is important to prevent over-stocking, over-selling, or acquisition of too many commitments).

7. Each company then makes a six-monthly short-term plan, divided into weekly figures, which are used for setting sales quotas, purchasing quotas, personnel targets, etc. With supporting figures it gives detail of organisation, capital expenditure, and a financial plan—in keeping of course with its five-year plan.

8. Control checks are provided by:

   (a) weekly operating result statements;

   (b) weekly financial statements (showing profit or loss),

   both of which are compared with the short-term and the long-term plans, and immediate action is taken if the results are not up to 100 per cent of the estimates.

9. While the availability of money has a great influence on these plans, the companies place great emphasis on research into design, sales techniques, layout of shops, and management methods.

10. An important aspect of Bata's planning is executive development, because the Company takes the view that plans are of no use without the right people to implement them. So they are continuously considering the executive manpower requirements of all the companies.

CHECK LIST

1. Is planning worthwhile, and is it possible?
2. Who has authority to make plans?
3. Are there company objectives in being?
4. Would M.B.O. help in setting lower-level objectives?
5. Study the present position, and ask, is it different from the objectives?
6. Is the obvious choice of action the best one to make?
7. Is all the information available to help make the choice of action?
8. Is the information available quickly or is it delayed?
9. Have we taken into account all the constraints in the circumstances?
10. Have we taken note of the established Board policies?
11. Are the plans in the right amount of detail?
12. Is there corporate planning, with the proper degree of co-ordination?
13. Is there sufficient participation in making plans so as to gain enthusiasm of the executives?
14. Is the plan feasible, or is it just "pie in the sky?"
15. Is it flexible, so that it can be adjusted in view of changing circumstances?

16. Is there a regular office system coupled with the right organisation?
17. Is the plan for the right length of time?
18. Is the plan when finalised based on facts and not on opinion?
19. How often should the plan be revised?
20. Do the plans include measurable targets, so that future comparisons can be made?

Chapter 14 Organisation

Basically, "organisation" is concerned with work—with how it is allocated, and what authority and responsibility is delegated, and with how many sections, and of what size exist. The bigger an enterprise becomes, the more important will organisation become.

This basic definition of organisation is sometimes referred to as the *mechanistic* theory, but there have grown up many other theories, which all have some substance, and the real nature of organisation probably contains elements of all of them.

There is the *human relations* theory, which stresses the humanistic aspects, and which states that the human relationships of people in a concern are the most important thing in organisation. This is partly true, because no matter how carefully devised the formal organisation, its successful working will depend ultimately on the calibre of staff employed and the morale inside the concern.

Then, there is the *systems* theory that organisation is based on office systems (to put it crudely), and methods employed. There is also some substance in this theory because, for example, when a business changes its information system to a computerised one, it changes the organisation totally.

Lastly, there is the *communication* theory, which states that organisation is based on the communications which flow from one section to another, and there is something in this theory, because the greater the volume of communication (formally or informally) the greater will be the influence on the type of organisation.

However, whatever view is taken, one thing is certain, that organisation is a dynamic flexible thing which varies not only from one concern to another, but also from time to time in the same enterprise. There can be no such thing as a standard organisation of different enterprises of different sizes concerned with different things. A golden principle of organisation is that it should always be dynamic and not static, and should change with the requirements of the concern.

Symptoms of bad organisation

While it is difficult to say what is a good organisation (because of its diversity), it is fairly easy to detect bad organisation. In Chapter 7 were listed some of the faults relating to *office* organisation, and in addition the following are often found in the overall organisation of an enterprise:

1. Insufficient delegation. Thus, the former chief executive of B.E.A. once stated that he even had to approve the employment of two extra staff, say in Istanbul—this in an organisation of 20,000 employees!

2. Failure to delineate responsibilities, or where they are so diffuse, that organisational sins of omission or commission go unpunished, and it is just nobody's fault.

3. Where specialists have too much executive authority. Thus, in one large publicly-owned company, a computer specialist succeeded in losing millions of pounds before management consultants recommended the company to keep to its main line of business (publishing).

4. Lack of co-ordination, whereby different departments follow different policies about the same things.

5. Too much central control (rather similar to (1)), where the result is bureaucracy and management by rules, thus deadening initiative and inhibiting improvements.

6. Little cliques within the formal organisation, that effectively destroy the team spirit, and make co-ordination of effort impossible.

7. Too little control, so that staff do not properly perform their duties, nor get reprimanded for not doing so.

8. Too few members of management allowed to make decisions. This, of course, is in keeping with 1 and 5 above, but concentrates on decision-making, instead of taking action. This applies particularly to middle management, which is most important for the successful working of any enterprise.

9. Failure to define authority, so that the subordinates only discover their limits when they exceed it.

In fact there are many more faults in organisation, but usually they are variations of one or other of the above.

Importance of organisation

It can be seen from the above that organisation is important because it is related to:

1. responsibility;
2. authority;
3. co-ordination;
4. control;
5. communication;
6. morale;
7. work.

The problem with a management services investigation is that what appears to be a problem of control or communication often reveals itself to be basically one of organisation. The difficulty is that while for academic purposes, management can be examined under all these different headings, in practice each is inextricably bound up with the others, and it is a question of close analysis to discover which is the main element at fault.

Furthermore, while, for example, a major fault may be lack of delegation, this is a human fault, and no matter how much training is given, to improve the situation may require replacement of an executive (however good he may be in other ways) by one who *can* delegate. This failure, unwillingness to delegate, is a common fault in organisation, and has repercussions in all directions.

Types of organisation

Brech has stated that there is only one type of organisation, *i.e.*, the line type, and that all others are elaborations of it. This is very true, although the elaborations in large concerns can be quite fantastic.

Nevertheless, as quoted in numerous management textbooks, there can be said to be four main types:

1. Line.
2. Functional.
3. Line and staff.
4. Committee.

What this means in a *functional* type, is that although there are line officers (*e.g.*, local supervisors) the organisation basically has managers in a functional capacity, such as O. & M., Personnel Officer, and so on.

Similarly, in a *committee* type of organisation, although there are line officers, the concern is run predominantly by committees (usually advisory to the managing committee, as in local government).

A *line* organisation is a vertical one, where there are seniors and juniors working in fairly watertight departments of the business, and executives in fairly powerful positions in charge of the separate departments or sections of the business.

The difficulty with a simple line organisation is that it may be very difficult to change it because of the powerful positions of the top executives, although it has obvious advantages of fixing responsibility. Another of its main disadvantages is that it usually suffers from lack of co-ordination.

A functional organisation can be said to be horizontal where managers are responsible for certain areas of work *throughout the concern*, and a *line and staff* organisation is one which consists of vertical and horizontal management.

The line and staff type should be ideal, having the simplicity of direct line management coupled with the expertise of functional management as well. But, in practice, it is rarely ideal. Perhaps one of the main difficulties is that if the specialists are made advisory only, their advice can be ignored (and as Joan Woodward reported, it frequently is), and if they are given executive powers, then there is schism with the line managers.

The management services department itself is a functional activity, and the only way out of the organisational dilemma is to make the functional experts advisory only, but responsible to the chief executive, who can give their findings his authority.

With the *committee* type of organisation, there is a panoply of advisory sub-committees to whom decision-making is delegated, and unless sufficient authority is actually delegated, such committees feel frustrated and there may also be inordinate delays in referring matters from one committee to another. The only answer here is a very tight timetable for committee meetings, so that decisions are not too long delayed.

While it is easy to talk about types of organisation, in practice, larger concerns are always a glorious mixture of line, functional, committee, and so on, but it is as well to recognise the influences at work in an organisation and to recognise the advantages and disadvantages of the different elements within it.

Specialists

The use of specialisation in office organisation was discussed in Chapter 7, but it is suggested that this is really different from the use of specialists. A specialist must be employed on a functional basis, without using the principle of rigid specialisation within the department.

Line managers are of course specialists in marketing, production, and so on, partly related to their employment, but the employment of specialist advisors (functional experts) creates the problem of how to use specialists.

This is related to the problem of line and staff organisation, mentioned above. Hooper once said that "specialists should be on tap and not on top," which from a management efficiency point of view is very true. Where specialists become too powerful, then management tends to become out of balance, because specialists have by their very nature narrow outlooks related to their specialisms.

Efficient management will ensure that it employs specialists and that it makes the best use of them, but if they are given too much authority, then (as with computer experts), management tends to be in their hands, and even their own particular language is a barrier to their proper use. It is management's job to balance the use of specialists, and to ensure that the best use is made of their advice, while not being in their hands. Management services experts are, of course, by nature, broad in their outlook, without any particular bias one way or the other.

Centralisation

One of the main problems in organisation in a large concern is centralisation. This does not necessarily mean putting all the typists into one room as with central typing, but in the broader context, means the emphasis on control from the centre. It is not a question of whether to have central control or not, because in a business with 1,500 shops like Boots the Chemists, it is necessary to have *some* central control; again, it is all a matter of degree.

Central control has in many cases been accelerated by the use of a Head Office computer, for even if it does not really exercise more control, the computer because of its insistence on deadlines for supply of data, appears to exercise control over all departments for which it performs.

Whenever management consultants are called in to examine the organisation of large concerns (B.B.C., Shell, Bank of England, etc.), the recommendations nearly always contain proposals for a degree of decentralisation. It seems, by the very nature of things, that large concerns tend to concentrate authority at Head Office.

Too much central control results in bureaucracy, frustration of staff, deadening of initiative, and a degree of rigidity in management style. Too little central control, and all control disintegrates, and co-ordination is impossible.

There should be some areas of delegated authority, subject perhaps to global financial controls, and there should be some areas of central control which are essential to co-ordination and overall management. This mixture of central and local decision-making and control needs to be worked out to suit the requirements of each individual enterprise, and no precise proportions can be laid down. It has been stated, with some truth, that the nearer the working level decisions are made, the better are they likely to be.

The problem of centralisation is also related to the number of levels of management, because the greater the number of levels, the more will authority be pared away at different levels, so that at working level or just above, there is next to no residual authority left at all. Even large concerns like I.B.M. have shown that with many thousands of employees, it is still possible to reduce the number of levels of management to half of what is found in much smaller concerns.

Working relationships

Some view formal, and human (or informal) relationships as being the basis of successful organisation, and it is certainly an important part of the total concept of organisation.

Apart from human groupings (*see below*), the following are some of the relationships which exist:

1. *Line relationship* of junior and senior, where the junior works subject to the direction and control of the senior for the performance of some of the delegated authority. But this simple relationship can be complicated by a state of full control (no managers above), or indirect control (with a line manager in between the senior and the working level), or partial control, when there are several line managers above.

2. *Functional relationship*, as mentioned above, which is usually said to be an expert giving advice; but because of their elevated positions in the hierarchy, functional officers often acquire executive authority even though it has not been officially given to them.

3. *Staff relationship* exists when an Assistant to a Manager is in an advisory position yet has certain specific delegated area of authority and responsibility, and it can be seen that by its very nature it is not the same as being Deputy Manager, nor yet a simple line relationship.

4. *Associate relationship* exists between employees on the same level in different departments, *e.g.*, supervisors in different departments, who are expected to co-operate and work together, yet

without forgetting their obligations to their respective line managers.

5. *Working relationship* exists where in the course of work an employee is required to give information or act on information received from other employees, perhaps in other departments. It is not a question of senior and junior, nor merely of being an associate, but a relationship arising from the exigencies of the work requirements.

6. *Service relationship* exists when a particular department is providing a service for all other departments. This occurs when a typing pool is established, and the officials in other departments are not necessarily superior to the typists, and it is perhaps one of the most difficult of relationships because it is one demanding co-operation from both sides, and one which can easily become upset.

Informal organisation

The human behaviourists would have us believe that informal organisation is the most important, and it is certain that communication, co-ordination, and even successful working of the whole organisation do depend on co-operation and human qualities.

Informal organisation can be said to consist of (*a*) informal grouping, (*b*) informal leadership, and (*c*) informal communication. Whatever formal grouping of staff exists, there will always be natural grouping of staff by reason of language, religion, the old school tie, or even unrecognised subdivisions of work, and although it aids co-operation, it can also help set up informal cliques.

Unless the formal leadership is effective, then informal leaders will be set up, and it is usually somebody with great technical knowledge and experience to whom workers go with their problems.

Informal communication is used all the time, partly as the result of human relationships. Nearly always, there is some kind of informal meeting between some of the committee members, before a formal meeting is held. In addition, there is always informal discussion on minor points before an official action is taken, particularly on personnel matters.

The difficulty of informal organisation is that it is most influential, yet difficult to detect, and cannot be shown on an organisation chart.

It is most important because it represents perhaps the true organisation, and as Robert Townsend in *Up the Organisation* discovered, very rarely does the real working of a concern correspond with its splendid official organisation chart.

Committees

Committees are a part of all large organisations today, and their effective use depends on:

1. Having not too big a committee, otherwise time is wasted on fruitless and detailed discussion.
2. Having the right people as members, *i.e.*, not those who enjoy the arena or playing to the gallery, or are brave but ignorant.
3. Having the right person as chairman, which means somebody who is business-like yet commands respect, not one who domineers, but is impartial and know what the chairman's job really is.
4. Having the right constitution regarding the fixing of a quorum, the giving of notice, and the taking of votes, etc.
5. Ensuring that the authority and responsibility of the committee is definitely laid down so that it is clear not only what it can do, but what it should be doing.
6. Ensuring the supply of proper secretarial service to provide agenda, minutes, etc.

Provided these rules are adhered to, committees can be a useful adjunct to an organisation, improving communication, co-ordination, education, and participation, as well as improving morale and team-work. But if badly managed, they can become "talk shops," which waste time, are too slow, and make weak decisions which are useless.

Analysing the organisation

Before it is possible to improve any organisation, it is necessary to:

1. analyse it to ascertain what it is, and
2. determine its faults,

before making suggestions for improvement.

Of course, the starting-point in analysing an organisation is to obtain a copy (or to draw one up) of:

1. the *Organisation Chart* which portrays the kind of organisation, shows how it is divided, how many levels of management, and so on.
2. Since the organisation chart only shows the formal organisation, to assess by discreet and wide inquiry, the *informal organisation*.
3. Since the organisation chart shows only job titles and not their content, to obtain or draw up the official authority, responsibilities and duties of each post (*i.e.*, Job Descriptions).

Improving an organisation

After analysing the organisation, and identifying faults (see beginning of Chapter), comes the process of improvement.

To help in assessing the organisation and what it should be, a check list can be used to examine it in detail (see example at end of Chapter).

Decide on the objectives of the enterprise, if not already laid down, and then decide on what work is to be done to achieve these objectives. Having done this, examine all the alternative methods of allocation of work and division of work to achieve the objectives, bearing in mind control, cost, co-ordination, and so on.

Having proposed tentative proposals for a new organisation, it might be advisable to call a meeting of executives to obtain their reactions (if there is likely to be strong resentment, such a meeting might be better called by the chief executive).

Once the new organisation has been achieved, draw up a fresh organisation chart, and new job descriptions, and circulate them so that everybody is informed.

Subsequently, frequent checks might be made to see if the new organisation is functioning as well as expected, or whether it needs amendment.

CASE STUDY

Organisation

JOHN MCLEAN AND CO.

1. BACKGROUND

John McLean and Company, building contractors of Wolverhampton, have grown in fifteen years from a one-man business to have a turnover of £1,500,000.

2. PROBLEMS

(a) There was great strain in the management, and lack of co-ordination.

(b) Too many staff had direct access to the Managing Director.

(c) No formal meetings were held.

(d) The real purpose of the Board (policy-making) had gone by default and had devolved on the two Managing Directors.

3. REVIEW OF ORGANISATION

Management consultants were requested to review the organisation, and from the reports received, it was obvious that there was:

(a) lack of a planned management structure;

(b) lack of effective delegation; and

(c) the organisation structure must be designed to do the work required, and not fit the skills and personnel available.

4. AREAS OF ATTENTION

The main areas needing attention were:

(a) the role of the board of directors;

(b) the position of the Managing Directors; and

(c) the activities of other executive Directors.

5. IMPLEMENTATION

(a) The consultants recommended the appointment of several outside Directors (the one recommendation that was not followed).

(b) The broad duties (particularly policy-making) of the Board were summarised and recorded.

(c) The main trouble in the organisation was the position relating to the joint Managing Directors. The solution here was that one was made Chairman of the Board, and the other the sole Managing Director.

(d) The position of the Managing Director was also clarified: he was to be responsible to the Board for the conduct of the Company. He was responsible for interpreting the policy made by the Board; for seeing that it was carried out; and for the co-ordination of the work of the other executives who were responsible to him.

(e) Another cause of difficulty was the executive Directors who were clear that their authority was delegated to them from the Managing Director; a start was made in defining their respective duties to eliminate overlapping.

(f) The administration was divided into six departments: office, research, planning, supply, production, and sales, and five departmental managers were appointed, responsible to the Managing Director.

(g) Another specific direction was that Departmental Managers should delegate to their subordinates.

(h) An appointment of Personal Assistant to the Managing Director was made, to co-ordinate the day-to-day activities of the managers, and to allow the Managing Director to concentrate on longer-term projects. Although resisted at first, this has proved to be a very valuable improvement to the organisation.

6. RESULTS

(*a*) The Company now has a clear-cut organisation structure related to the work requirements.

(*b*) There is better co-ordination.

(*c*) Responsibility and authority are much more clearly defined.

(*d*) Delegation is seen to be the keystone of good organisation.

(*e*) Even site management has improved owing to reorganisation at site level.

[*Business* February 1961

CHECK LIST

1. Have objectives been formulated, and does each person know them and understand them?
2. How are the departments or sections divided, is it the best division (*e.g.*, by product, should it be by function, or vice-versa)?
3. Is each of the units in the organisation justified at present (sometimes old units are really superfluous)?
4. Is there sufficient centralisation to give adequate control?
5. Is there sufficient decentralisation to make the best use of staff?
6. Is responsibility properly defined for all work areas?
7. Is authority sufficiently delegated to allow proper work performance?
8. Moreover, does each person know of his authority and responsibility?
9. Is there the right balance between authority and responsibility of different work units?
10. Is the best use made of specialists, or are they ignored?
11. Is there sufficient flexibility in the organisation, so that adjustments can be quickly made for changes in nature or volume of work?
12. Are the right decisions being made by the right persons?
13. Is the span of control of executives too wide or too narrow?
14. Do duties and responsibilities include the exercise of controls?
15. Is there adequate provision for co-ordination?
16. Are there too many time-wasting committees, or should there be more?
17. Is the informal organisation too much out of line with the formal?
18. Are job descriptions in use, so that the authority and responsibility of different executives is clear?
19. Is there a clear line of communication and accountability from one level of management to another?
20. Above all, is the organisation so complex that it fails to achieve its tasks, because nobody understands it?

Chapter 15 Command, authority, and decision-making

The word "command" is often viewed as being too strong in meaning for what it is really concerned with, *i.e.*, the achieving of action. It connotes the giving of orders, when in fact a good deal of action is achieved by quiet suggestion, by advice, and even by calling for volunteers. It depends on the subject-matter of the "command."

This achieving of action will, of course, greatly depend on the authority of the person giving instructions, etc., and "authority" in its classical or mechanistic meaning is *the right to make decisions and/or the right to take action*. This has been called "legal authority" for it is that authority conferred by a senior body. There is little doubt that however much legal authority a person may have, it is not likely to be effective unless it is also accompanied by some personal authority, and perhaps with some reputational authority (sapiential).

Since authority includes the right to make decisions, it is therefore closely concerned with decision-making.

Importance

Command and authority are important for many reasons. In the first instance, they will be relevant to action taken, decisions made, and results achieved.

Secondly, authority is a part of organisation, and the right authority in the right degree should be allocated, so that personnel are permitted to take action and make decisions. A common failure, particularly in large enterprises, is the under-delegation of authority, so that action is not taken at all.

Thirdly, they are basically concerned with communication, for the giving of effective instructions, etc., depends on how the order is communicated.

Fourthly, they are related to control for if there is too much authority delegated, then there is a loss of control and a basic principle of all delegation is that since the delegator is ultimately responsible for what

132

is delegated, he should exercise a degree of control over what is performed in his name.

Lastly, since it is concerned with decision-making, it is of such vital importance that the wrong decisions may influence the whole future of a concern.

Achieving action

It is useful to recognise the different ways of achieving action, the foremost being:

1. *By command:* when management has already made a decision.
2. *By request:* to experienced staff, to a person on equal footing, to an older man, etc.
3. *By suggestion:* where something new is being tried out as a trial run, particularly with experienced workers, and when it is wished to develop initiative.
4. *Call for volunteers:* for extra-heavy work, dangerous work, or for an extra amount of overtime.

If the wrong style is adopted for a particular communication, it can upset morale, and may not achieve the action hoped for. Thus for special extra duty, a command might simply result in the employees (just coincidentally) going on sick leave!

In a survey made by Dr. G. Copeman, it was found that about 30 per cent of instructions passed to subordinates were "firm instructions," another 30 per cent were requests, and the remainder were points of broad guidance.

The "law of the situation" (M. P. Follett) should not be overlooked; this states, more or less, that workers take action indicated by the circumstances, without waiting for a superior to give them instructions at all.

Directives

Directives can be described as written instructions to staff, and which can be said to be of three types:

1. *Procedure directives:* deciding what operations have to be performed, what forms have to be completed, and how and when.
2. *Policy directives:* outlining policies, giving guidelines to action.
3. *Combinations of* 1 *and* 2: concerned with both policy and procedures.

Sometimes, a procedure directive is circulated, which involves a change of policy, and management does not even bother to explain any reasons for the change. But it is suggested that employees will accept change much more readily if reasons are given, particularly if the advantages to the employees themselves are emphasised.

Where a concern issues an information bulletin to its staff, it often merges important policy directives with temporary less-important information (say, about sports meetings, etc.), and it would be better if the two were clearly separated (perhaps on different coloured paper), so that it is clear to the recipients which are important, and which are less important.

Issuing directives

1. They should be clearly written and concise, without the need for redundant summaries of contents.
2. It should be clear who has authority to issue duty instructions, and responsibility should be assigned for doing so.
3. It is useful if the directives have a classification, *e.g.*, numbers and dates, so that they can be identified.
4. Distribution should be stated at the top, so that there is no doubt for whom they are intended.
5. If important, then they might be pre-punched, and even folders issued for filing them.
6. If a directive countermands a previous one, it should state which one is repealed.
7. Checks should be made that they are taken note of, because if they are derided and are ineffective, then some other or additional method of communication might be advisable.
8. Groups of directives on related subjects might be issued as separate manuals.
9. Wherever possible, the illustrated sample method should be used showing how a form is completed, etc.

But no matter how important a directive is, its effectiveness will only be as good as its users wish it to be, so general morale is related to effectiveness. If too many directives, or too much information, is issued, it tends to become increasingly ineffective.

Decision-making

Decision-making has become so important in management that it has been called the new science of "praxeology." Decisions can be based on:

1. Past experience.
2. Research.
3. Tests.

In practice, all three methods are often used simultaneously, thus in sales forecasting, a business will examine its past statistics, undertake market research, and perhaps have some test-marketing.

The tendency in the past decade has been for decision-making to become more scientific, and numerous techniques can be used, some of which are mentioned here, but it is doubtful whether precise methods always lead to precise solutions.

The four steps in any decision-making process are:

1. Collate information, and analyse, categorise, etc.
2. Examine different actions which could, must, or ought to be taken, and examine the pros and cons.
3. Make a decision—which depends on how much legal authority is conferred.
4. Execute the decision, *e.g.*, by the issue of directives (*see above*) to see that it is effected.

The B.I.M. in its Checklist No. 19 gives as its first step "identification of the causes and extent of the problem," and in fact Professor Drucker has stated that the first step in decision-making is identifying what the real problem is. Thus, a problem apparently about clash of personalities, may be one of organisation, one of cost controls, may really be of policy, and so on. The content of the B.I.M. Checklist (in shortened form) is:

1. *Identify causes and extent of the problem:* all the factors, why is a decision needed; what are the critical issues, etc.?
2. *What circumstances affect the method of dealing with it?:* can it be delegated? are there limitations of time, cost, etc.? have similar problems arisen before? and what is the degree of urgency?
3. *Identify the long- and short-term objectives:* are they feasible? in the interests of the organisation? what about future plans?
4. *Collect and analyse all relevant information:* what degree of accuracy, where? what information? can external help be used? is the information reliable, sufficient?
5. *Explore all possible alternative solutions:* with possible actions; can scientific methods be used? have critical areas been obscured by minor problems?
6. *Take action to implement your decision:* what action? how long should it take? who will implement it? and what effect will it have on others? and what is the follow-up and control?

1. SCIENTIFIC TECHNIQUES

The reduction of problems to quantitative terms and the use of mathematical and statistical devices is on the increase, as it should be if it relieves management of decision-making, and if it makes the decisions taken more reliable. Unfortunately, the best that can be said about the use of such methods is that they offer a "navigational aid" to assist decision-making, while some of the protagonists claim 100 per cent accuracy for their techniques. The main reasons for the lack of precision are that the premises which are used and quantified, are not inviolable, and must be based on past experience (*e.g.*, usage in stock control), but is not necessarily reliable in future calculations; there are so many things which defy measurement (such as influence of fashion); and, however accurate a forecast may be, it can be so easily upset by external factors (thus, a change in rates of taxation can make nonsense of the most carefully devised D.C.F. calculation).

Operational Research is dealt with in other Chapters, so mention is made here only of the different scientific techniques which can assist decision-making.

1. *Decision trees:* this is where a diagram depicts different courses of action, quantifies the results of such action, and where by simple mathematical calculation, the results of each line of action can then be compared.

Example:

Problem: to close down a production line (and so reduce production), normally 80, to 60 a week, or to continue with it in the hope that sales will improve?

Answer:

The top arm of the decision tree in Fig. 6 represents a cut in production (60 a week), and the most optimistic and most pessimistic sales forecast of each course of action are also drawn in as an extension. The same is also done for the lower arm—*i.e.*, keeping the production line (80 a week). The two extensions of each course of action, *i.e.*, optimistic (say, 20 per cent), normal (say, 60 per cent), and pessimistic (say, 15 per cent) can then be calculated.

Then, by multiplying each of the cash flows by its relative percentage and calculating an average, it can be found that Course A will give £86,200, and Course B £78,200 net cash flows, so that with a difference of a mere £8,000 it is not worth losing morale and good workmen involved in closing down the

NET CASH FLOWS (£)

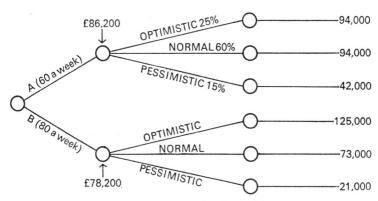

FIG. 6.—An example of a decision tree.

production line. The decision is made to retain the production
as it is.

2. *Algorithms:* the word means "orderly procedure," and seeks to
reproduce all the decisions inherent in a system, so that all that
is necessary is to read what is relevant to your problem, and the
answer is indicated (*see* Fig. 7). It is not as much concerned with
quantitative results, as with the progression of decisions and
their sequence.

Example:

To decide the rate of National Insurance Contribution (*see*
Fig. 7). (This is now changed by current legislation on N.I.)

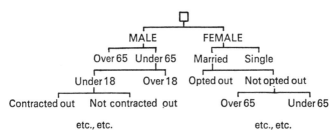

FIG. 7.—This algorithm shows the factors in deciding rates of National
Insurance.

3. *Decision tables:* a formal method of recording the conditions
applying to a particular action and to the actions which result
from these conditions.

The tables were devised for use in connection with computer

systems, and they reduce the conditions to a table so that it is immediately clear which will be accepted, and which will not. Figure 8 is a simple example, but it demonstrates the theory.

CONDITIONS		RULES					
	1	2	3	4	5	6	7
60% plus in Examination	Y	Y	Y	N	N	N	N
Satisfactory Interview	Y	N	N	Y	Y	N	N
Good reports	–	Y	N	Y	N	Y	N
ACTIONS							
Accept	X	X		X			
Reject			X		X	X	X

(Y = Yes   N = No)

The Action thus depends on Examination Result, Interview and Report.

FIG. 8.—A decision table.

2. TECHNIQUE OF DECISION-MAKING

Decision-making is important, because it affects, and in fact often makes, the policy involved in the decisions, because it is an aspect of authority, and because it is related to controls. It is exercised at all levels of management, but the important decisions are usually handled by a select few of the top managers of a business concern.

There are four main stages in decision-making:

1. *Information* is gathered on all circumstances which affect the decision; it needs to be analysed and categorised, and reduced to simple terms so that it can be easily assimilated.
2. *Findings*—considering alternative decisions, with all the parameters, and looking at:
   (a) action which *could* be taken;
   (b) action which *must* be taken;
   (c) action which *ought to* be taken.
3. *Decision* on the action which should be taken, and here, the structural authority may decide on what kind of action.
4. *Execution*—concerned with the proper way of executing the decision.

These various stages may be undertaken by individuals or by committees. In fact, in some concerns 1 and 2 are performed by individuals, 3 by a committee, and 4 by individuals again.

3. DISTRIBUTION OF DECISION-MAKING

How authority to make decisions is distributed in an enterprise will have a great effect on its efficiency. For example, in a highly centralised concern, where there is little delegation of authority, there is more likely to be bureaucracy and red tape in evidence.

In a more informal organisation, not only is it not clear who makes decisions, but any difficult decisions may be just passed from one manager to another, without any action being taken at all.

Even in a formal organisation, very often decisions are made by the wrong people, at the wrong level, which of course is a sign of bad organisation.

But perhaps the commonest fault is where too many decisions are made at top level, leaving lower levels of management constrained and with minimum authority.

4. CLASSIFICATION OF DECISIONS

After identifying the areas where decisions have to be made, comes the problem of classifying the decisions for different levels of management.

Classification of decisions has been attempted by many management writers varying from (*a*) simple policy decisions, and (*b*) problem-solving (*i.e.*, the rest), up to six-level stratification by Paterson; in between is Dr. Simon's (*a*) non-programmed decisions, (*b*) partially-programmed, and (*c*) highly-programmed decisions.

Lastly, there is Professor Jaques's "time span theory" which is based on the emphasis on the futurity of the decision-making, although it is suggested that this is really only one element of decision-making.

On a more pragmatic level, Dr. Copeman in recent years has suggested a division of management decision-making into:

1. the right to increase staff working under them;
2. the right to employ and dismiss staff;
3. the right to increase wages and salaries of their subordinates;
4. authority to order raw materials and supplies, and
5. authority to order capital equipment.

This leaves out main policy decisions (*e.g.*, which product to make, and at what price), concerned with the spending of money, and of course a very important area of decision-making.

5. COMPUTERS AND DECISION-MAKING

Management can (for the sake of convenience) be divided into three levels:

1. top management, concerned with strategy (what shall be done);
2. middle management, concerned with administration (how it shall be done), and
3. supervisory management concerned with operations (actually doing things).

The computer does not make decisions (apart from doing so according to its programme), but it does provide management with the information on which decisions can be made, and for 2 and 3 above, a computer can give useful information on sales analysis, costings, production control, etc., which are an obvious aid in making decisions at those levels. There is no doubt that the computer has thus saved many levels of management from making decisions which previously would have been little short of "guesstimates."

However, there is little doubt that the greatest areas of specialisation where computers have valuable potential is in strategic decision-making. By the use of storage and retrieval of data environmental to the decision, comparison with internally generated data, and the use of simulated models, much can be achieved.

For example, a businessman is faced with the problem of whether or not to invest in a new technological development of relevance to his product. He is able to identify the four environmental areas which would most likely affect his decision: 1 the chance of successful production with the new technology, 2 the advent of Government legislation affecting his processes, 3 the possibility of shortage of existing material, and 4 the chance of price increases adversely affecting the new material. On each of the variables, a statistical range is drawn up (say, price increase ranging from 1–20 per cent), with the probable expectation being employed. All the variables at different values are then built into a computer model, and after a computer run, the results are summarised, so that he has a table of alternatives, with the likely results of their employment.

It will be noted that the success of such a simulation method requires: 1 correct identification of the parameters of the decision-making, 2 still requires emphasis on the probable environmental happenings, and even then, 3 leaves the manager with the job of making the decision between the alternatives presented.

A problem with the use of computers is that there may be more figures produced, but less really relevant information. This is downright bad management and a failure to evaluate the factors involved in decision-making.

CASE STUDY

MARKS AND SPENCER LTD.

Policy

1. OBJECT

To reduce paperwork, to simplify the work, and generally to improve Company housekeeping and make the best use of staff.

2. RECOMMENDATIONS

1. *Sensible approximation*—the price of perfection is prohibitive. Where it is costly to account precisely, an approximation is likely to do just as well and give considerable economies. For most purposes, quantities of stock, sales, etc., are expressed in terms of sterling selling price in round figures.
2. *Reporting by exception*—it is assumed that events will occur as arranged or anticipated. For example, the arrival of stores of goods offered by Head Office is not reported to headquarters, only non-arrivals and discrepancies are reported.
3. *Manuals*—No attempt is made to legislate for every contingency and every eventuality. Before simplification, there were thirteen instruction manuals, now there are basically two small booklets, a Guide to Staff Management and Store Regulations. Officers in charge are now left to make most of the decisions themselves and to settle their own problems.
4. *Decategorisation*—The number of different grades of staff in stores has been dramatically reduced; people's work is no longer classified in watertight compartments but has been placed in general categories. They are used where and when needed; at busy periods everyone is required to man the counters irrespective of his or her grade or position.
5. *"Most people can be trusted"*—Once this principle is accepted, a host of checks and cross-checks can be eliminated. This in turn saves time, staff, and money, and leads to increased self-confidence and a sense of responsibility among staff. Management control can be effectively exercised by selection and occasional spot checks which are usually more satisfactory and productive, and certainly cost less than a whole series of permanent control systems and continuous routine checks.

3. BENEFITS

(*a*) Saving in paper—about 26 million pieces a year.
(*b*) Reduction in staff—about 2,000.
(*c*) Greater flexibility in organisation.
(*d*) Lower costs.
(*e*) Staff not tied to desks or bogged down with paperwork.
(*f*) Elimination of a great deal of checking.

[*O. & M. Bulletin* May 1969

CHECK LIST

1. Who has authority and how much is decision-making in their hands?
2. Do the right people have authority?
3. Is the right amount of authority delegated?
4. Is it clear to the person who has it, and to others, what authority there is?
5. Who issues instructions and general directives?
6. Is it clear if a directive is mandatory or merely advisory?
7. Is there a difference between what is policy and what is system?
8. Is authority distributed correctly, to the right people?
9. If a person is made responsible for a job, is he given sufficient authority to perform it?
10. Is a person exceeding his authority?
11. What are the decision areas?
12. If a problem arises, has the real problem been identified?
13. Have all the factors involved in the problem been identified?
14. Which would be the best technique to use in the decision-making?
15. How much of decision-making is delegated, or could be, or should be?
16. Are there limitations of cost or time (will a computer be helpful)?
17. Has all the information been specified, necessary for decision-making?
18. Is the information presented in suitable form?
19. Has a list been made of all possible courses of action (*e.g.*, decision trees)?
20. What action must be taken, by whom and when?

Chapter 16 Control and management information

After forecasting and planning and making decisions about future operations, instructions are issued to ensure the taking of action, after which comes the need for control, for this important element of management is concerned with seeing that there is continuous follow-up to ensure that policies are correctly interpreted and implemented.

A great deal of office work and a great deal of management work is concerned with exercising control, and it should be clear exactly what it is. Control is simple enough in concept, for no matter whether it is stock control, financial control or control of personnel, it always contains the same elements:

1. Setting up *standards*.
2. Making regular periodic *comparison* of physical events with these standards.
3. Taking *corrective action* if events do not comply with the standards.

In practice, however, control becomes more difficult, because in the first place, it is not always easy to set standards which are fair, and furthermore they are often the result of policy decisions made by top management. Making regular comparisons with these standards means *after* the events have happened, and control must be exercised quickly if it is to be of use, and very often controls are exercised too late in the day. Corrective action is in any case not always possible, in fact (*e.g.*, with budgetary control) there appears to be more an explaining away of the divergencies from the standards, and as with rising prices and wage rates, there often seems little corrective action that can be taken anyway.

Importance

Control in management is very important, because it represents the "steering of the ship," and unless it is exercised, the ship may easily go on the rocks. It is no good blaming the strong winds if the steering is not adjusted to allow for them.

First, control is related to forecasting and planning and policy-making, because it is through the medium of control information that it is possible to assess the adequacy (or otherwise) of the previously-formulated plans and policies.

Secondly, control is very much an integral part of organisation, because if work is not being performed, it should be built into some-body's job responsibility to exercise control to see that all work requirements *are* being performed. It used to be the fashion of some large business concerns to appoint executives known as "controllers," but while it can be said that all managers need to exercise control, it is foolish to appoint a controller external to the duties being performed. Controls must be *built into the duties* of the post.

The basis of all organisation is delegation, and since the delegator is ultimately responsible, he must exercise control over the delegated work, however experienced and competent the staff may be. There is little doubt that the older-established businesses with experienced staff need less controlling than otherwise, but the need still remains.

Thirdly, control is related to command and the giving of instructions, because there can be little control over events if instructions are badly given, and things happen differently from what was intended.

Fourthly, control is related to co-ordination, because without co-ordination, different sections of an enterprise follow different policies, and there is obvious lack of control.

Control is fifthly concerned with communication, because all these management elements depend on good communication to function effectively, and the reporting back of control information is one of the biggest functions of the office.

Lastly, excessive control of the wrong kind, only upsets employees. One of the perennial problems of management is how to excercise control without appearing to be doing so. Every human being likes to feel that he is held responsible for a particular task, and he resents external control of what he views as his personal job.

Management information

The role of management information is thus to enable comparisons to be made with the previously established standards. The role of administration therefore is to ensure that management receives all the information needed, and no more. Information which does not lead to some corrective action being taken is usually useless, although as stated above, there are occasions where no action is possible.

Management information therefore should give guidance on decision-making and the framing of future policies and plans; if it does not, then it is not management information. It is not the volume of information that matters, but its relevance, and in many companies the advent of the computer has aggravated the problem by providing more and more figures, but less and less real control information.

So, the job of management is to decide:

1. What control information is essential?
2. How is it going to be produced?
3. At what intervals?
4. Who is responsible for reporting the information?
5. Who shall be responsible for taking corrective action arising from it?

One of the problems of management information is that it can be divided into "specified" and "discretionary." Thus, there are certain statistics which must be compiled, *e.g.*, for the preparation of the annual accounts, for the Government, for a trade association, and so on. This should be clearly stated as the minimum which *must* be compiled, and then the extra discretionary area should be decided on. It is not possible, nor even desirable, to separate these two because if they can be produced simultaneously, then it will be with greatest efficiency, but the difference between the two should be recognised.

There is not one standard system of management information suitable for all concerns, because it depends on the type of business, on its size, and on its peculiar needs. But in a business concern, it is necessary to isolate the key profitability factors, and to decide who is responsible for each of them, and what management information is required from each, and at what intervals.

Financial control is perhaps the most important control in a business, and monthly profit and loss figures are meaningless in themselves unless they are compared with standards (*see above*), and there are three possible standards with which comparisons can be made:

1. with the previous year's figures (still used in many businesses, and with increasing inflation this can be very misleading);
2. with the forecast results (as in budgetary control, which is better than 1);
3. with I.F.C. (Inter-Firm Comparison) ratios, *i.e.*, with *external* standards, so that comparisons can be made with other companies of similar size and of similar business interests.

There are dozens of I.F.C. ratios obtainable, and a business must decide which ones are relevant and strictly necessary to give it the required financial control.

Some examples of prominent I.F.C. ratios are:

1. profit (after tax)/capital employed.
2. profit (after tax)/sales.
3. sales/capital employed.
4. cost of production/sales.
5. cost of marketing/sales.
6. cost of administration/sales.

Standards

As already mentioned, standards are a very important part of exercising control, but there is often difficulty of setting standards.

One of the problems with scientific management is that because a thing is set down in precise measurable terms, it is often thought to be reliable, but there are many factors which make standards difficult to establish. To take budgetary control as an example, the standards (or budgets) may contain a strong subjective bias of the manager setting them.

Standards may have measured work that is not 100 per cent the same as is being measured now, and may include slightly different material.

There are external, and cyclical variations, which may make the standards not really typical. Standards might even be based on extreme situations, and not be representative at all.

Standards may be applied to situations so complex that they lose their applicability.

It is very important to examine the standards beforehand, and to take great care in fixing them, for if they are not genuine, they may be definitely harmful in their use for control purposes.

Cybernetics

Stafford Beer is probably the greatest authority on cybernetics, which can be loosely defined as the setting up of self-controlling systems. As the fly-wheel and escape valve on a steam-engine regulate the smooth running of a machine, so (it is claimed) can mathematical models and systems provide automatic controls over management operations.

A simple example would be the use of the principles of "management by exception," whereby only the exceptions to a standard are reported, so that, for example, in credit control only those debtors who owe more than £20 for more than two months would be reported. Such a system can easily be built into a computer programme, and certainly does reduce clerical work, but it does not mean that the control is automatic, although the subsequent control procedure would be automatic. The trouble with automatic control is that the indication of a need to change policy may not even be noticed. Like all machines, it works all right when running smoothly, but a major breakdown may gradually build up and not become evident until the machine virtually disintegrates!

Principles of control

1. All different controls should be integrated (thus financial control should be integrated with, say, control of personnel).
2. Controls should be flexible to allow for changing circumstances.
3. Controls should be simple and easy to understand (if too complicated, they often become useless and undermine authority).
4. Controls should be essential, otherwise they assume the proportions of mere exercise of power.
5. Controls must be in accordance with laid-down policies (particularly the established standards).
6. Controls must be in the right quantity (too many controls lead to bureaucracy, and too few means failure to co-ordinate and failure to give a feedback on policy).

Kinds of control

Although accountants are apt to think there is only one kind of control, and that is financial, there are many kinds of control which affect finance, without being primarily financial controls, *viz.*:

1. Costing and budgetary control (which is financial).
2. Stock control.
3. Production control.
4. Credit control.
5. Quality control.
6. Work study and O. & M. (control over efficiency).
7. Internal audit.
8. Investment control.
9. Personnel control.

Methods of control

Many management textbooks mention only reporting as a method of control, and while this is probably most important (particularly with financial control), it is not the only method.

1. Reporting (oral reporting should be used for some things, *e.g.*, the state of the filing) and it is stressed that whether oral or in writing, reports should be at regular intervals—control should be a continuous dynamic affair.
2. Visual and personal control (*e.g.*, over timekeeping) is the kind most often used over staffing.
3. Control by exception, as mentioned above, is a method involving the least amount of paperwork, but needs to be carefully set up, and the standards reviewed from time to time.
4. *Ad hoc* decisions—the method used in a developing organisation, still trying to establish policies, or for less important matters.
5. Rules and regulations. Not always a successful method of control, because even if communicated successfully, they become self-defeating if too voluminous (witness sections of the community when they "work to rule," *i.e.*, rules which are out of touch with reality).
6. Use of mathematical models (such as network analysis) for giving control over the sequence in which work is performed, as well as the time taken by the different operations concerned.

CASE STUDY

Control

A WHOLESALING COMPANY

1. BACKGROUND

A wholesaling company dealing with about 30,000 different products with various profit margins. Basically, the company bought goods at a high "price-break," and then sold them in smaller quantities at a better margin.

2. PROBLEM

The company was never quite sure what its total profit margins were, because of the variety of goods, and the fast-changing market.

3. PROCEDURE

Several hundred invoices had to be prepared each day, which in a relatively small company was a major clerical operation—and speed of reaction to market conditions and prices was a key factor in the competitive situation.

4. O. & M. SOLUTION

(a) changes were made so that customers' orders were priced at both selling price and net buying price;

(b) the total range of products was divided into about one hundred different product groups, with various codes which were reproduced on the invoices;

(c) the extension of sales at buying prices (as well as selling prices) was an additional clerical task; but it did give

(d) regular monthly total profit margins from each of the one hundred different product groups.

5. RESULTS

(a) The change in the procedure gave management much tighter control on its pricing policies and on its profit margins.

(b) The information gained also gave most valuable data for planning how to deploy the capital available to the best advantage across the existing and potential product ranges.

(c) Better and more economical stock-holdings of the different product groups were possible.

CHECK LIST

1. What are the decisions that top management has to make?
2. What information is required in order to make these decisions?
3. How could the information be presented in the simplest way?
4. What kind of records need to be kept to provide such information?
5. How should the records be maintained?
6. Who should keep the records?
7. Who is responsible for taking corrective action?
8. What kinds of control are essential in the enterprise?
9. What are the best methods suitable to each control?
10. What information is required by law or other external agency?
11. What controls are required to prevent internal fraud?
12. What other discretionary control information is necessary?
13. Are the standards the best ones, or representative?
14. How often should different controls be exercised?
15. Is the control information actually fed to the policy-makers?
16. Is there too much control, leading to deadening of initiative and red tape?

17. Is there too little control, leading to duties not being performed?
18. Could "management by exception" be instituted, so as to save in clerical work and paperwork?
19. Are controls really defined in job specifications?
20. Are certain controls (even if viewed as necessary) costing more than they are worth?

Chapter 17 Co-ordination

When an organisation grows in size, it usually establishes an increasing number of functional specialists—in personnel, work study, market research, and so on. Furthermore, the authority of such specialists is often ill-defined, so that there develops friction between the specialists and the line managers. The larger the concern, the more is this likely to happen.

Even in small concerns, there is often a clash of personalities, and of course even if there were not, there is always a clash of interests between, say, the sales manager and the credit controller, between the stock controller and the buyer, and so on.

In these days of computers and scientific management, there are more and more experts who give advice to management, and who unfortunately are rather narrow in their outlook.

These are some of the reasons which point to the great need for co-ordination, one of Fayol's management elements laid down at the beginning of the century, and to some observers is the most important management element of all.

It should be clear what co-ordination really is:

1. The deliberate and planned unification of effort, e.g., with systems which dovetail, so that the lowest running cost is achieved, without duplication of effort.
2. Above all, the following by different departments of common policies, or the following of different policies in different areas (sales, personnel, etc.) which do not conflict with one another.

Importance of co-ordination

Perhaps the first and most important reason for the eminence of co-ordination is because of its relationship with organisation. In so far as organisation is the allocation of duties and responsibilities then it can by itself ensure a degree of co-ordination.

Then, it is related to communication, for there would often be better co-ordination if more information were made available to the different sections of the whole concern—particularly on what is happening in other departments.

Of course, it is related to control, especially financial control, because with budgetary control, the master budget is one of the greatest co-ordinating agents there is, and it forces different departments to confer and agree on a common approach.

Co-ordination is important because it affects all individuals in a concern, and is related to their co-operation and to their morale. Sometimes, the basic objectives of a business are not reached owing entirely to lack of co-ordination.

Lastly, unless there is full co-ordination, it often means a waste of money, time, and effort in all directions.

Co-ordination, co-operation and integration

Some management writers define co-ordination as being synonymous with co-operation, and the two are certainly related. But while co-ordination is a deliberate, planned affair, co-operation is a matter of state of mind, and is a matter of willingness. However co-operative staff may be, if there is lack of co-ordination, it is doubtful if there will really be a following of common policies or a unification of effort.

Alternatively, it can be said that whatever steps are taken by management to improve co-ordination, if the staff are not co-operative, then the management intention is likely to be defeated.

So that while co-ordination and co-operation are separate things, they are interwoven, and while co-operation can improve co-ordination, it is doubtful if co-operation in itself can produce co-ordination.

Integration, on the other hand, is a joining together, and the classic example is I.D.P. (Integrated Data Processing), by means of which a computer, while it is processing the sales invoices, produces information for credit control, and while it is processing the pay-roll, produces information for costing and budgetary control, and so on. The British Government often reshuffles its departments, and by joining different departments, attempts to achieve better co-ordination. The fallacy with following the integration policy in organisation is that ultimately all departments would be abolished and be contained in one corporate body, so that specialisation would be lost and responsibility and authority be so blurred as to spoil any vestige of good organisation there existed before.

1. PRINCIPLES OF CO-ORDINATION

To achieve co-ordination, various principles should be borne in mind:

1. Co-ordination must begin at the earliest possible stage of any system or organisation. Once established, it may be very difficult to effect change when it becomes apparent that co-ordination has been lost.
2. Co-ordination should be seen as a continuing process, and not something which is done once and for all. Like control, it is dynamic, and constant vigilance is needed to see that it is working.
3. As far as possible, people should meet face to face in order to achieve co-ordination, and not through the medium of memoranda and reports, etc.
4. Differences of opinion should be brought out in the open and examined, and not be nursed resentfully.
5. The common objectives and common policies must always be reiterated, for they are the essence of what co-ordination is really about.

2. METHODS OF CO-ORDINATION

It cannot be said that achieving co-ordination is simple, for it is rather like getting members of a family to work together, instead of pulling in different directions. Co-ordination is also required vertically (say, inside a department), as well as horizontally between departments, and sometimes vertical co-ordination is the most difficult of all to achieve.

Most management writers refer to the holding of conferences and meetings as the only method of co-ordination, but such meetings will be abortive if there is no common policy to bind together the different sections.

1. The most important step is to *have objectives and policies.*
2. For management to *communicate them* to the people concerned.
3. Then, the holding of regular *conferences*, where common action can be agreed (but *see below*).
4. As mentioned above, co-ordination rests on co-operation and goodwill, so *good leadership* can contribute to that goodwill, and to be effective, there should be frequent communication between the leader and his subordinates.
5. By good organisation and the clear allocation of duties and responsibilities; and in this connection bear in mind:
   (*a*) decisions which a person can make for himself;

(b) decisions about which he should formally consult others (and which persons to consult);

(c) decisions about which he should consult *informally* (and which persons); and

(d) decisions which he should *not* take, but refer elsewhere.

6. By the appointment of functional officers, who can ensure co-ordination or the following of common policies. But care should be taken with the terms of their appointment, and the personalities of people appointed, for this can so easily spoil morale and impair co-operation, without which co-ordination is impossible (this, of course, includes O. & M. officers).

7. By good leadership, which of its very essence means getting people to do things willingly, without compulsion.

8. By budgetary control, because, as explained above, nothing is so co-ordinating as the master budget, when the rival claims of research, advertising, and other departments have to be reconciled.

9. By the issue of regular information bulletins or house journals, in which policy and information about other departments is promulgated.

10. Sometimes co-ordinating officers, or liaison officers are appointed, *e.g.*, a representative from the production department on the R. and D. Committee.

11. By the regular interchange of personnel between departments, certainly a means of increasing awareness of the problems of others.

3. CONFERENCES

The holding of regular meetings can be a great aid to co-ordination, but it can also be the opposite! One of the classic management writers Mary Parker Follett recognised that at meetings, differences of opinion can be settled by (1) domination by one side over the other (which frequently happens in practice, and is worse still when endorsed by top management); (2) by compromise, by which each side surrenders some of its position, and only waits for the day to get its own back. Miss Follett suggested that effective settlement could only be by what she called "integration," which is really the proposal of a *third course of action*, different from that desired by either side, but acceptable to both of them.

A conference of course obeys one of the principles of co-ordination, *i.e.*, by bringing staff face to face, to argue out differences, but its measure of success depends on several things:

1. Such a meeting must be properly constituted, *i.e.*, regarding number of members, notice of meeting, etc.
2. The appointment of a good, strong and to some extent impartial chairman, who is respected by all at the meeting.
3. The support of proper secretarial services, and the provision of proper agenda, minutes, etc.

If strong personalities shout down discussion at meetings, it might make co-ordination impossible, and a strong chairman is needed who can control the meeting and ensure the right of speech to everyone, as well as keeping discussion to the point.

It is essential at such meetings that if the chairman is not a member of top management (as he usually is), that he is able to spell out common objectives and policies. If a member of top management, he should not only spell these out, but also try to persuade staff of their wisdom.

Regular meetings can be expensive in time and clerical costs, and there is the possibility of such meetings being held regardless of whether there are really topics for discussion. Unnecessary meetings which just waste time only spoil co-ordination.

4. LACK OF CO-ORDINATION

The first and most obvious sign of lack of co-ordination is when different departments follow different policies about the same things (*e.g.*, supplying and stocking of certain goods).

Then there is the duplication of effort, in so far as the departments are so self-contained that they keep the same records, and produce the same information. In other words, there is a lack of integration of systems.

Again, there is often a lack of synchronisation, even if there is no wasted effort, so that the timing of operations is out of step in different sections of the business, and there are inordinate delays (say, in attending to customers' orders).

If there is a common policy, because there is a lack of communication it is interpreted differently in different places.

As mentioned above, vertical co-ordination is probably the most difficult problem, and here it may be due to failure to delegate, or even of delegating too much; certainly, there is a general lack of control.

Until overall forms control is established, it is well known for almost identical forms to be printed for different departments, and excessive expenditure in paper and clerical costs might be the result of bad co-ordination.

CASE STUDY

Co-ordination

1. Co-ordination is not only concerned with people meeting, but more with the proper flow of information.
2. In a toy-manufacturing concern in America, the data-processing manager was a first-rate technician and extremely conscientious.
3. He attended a D.P. Management Association seminar which quite startled him, for it outlined how E.D.P. can assist the marketing and sales function of a business, and he was introduced for the first time to several new techniques for obtaining the information—on a computer.
4. Back at his office, he consulted the Sales Manager stating what his equipment could do in this respect. The manager was most enthusiastic, stating "We've been trying to do some of this on our own, and you have no idea what we've been going through, nor how much it costs."
5. A new programme was launched straightaway to produce the required marketing control information.

Comments

There is nothing very startling about this short case study, but it is a simple example where technical knowledge and skill were translated into concrete terms which were meaningful to management.

It is an example of how the co-ordination could have been achieved if there had been a conference, with a flow of communication on:

(a) what control data was needed (or fumblingly produced); and
(b) what E.D.P. could do for the marketing division.

CHECK LIST

1. What are the signs of bad co-ordination?
2. What are the causes?
3. Are policies clear and stated?
4. Are they communicated to the people concerned?
5. Is not policy, but unification of effort, at fault?

6. Is this due to lack of co-operation?
7. Are staff co-operative, but systems not co-ordinated?
8. Is there an O. & M. or other co-ordinating office?
9. What is the best method of improving co-ordination?
10. Would a regular conference really improve it?
11. Is it a question of morale, which depends on other things?
12. Are there frequent face-to-face meetings?
13. Is it a problem of vertical or horizontal co-ordination?
14. Would the publication of regular information bulletins to all staff improve the situation?
15. Is it the fault of systems or of policies?
16. Would the appointment of liaison officers be useful?
17. Would it be better to combine some sections, so that insular feelings are removed?
18. Is poor co-ordination due to clash of personalities?
19. Would interchange of staff between departments improve the situation?
20. Have we identified the real causes of poor co-ordination, and have we postulated the correct solution?

Chapter 18 **Communication**

Communication is a comparatively new element of management (although doubtless Fayol would have included it with "command"), and to some, it is the most important element of all. Communication involves not merely the transfer of information, ideas, facts, advice, etc., to another person or persons, but, more important, it involves their *understanding* of the ideas transmitted, so that they *act in the way* intended. Thus, if a reprimand is intended to remind somebody of the rules, to improve behaviour and not to build up resentment, then it is important how, when, where, and what is communicated.

In fact, it can be said that an attitude of mind can be communicated, even if nothing is said at all, and management is often guilty of failing to communicate, when it has an obvious obligation to do so.

In management theory, communication is a much wider thing than command, which has an implication of giving orders; in its full meaning, communication includes the giving of suggestions and the feedback of ideas. It is both a giving and a receiving of information.

Importance of communication

There are usually stated to be three kinds of communication: 1 *downwards*, from top management, 2 *upwards* to top management, and 3 *laterally* between different departments. Most managements give attention to 1 and often forget that 2 and 3 are equally important.

Downwards communication is important because it is related to obtaining action, through the exercise of command and authority; because it is related to control; and because it is the main method of letting people know about objectives and policies. Some management writers go so far as to say that organisation is based on a communication network, and it can certainly aid or destroy motivation and morale.

Upwards communication is important because it is related to participation of workers (morale), to feedback on policies, and to innovation.

Lateral communication is that which takes place on the same level between departments, and is essential to good co-ordination.

It has been stated that communication is the lubricant to the working of management, and that it facilitates the exercise of forecasting and planning, organisation, control, and so on.

Principles of communication

Lines of communication should be as direct and as short as possible; if, for example, there are too many levels of management, it will interfere with good communication, which may not only get distorted, but lost altogether.

Secondly, since communication involves understanding, it is often useful to test that although communication has been received, it has in fact been understood.

The third test of communication is the impact that it has, in the action induced, so an assessment of the action may also be an assessment of the effectiveness of the communication.

Fourthly, only *the right amount of information should be given.* A common fault, aided by the potential of computers, is for management to be given far more information than is really needed, and nothing is more expensive in overhead costs than this unnecessary proliferation of management information. Too little can be just as dangerous, for many a workers' strike has been caused by the failure of management to inform workers about things which vitally affect them.

Fifthly, information should be given in the right form—appropriate to the occasion, to the kind of message, and to the receiver of the communication.

Sixthly, it is advisable to give reasons for the ideas conveyed, for not only does it make the communication easier to remember, but it makes the ideas more acceptable.

Communication should always be given to the right people, and it should be clear who those people are.

Information should be given at the right time. To give information when it is already out of date, or to give it too far in advance of an event, is bad communication, no matter how good the content or method chosen.

Lastly, information should be in the language suitable to the receiver, and not that most convenient to the giver, although this is very much related to the understanding mentioned at the beginning.

Methods of communication

Some specialist books on communication concentrate on the *style* and the English used, etc., which are important, but even before this, comes the fundamental question of the *form* of the communication.

There are basically three methods of communication:

1. *Oral.*
2. *Written.*
3. *Visual or pictorial.*

1. ADVANTAGES OF ORAL METHOD

To discuss a problem with a head of department is the better way to encourage co-ordination, than it is to resort to memoranda, which can cause relationships to become cold and formal.

In oral discussion, it is possible to elaborate at any length, which would be unreasonable in writing, as well as affording an opportunity to give emphasis to important points.

If wrong information or wrong impressions are given (which is faulty communication), then it is much easier to put this right orally than it is in writing.

Lastly, if there is a difference of opinion, agreement is much more likely to be reached and much more quickly than by writing.

2. ADVANTAGES OF WRITTEN COMMUNICATION

It provides a record of what was said, and can avoid misunderstanding, in fact a speaker may himself not be sure of what he said, so it may be useful to have it in writing.

Written communication is often more convenient and may take less time, for a discussion with another person may mean travelling long distances to see him.

When committing oneself in writing, it is likely to be more precise and carefully prepared than when talking to a person. Oral instructions are often much less precise than written ones, in fact what is left unsaid may be more important than what is actually stated.

There are some managers who are careful to never put anything in writing unless they have to, so that they can change their minds as often as desired, and they then misuse their authority in asserting whatever they wish. On the other hand, there are those who are afraid of being misunderstood (probably bad at oral communication anyway), that they put everything in writing. The ideal, as always, is somewhere in between these two extremes—to put the important, the abstruse, and the difficult in writing, but not cause unnecessary clerical work by putting everything in writing.

It is not always a matter of choice between oral and written, and in fact it is often advisable to use both, *i.e.*, to discuss a problem orally, and when agreement is reached to confirm it in writing.

3. ADVANTAGES OF VISUAL COMMUNICATION

Sometimes it is better to communicate by means of charts, cartoons, moving films, posters, and so on. This has the advantage of simplicity, and more immediate impact on the receiver than anything else. That is why such methods are chosen when presenting statistics in pictograms, pie-charts, etc., and why posters are used for safety campaigns, and as a part of induction training, and so on. People remember much more vividly what they have seen in a cartoon, in an action film, or on television, than in all the newspaper write-ups ever devised.

Informal communication

The "grapevine" is well known in all organisations, and it consists of the informal as opposed to the formal communication which has been discussed so far. To the workers, it is a way of gaining information in advance of its official release by management, and it can be very useful to them for very often it is their only means of learning about, say, an impending takeover bid.

It can also be useful to management, for by informal communication, it can get advance warning of a possible strike in the works, of staff looking for other jobs, and so on.

But while it has its uses, it can be a disadvantage to both worker and to management. Workers who rely on informal communication (sometimes it is all they get), may be listening to nothing but garbled rumours and in reality nothing but distorted facts about what is really happening. Equally, management might be stampeded into taking an unwise course of action because of unrepresentative facts communicated informally.

Informal communication can be useful, but it should be recognised as being a potential scandalmonger, often with little real importance.

Barriers to effective communication

Perhaps the biggest barrier is the lack of will to communicate where managers question the need to give information at all.

This may be partly due to bad morale in a concern, where there is a "couldn't care less" attitude.

There is also often a failure to realise the emotional barriers to understanding. If a man is likely to become redundant, his emotions may preclude his understanding the need for it, let alone accepting it as inevitable. This is a very formidable barrier to communication, and one which is not always given sufficient attention.

Then there are the semantic barriers, *i.e.*, of language, which preclude real understanding. This is particularly evident between computer personnel and top managers, who may in effect be speaking different languages, one of technical and one of business jargon.

There may be faults in listening on the part of the receiver, and there may be faults in assessing effectiveness of communication on the part of the giver.

Often, the wrong method of communication is chosen (*see above*) for the subject, and the giver of information is then surprised that he has not communicated (*e.g.*, not many people read notice-boards, although they are still used for important communications).

CASE STUDY

Communication

MIRRLESS, BICKERTON AND DAY LTD.

1. BACKGROUND

The Company manufactures industrial and marine diesel engines.

2. PROBLEMS

   (*a*) Production was not keeping pace with orders.
   (*b*) The workers were apathetic and unsettled.
   (*c*) Morale was low.
   (*d*) There was a general failure of communication between management and the workers.

3. ACTION

A series of meetings was arranged for all levels, so that workers, supervisory staff and representatives of office staff could meet the management regularly. At any time, a department was entitled to call a "production development" meeting at which management was represented.

   (*a*) The first of the meetings arranged by the Managing Director was with the shop stewards once a week in the board-room. The meetings were completely informal, without formal agenda or minutes.

These were very successful, but the Managing Director soon realised his mistake that he had inadvertently by-passed his senior staff who felt resentful at the Managing Director telling shop stewards things which they did not know.

(b) So the Managing Director then started a senior staff forum every two months, when he was careful to give all the information he had been giving to the shop stewards. The senior staff took even longer to realise that they had "carte blanche" to raise any criticisms they wished.

(c) Thirdly, the Managing Director introduced what he called the turning-point of his campaign, the introduction of "production development committees." The function of these is to encourage suggestions, criticism of management, and even a shop steward can ask for such a meeting of his section. Such a committee is composed of four representatives from the section (including the shop steward), the Works Manager, the foreman of the shop, and any other person the M.D. feels can contribute to the discussion. Although at the beginning, the complaints were mostly about draughts and cold tea, more important issues were eventually discussed.

4. RESULTS

The results have had effects reaching far beyond management–worker relationships.

(a) It has thrown up definite weaknesses in management, particularly in shop floor supervision.

(b) Since the foremen agreed to have their meetings, partly in Company time and partly in their own time, the M.D. has arranged for:

(c) all shop foremen to be given staff status, not needing to clock in or out, and qualifying for other staff privileges.

(d) Output per man since the scheme started has increased 21 per cent (taking into account inflation, this really amounts to 47 per cent increase).

5. COMMENTS

Again, the impetus for this exercise in communication came from top management. The Managing Director had a great faith in the British worker: he says they do not moan for nothing. He is also of the opinion that every worker knows more about his job than other people, and that he can make important contributions to running the Company efficiently, and should be given opportunity to do so.

[*Business* August 1957

CHECK LIST

1. What are the ideas I wish to communicate?
2. To whom should I communicate?
3. What impact do I wish the communication to have?
4. What is the best method of communication?
5. What is the best language and style to use?
6. Shall I communicate by more than one method?
7. Have I checked on the effectiveness of a particular method?
8. Would informal communication be preferable?
9. What methods of upwards communication are there?
10. Have I communicated too much information?
11. Have I communicated too little?
12. Is this the best time to communicate?
13. Why do I need to communicate at all?
14. Have I taken account of emotional barriers?
15. Is lateral communication in order?
16. Have I considered the cost of the communication?
17. Have I given reasons for my proposals?
18. How can I improve my methods of communication?
19. Have I roused interest in what I want to say?
20. Am I the right person to be communicating anyway?

Chapter 19 Motivation

Some writers divide management into "mechanistic" (*i.e.*, the classical theories of organisation, control, authority, etc.), and "behavioural," while others divide it into "quantitative" (*see* Chapter 29) and "qualitative." Under the heading of "qualitative" comes "behavioural science," which is concerned with the psychological aspects of management.

So much attention has been lavished on this aspect in recent decades that it has now become almost another element of management, and who would deny that personal relationships, for example, are important in organisation, or morale in communication, and co-operation in co-ordination?

Motivation refers to the driving force from within a person, but although some treatises attempt to make it scientific, thêre is no doubt that the same motives produce entirely different actions in different people. This is not to say that it is not worth while studying them.

It is unfortunate that the word "incentive" has become (particularly by cost accountants and work study men) associated with "incentive bonus" payments, or the provision of tangible things (particularly money) as an incentive to do more and better work. Motivation, on the other hand, is more concerned with the intangibles, with discovering what it is that prompts people to act in a certain way. It is psychological, and every supervisor and manager should have a knowledge of its fundamentals.

Importance

The importance of motivation is self-evident to some extent because it is the main ingredient of morale. However, from a management point of view there are many reasons for its importance, not least that a well-motivated group of workers can produce twice as much as one which is badly motivated.

It is related to leadership, for good leadership is one of the prime motivators. Workers who respect and like their manager will be more

165

highly motivated than they will by a draconian, dehumanised admini-
strator who has forgotten how to get the best out of people.

The famous Hawthorne experiments in the 1920s proved that when
staff are consulted about changes, they invariably produce more and
better work than previously. In other words, involvement has a direct
causal relationship with productivity.

A study of motivation means a study of human behaviour, and many
an industrial dispute could have been prevented if there had been better
motivation of employees in the first place.

When management is framing policies (particularly in the personnel
field), it would be advised to bear in mind the motivational factors
involved.

Motivation theory also states that workers work for more than
money, and if they are treated as if that is their only interest in life:
it is likely to become so, and we cannot hope to understand them,
earn their respect, or call for the reactions that we often want from them.

Maslow's hierarchy of needs

In 1954, Professor Maslow enunciated his hierarchy of needs theory,
which delineates human needs in the form of a pyramid (*see* Fig. 9).

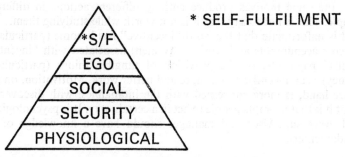

FIG. 9.—Maslow's hierarchy of needs.

In this important theory, there are thus five basic levels of human
needs:

1. *Physiological:* related to having a fair income, sufficient to provide the material necessities of life such as clothing, food, shelter,
   etc.
2. *Security:* related to knowing that there is security of employment, sick pay, pension rights, etc.

3. *Social:* related to being a member of a happy working group, so that one receives respect and can respect the others in the group.
4. *Ego:* concerned with the need to have identity, and to have one's work recognised as personal, the need for receiving praise, the need for promotion, and high-sounding job titles, etc., as well as simple satisfaction in doing a job well.
5. *Self-fulfilment:* related to the satisfying of one's innermost psychological needs, even if the individual is unaware of them, such as a need to become a singer, etc.

The importance of Maslow's theory lies in the following:

1. it is little use trying to satisfy one of the levels unless the one below it has first been satisfied;
2. having satisfied one level, the one above it then has increasing importance;
3. failure to satisfy any one level may result in frustrated behaviour (*see below*);
4. the base of the pyramid represents the most important needs, with decreasing importance up the pyramid.

This is not to say that all human beings are the same, and have the same proportions of these needs, for undoubtedly some require, say, a greater degree of security in employment than others, and the age and sex of workers must also be taken into consideration.

The ambitious employee will lay emphasis on his ego needs, but management's problem is not so much with motivating him, as with retaining him. Most people do not have soaring ambitions, nor very great abilities, but there is still a need to provide them with sufficient motivation.

McGregor's Theory X and Y

In 1960, Professor McGregor propounded his Theory X and Theory Y, which is a psychological variant of Maslow's theory. He stated that some managements believe in either:

Theory X: that the average human being dislikes work, needs to be controlled and threatened to make him work (carrot and stick theory), and that he dislikes responsibility, is unambitious and just desires security above all else.

Theory Y: that the performance of work is natural, that a man prefers to direct himself, that job satisfaction gives commitment to the organisation, that man seeks responsibility and that the intellectual potential of the average man is only partly utilised.

The importance of this theory is that the Theory X management gives rise to tough management with punishment and tight controls. Theory Y, on the other hand, is the one in favour of a greater degree of worker participation, of job enrichment, and treating employees as responsible, intelligent human beings.

As with Maslow's theory, it is half-true, because it depends on the individual concerned, for there are some who dislike responsibility and prefer to be controlled, while there are an increasing number of responsible, intelligent workers who can contribute a great deal. General Motors of America has found that girls come more within the Theory X category than the Theory Y category, and management should adapt the philosophy according to the staff employed.

Herzberg

In 1968 Professor Herzberg's hygiene theory was published. This states that there is a difference between the hygiene factors (environment, and so on) and the other factors to do with the job itself. The second group of factors is based on Maslow's theory, and includes such things as achievement, resignation, advancement, and responsibility (all ego factors). Herzberg then stated that when management gave attention to working conditions, etc., it only improved the hygiene, and did not prevent disease (or psychological unrest), only made it less likely, and that disease can be best treated by giving attention to the second set of factors.

In a way, this is a restatement of Maslow, asserting that the physiological needs are the first and basic needs of human beings.

Frustrated behaviour

The behavioural scientists have thus given us theories concerning what it is that motivates human beings, and furthermore have given us guidelines on what sort of behaviour to expect if these needs are not satisfied.

There are several expert classifications of frustrated behaviour, but Professor Munro Fraser has summarised them into four basic groups:

1. *Aggression:* resulting in hostility, even if only a mild habit of swearing, etc.
2. *Regression:* a return to childish behaviour, with loss of emotional stability, and the creation of childish cliques.
3. *Fixation:* continuing with a stubborn behaviour, resisting all change, and rejecting rational argument.

4. *Resignation:* giving up, becoming extremely cynical, which easily becomes resignation and lack of interest.

Again, this theory must be used with caution, because some people are actually aggressive, and some are irrational anyway, but it does undoubtedly help to explain the behaviour of others, even of some top managers.

Irrational behaviour

Although the psychologists have given us reasons for human behaviour in terms of human needs and frustrated behaviour, there is still an area which they find difficult to explain, and this is called irrational behaviour.

There are intelligent businessmen who continue with a belief (perhaps borne of past experience) that if they apply for passports for foreign travel, then the income tax authorities will catch up with a previous financial misdemeanour.

In such cases, it is useless trying to explain that the Inland Revenue has no connection with the Home Office (he knows that), but such persons still persist in their irrational belief. Such irrational behaviour is based on a deep-seated fear, and in fact this example is based on an actual case.

Conclusion

All these psychological theories about motivation are very interesting and very useful to management, but what is their contribution in practical terms? Perhaps the greatest is that an employee needs:

1. Satisfaction in doing his job (this is related to organisation and the use of specialisation).
2. To be happy in the company of fellow workers (related to informal organisation and grouping of workers).
3. To be appreciated by his superiors (a golden rule of good supervision is to give praise as well as finding fault).
4. A challenge from his work (management should prevent a worker getting stale on a job). This is coupled with a need for new experience and adventure.
5. To gain responsibility (to satisfy ego needs).
6. To be informed about things that affect him (the importance of downwards communication).

CASE STUDY

Motivation

I.C.I. LTD.

1. STAFFING

In a research establishment of I.C.I., morale was very low. The proportion of the workers over fifty had risen to 23 per cent, a quarter of them had reached their maximum salaries, and the traditional road to promotion (plant management) was now barred to them. Technology had become more complicated and only qualified graduates were being recruited. The bulk of the staff did not take time off, or leave—they just stayed, disinterested and contributing little.

2. EXPERIMENTAL PROGRAMME

Dr. Paul, an American consultant who was a colleague of Professor Herzberg, was called in to carry out an experimental programme to improve morale.

3. INCENTIVES

The criteria chosen for the motivators were: sense of achievement (and its recognition), qualities of the work itself, responsibility, advancement and self-development. Financial incentives were not viewed as prime motivators.

4. CONTROL GROUP

Dr. Paul chose a group of fifteen research officers, and a control group of twenty-one similar officers remained on the old conditions, but eight proposals were implemented:

(a) A minimum of one-tenth of working time could be claimed to pursue research of their own devising.

(b) They could requisition services or materials on their own authority.

(c) They could write and sign their own requisitions.

(d) They could take greater management responsibility for their juniors—the laboratory assistants.

(e) They could devise and start a training scheme for them.

(f) They would be involved in interviewing candidates for the lower-level jobs.

(*g*) When staff were appraised, they would be the first ones consulted.

(*h*) The staff would be involved in planning at an earlier stage than previously.

5. RESULTS

After a six-month experimental period, the results were:

(*a*) Morale was higher.

(*b*) The regular research reports improved, and in fact those received from three staff were as good as the graduate reports.

(*c*) The research officers produced a valuable training scheme for the assistants.

(*d*) Of the three people who claimed time for personal research, one of them made a research finding which led to a patent application, judged by the then Ministry of Technology as the most promising of two hundred ideas submitted to them on the subject.

6. COMMENTS

Nobody demanded a rise in pay for the increased responsibility and only three complained that they did not want the extra responsibility given to them. The research department is pleased with the results, so is Dr. Paul, who stated that people of all levels "have an enormous contribution to make, and desperately want to give it provided the company gives them the framework."

[*The Guardian* 27th June 1968

CHECK LIST

1. Have I analysed the basic needs of my employees?
2. Are Maslow's five levels given attention?
3. Are individual differences taken account of?
4. How do the personnel policies affect these?
5. Is there too much attention given to financial rewards?
6. Is there good leadership to help motivation?
7. Have we examined the relationship of communication and motivation?
8. Is decision-making too centralised, without any participation?
9. If we wish to change things, have we studied motivational needs?
10. Is conflict a motivational need or sign of frustration?
11. Which one of McGregor's theories do we follow?
12. Does the organisation allow of delegation of authority?
13. Is low morale related to frustration of needs?

14. Have we given attention to job enrichment?
15. Do we have over-specialisation?
16. Have we got personality appraisal of our employees?
17. Is the behaviour of staff related to frustration?
18. Do we get the best from our employees?
19. If not, is it the failure of bad motivation?
20. What are the faults in our motivation?

Part Four: O. & M.

Chapter 20 Organisation of O. & M.

As stated in Chapter 2, O. & M. is concerned with improving office efficiency, and so it is also concerned with everything that affects office efficiency. This, therefore, must include much more than just systems and forms design.

Personnel is certainly one of the great factors in office efficiency, and yet, how often are the personal factors denied O. & M. attention just because there is a Personnel Officer in the organisation? Admittedly, the position is difficult, but that is all the more reason why O. & M. should have sufficient authority and have the full-hearted support of top management:

Perhaps the main things to be considered are:

1. The function of O. & M. in the enterprise.
2. To whom should it be responsible?
3. The authority given to O. & M., and preparation of the climate in which it works.

A functional authority

Undoubtedly O. & M. should be advisory only, in the same way as other specialist functions, but the old broad organisational difficulty arises of what to do if the advice of such functional officers is ignored. And what to do, on the other hand, if he becomes such a power that he is viewed as an executive? Joan Woodward in her admirable book *Industrial Organisation* stated that she found both of these extremes existing in industry. On the other hand, she could not understand the employment of an officer whose effect was negative, nor the fact that he often assumed authority far above any line officer.

It is, as usual, a question of balance, so that while the O. & M. officer is acknowledged to be advisory, he is nevertheless given such authority that his advice is not ignored, but on the other hand, his authority should not override that of the line managers.

A great deal will depend on the personality and diplomacy of the

O. & M. officer and his staff. Thus, if a new system is recommended, it is ideal if the real agreement and support of the line officers is obtained before recommendations are made to management. This is particularly important when, as is usually the case, the O. & M. unit is expected to not only install a system but also to supervise it and to see that it is working. There is an obvious area of conflict here, since it is the line manager's job to supervise his own systems. But, again, it is mainly a matter of diplomacy and tact. In fact, frequently an O. & M. recommendation will have the support of staff, against the wishes of the departmental manager, and it is then a matter of persuading the departmental head of the wisdom of changes recommended.

Normally, the O. & M. department makes a report recommending certain changes, a copy of which goes to the line manager of the department concerned, so that he can also make his comments on the recommendations to top management. If the O. & M. department has done its job properly, any comments on its reports will be minimal and concerned only with minor issues.

Where there is a specific project in hand, management often gives the O. & M. department executive authority, for the purpose of that specific project and for a limited time.

The important issue is to ensure that it is clear who has responsibility, and generally speaking, O. & M. cannot carry responsibility since it is only advisory.

The ideal situation is where, for example, a successful O. & M. department has been established for many years, and has become so *accepted and appreciated*, that a department even calls it in for advice when wishing to change an old system or start a new one. Then there is not likely to be any difficulty with implementation of its recommendations.

Accountability

To whom, then, should O. & M. be responsible? There is not, and there cannot be, any standard organisational position here, because a great deal will depend on the requirements of the business, and of the historical growth and emergence of O. & M.

In some companies, it has grown out of work study in the factory, being concerned mainly with production planning and control systems. In fact, some prefer the term "work study." In others (as at the B.B.C.), it grew out of the need to assess staffing numbers and grades.

This last situation is an interesting one, because it is not possible to relate staffing numbers merely to the amounts of work performed. It is possible that one method of performing work will be six times more efficient than another, and this will have a considerable impact on the numbers and types of staff employed. This is not to say that the personnel function should be usurped by the O. & M. department, but it should be recognised that after an investigation of clerical work the job contents may alter, and it is then the function of the personnel office to grade the job (or the O. & M. officer can do the Job Evaluation).

It can be seen that whether O. & M. grows out of internal audit responsible to the Accountant, to the Production Manager, or to the Company Secretary, it is still likely to have a departmental bias. This will not only colour its recommendations and the stringency of its investigations, but will make it highly suspect in the eyes of other departments. This will lose it "credence," which is one of the main requirements of successful O. & M.

Ideally, therefore, O. & M. should be responsible only to the chief executive, by whatever name he is called, whether it be General Manager, Managing Director, or Company Secretary.

This may well give the O. & M. department authority, respect, and indeed instil a certain amount of fear in the staff of other departments. If the O. & M. staff work only on the instructions of the chief executive, it may be accused of spying, and "wielding the big stick" (and be tempted to do so).

The best way out of this difficulty is to appoint an O. & M. Committee to meet, say, once a month, not only to receive the O. & M. reports, but also to give new assignments.

Such a Committee will probably have the chief executive as chairman, but will also include all the line managers of all departments. Such a committee not only ensures impartial assessment, but it also ensures that the line managers give the necessary attention to O. & M. activities and should improve the climate in which it works.

Commencing O. & M.

In the first place, O. & M. must have the active support and goodwill of top management. Thus, the Board of Directors or Committee of Management must *really* approve the setting up of such a department. Secondly, its position in the organisation, and its function, its authority and its responsibilities must be clearly defined (*see above*). Then, thirdly, it must be introduced properly.

It is very important to get the terms of reference right from the beginning, and this might well take the following form:

"To investigate, advise and report on office efficiency, and all things conducive to it, in any area of the company's activities, as requested by Company officers, or as directed by the O. & M. Committee."

The ground should be prepared by informing all departments beforehand of the setting up of O. & M., and of its functions, authority and responsibilities.

When an O. & M. officer is appointed, meetings should be held of supervisors and top managers separately, so that he can be introduced to them, and when they can ask questions on his future activities.

This, however, is not enough, for as stated at the beginning of the Chapter, a very important issue is to establish the right climate of operation. An O. & M. appointment is nearly always feared because it means change, because of anxiety that an outsider will meddle and misinform management, and expectation that staff will be declared redundant. This last point is of course a very real fear, because unless an O. & M. officer can show savings, his appointment is often viewed as a waste of time. Not that this is necessarily true, however, for efficiency means more than just reduction in costs.

What can management do to allay these fears? Management (at Burroughs Wellcome Ltd. a few years ago) gave two specific promises to staff before the O. & M. appointment:

1. There would be no staff dismissed as a result of recommended redundancies. In a large concern, it is always possible to absorb redundant staff as the result of normal retirements, etc.
2. There would be no recriminations about any faulty methods or systems, and there would be no "court of inquiry" on malpractices.

Policy statement

Such a policy statement is invaluable in setting the right climate for the exercise of O. & M., and it might be advisable to stress, perhaps in writing as well as verbally, that increase in efficiency does not necessarily mean a reduction in staff.

1. Efficiency means the achieving of the purposes of an office at the lowest cost.
2. Efficiency can therefore mean achieving the *same* purposes at a lower cost.
3. It can also mean achieving *better results* at the same cost, and with the *same staff*.
4. Efficiency can mean the achieving of better office purposes, or *better results at lower costs*.
5. It may even mean achieving *better results* than previously at *higher costs*, and with more staff.

Since the main function of an office is to achieve its purposes at the lowest cost, O. & M. might, for instance, make more management information available than previously, without saving any money. It might even recommend the employment of more staff and the spending of more money. It is foolish, therefore, to judge the efficiency of an O. & M. unit merely on the savings it recommended. If this attitude is taken (and it is a common one, and financial savings are often quoted as its main justification), then the O. & M. staff will tend to concentrate on how they can reduce expenditure, regardless of the real efficiency of the concern.

O. & M. conflict

Supposing, however diplomatic and persuasive an O. & M. officer, his recommendations are totally rejected? Supposing there is one particular departmental head who has been opposed to the O. & M. department from its inception?

Here, of course, is where it is essential for O. & M. to be accountable to the chief executive; if he really believes in O. & M., he should support it, even in face of obstreperous line managers.

One O. & M. officer, to the writer's knowledge, reported on his inability to assess the accumulated records of a certain department because of opposition. In consultation with the chief executive, a strategy was then worked out, and a directive issued stating that no new filing cabinets would be supplied in future to any department unless it first submitted to an O. & M. inquiry into its accumulated records. This achieved the action required, and not only were thousands of records cleared out of the obstructive department, but the working staff of that department clearly supported the O. & M. in its inquiries.

It must not be forgotten that O. & M. is, or should be, a part of top management, even if it is only advisory.

CASE STUDY

Starting an O. & M. department

BURROUGHS WELLCOME AND CO.

1. BACKGROUND

Burroughs Wellcome is a very old-established firm of manufacturing chemists, who wanted to improve office efficiency without spoiling staff morale.

2. CONDITIONS

The Company therefore applied the following conditions:

(*a*) O. & M. should be applied sensibly and resourcefully by men of the right calibre;

(*b*) its purpose should be understood and approved by the people whose jobs are being examined; and

(*c*) the project should be actively supported by all levels of management.

3. METHOD

The Company appointed an O. & M. officer (called, incidentally, a Work Study Officer) with no executive authority, and at the same time, the Managing Director set up a three-man committee consisting of:

(*a*) The O. & M. Officer;

(*b*) The Company Secretary; and the

(*c*) Chief Accountant.

This committee is responsible to the Managing Director, and it meets informally about once a month (*a*) to assess the progress of its operations, (*b*) to plan fresh assignments, and (*c*) to consider matters of policy arising from current investigations. After the O. & M. Officer makes his report to this committee, it is approved or modified, and passed for acceptance to the Managing Director, who also receives regular progress reports.

4. PREPARING THE WAY

When O. & M. was introduced, the Company organised a number of three- and five-day "appreciation" courses for departmental managers, section heads, supervisors, foremen, and employee representatives. At these meetings, the purpose of O. & M. was explained, and questions were answered frankly. In addition, the following assurances were given:

(a) Employees who became redundant as a result of investigations would be absorbed through normal wastage in their own or other departments.

(b) The function of O. & M. was advisory and not executive. No changes would be made in a department's system without the approval of its manager.

(c) The investigations were concerned with the efficiency of future routines, and there would be no inquests or recrimination.

5. STARTING

It was thought diplomatic not to start on any particular department, and yet a project which would yield recognisably good results ought to be chosen.

So the routine for dealing with overseas orders was studied and which eventually saved 188 man-hours a month, and subsequent investigation into filing made thirteen tons of paper redundant in one week, and 88 four-drawer filing cabinets were reduced to 46.

[*Business* November 1955

CHECK LIST

1. Is it clear what is the function of O. & M.?
2. What is its position in the organisation?
3. To whom is it responsible?
4. What authority will it have?
5. What relationship with line managers?
6. What relationship with the Personnel Officer?
7. Is it clear, to whom O. & M. is accountable?
8. What has been done to build up a proper working climate for O. & M.?
9. Has management a policy on redundancy?
10. How do we measure the effectiveness of O. & M.?
11. Has O. & M. really got support of top management?
12. Is there an O. & M. Committee?
13. Is the O. & M. officer able to sell his ideas to line managers?

14. Do line managers recognise their right of challenging O. & M.?
15. What if O. & M. recommendations are not accepted?
16. Does O. & M. have the job of installing new systems?
17. Do they have to see that their ideas work?
18. Supposing there is conflict with line managers?
19. Do we have a regular report on O. & M. activities?
20. Is O. & M. justified?

Chapter 21 Techniques of O. & M.

O. & M. assignments arise in many ways, so that it is not possible to lay down empirically the steps to be followed on all occasions. Thus, assignments can be:

1. to improve an existing system;
2. to reduce the cost of operation;
3. to reduce the cost of staffing (not necessarily the same as 2, and this might not mean a reduction in numbers either, although it usually does);
4. to examine the replacement of forms (and their incidence with systems);
5. to install a new system;
6. to avert a Parkinsonian increase in staff (*i.e.*, a preventive function);
7. to improve the methods, particularly recommending the use of better mechanical methods;
8. to study and improve the organisation of a section or department;
9. to improve the layout and flow of work in an office.

To some extent, the techniques will vary according to the type of the assignment, although whether it is to install a new system or to improve an existing system, it is still necessary to examine the purposes, to carry out interviewing, etc., but the avenue of inquiry, and the depth of inquiry will vary.

O. & M. assignment

It is important that there should be a systematic approach to all O. & M. assignments, and in general, the steps will be as follows:

1. Preliminary survey.
2. Deciding objectives of the assignment.
3. Planning the assignment.
4. Collecting the facts.

5. Recording and charting the facts.
6. Verifying and examining the facts.
7. Developing new or improved systems, forms, organisation, layout, etc.
8. Evaluating the new proposals and assessing efficiency increases.
9. Presenting recommendations.
10. Implementing (or helping to implement) the adopted recommendations.
11. Follow-up and maintaining the new proposals—to see that they are working.

1. PRELIMINARY SURVEY

This is a most important part of the assignment, for on the preliminary survey may depend the terms of reference, and the whole conduct of the assignment. It consists of discussion with top management and supervisors and the weighing up of all the factors involved. It is the diagnostic stage, and, as any doctor knows, correct diagnosis is half the battle. Thus, a manager might well think he has a system problem, whereas in reality it is bad organisation. Or, again, a proliferation of paperwork might be thought to be a system fault, whereas in reality it is a fault in management policy.

It is necessary at this stage to assess what the purposes of a system are thought to be. Often, they should be more, and sometimes less, than they are understood to be.

Having identified what the problem is, it may be useful here also to define the boundary lines of the assignment, for if anything unpalatable is uncovered, it is often suggested that the O. & M. inquiry went beyond its terms of reference (with implications of being power-drunk, prying, etc.).

The preliminary survey is also an opportunity for O. & M. to obtain first-hand experience of the operating environment, which will be of assistance in planning the subsequent inquiry.

It might be advisable at this stage, if the assignment has been agreed, to call meetings of the staff to let them know what has been agreed, and to call for their co-operation. This also gives opportunity to introduce the O. & M. officer if he is not already known.

2. OBJECTIVES OF THE ASSIGNMENT

During the preliminary survey, it is possible to draw up terms of reference, which may be only tentative and subject to amendment, but at least they give a basis on which to work. It is most important to define what the objectives of the assignment are, for this will shape the

O. & M. methods, and its findings can ultimately be compared with what it was supposed to be doing.

Here, great caution is advised, because it is frequently impossible to separate system from staffing, or from organisation, and if the terms of reference are too narrow, they may be found to be not only restricting, but preclude the investigation of the real cause of trouble.

3. PLANNING THE ASSIGNMENT

While the preliminary survey will be made by the chief O. & M. officer or his deputy, it is advisable if O. & M. working staff are brought in as soon as possible, not only as a means of making them known, but so that they participate in the assignment from the beginning.

Planning will, however, involve allocation of staff, and giving them full briefing on the purposes, scope, objectives, policy, and boundary lines of the assignment, together with details of the problems.

It also entails deciding on the methods to be used (*e.g.*, systems charting, machine operation chart, layout diagram, activity sampling, organisation charting, and so on), and the date on which the inquiries will begin. When staffing, methods, and commencing date have been decided, this detail must be communicated to top management (to whoever O. & M. is accountable), and to the manager of the department concerned in the inquiry. It might also be desirable to set a time schedule so that a finishing date can also be determined.

The O. & M. staff allocated, if not already introduced, must then be introduced to all management staff, from supervisor upwards, so that they are known.

4. COLLECTING THE FACTS

This is an important part of an assignment, not merely because it takes so much time, but because the O. & M. recommendations will be based on the accuracy of the facts collected. So important is it, that the whole of the next Chapter is devoted to it.

5. RECORDING THE FACTS

This is where the detailed knowledge of charting is very useful, for it enables most complicated details to be recorded succinctly, as well as facilitating subsequent analysis and assessment. To a great extent, this is subjective, and the O. & M. officer has to decide which facts are important and relevant to the inquiry.

The facts recorded must be pertinent to the issue, whether it be organisation structure, methods of work, work load, or even customer and statutory requirements.

Recording too much information will be a waste of time and may well cloud the real issues, but recording too little may be disastrous and leave out the really important things which are relevant to the inquiry.

Proper notebook and chart recording methods are most important, and staff should receive adequate training in the best methods to use.

6. VERIFYING AND EXAMINING THE FACTS

This is the activity of examining the facts collected to see if they are relevant, and to see if they are adequate. It may well reveal that further inquiries are necessary to corroborate or to fill in some of the missing picture.

This is also the opportunity for testing the logic of the sequence of operations in a system, in the distribution of duties in organisation, and so on. It may well reveal that the facts are not in accordance with what top management believes them to be, and it might be necessary to confer again both at lower and upper levels to confirm the reality of the situation.

There may have been wrong interpretations at the beginning of the assignment, and this is the opportunity to check on them.

7. DEVELOPING SOMETHING NEW

Then, there is the job of developing alternative methods, systems, organisation, forms, etc., and proposals will arise after intensive study of the facts of the situation. The new proposals must not only be better, but they must be seen to be better, and charts of the alternative proposals should be prepared for comparison with the old.

The new system, organisation, etc. must bear in mind:

1. purposes of the office;
2. management control;
3. prevention against fraud and theft;
4. costs.

8. EVALUATING NEW PROPOSALS

Here, it is important to assess dispassionately all the advantages which should accrue from the new proposals. As mentioned in the last Chapter, it may not necessarily mean a saving in cost, or in staff, but may simply mean more management control information, or quicker compilation of previous information. Whatever the advantages, they should be spelled out and itemised.

This is so that not only are the proposals made acceptable to management, but also so that subsequently, if proposals are put into effect, the improvements can be measured against the expected benefits.

An O. & M. officer should be careful about being too optimistic, and, in fact, it is advisable also to examine the difficulties and the disadvantages of the proposals. It is often found that new proposals would be ideal if adopted properly, but because of working difficulties the full advantages do not materialise.

When the O. & M. report is being considered, the O. & M. officer should be present to answer any questions and the line manager's comments, and the line manager himself should also be in attendance. This finalising of the acceptance of recommendations, and reaching of amicable agreement, can have a great effect on the subsequent successful implementation.

9. PRESENTING AND IMPLEMENTING RECOMMENDATIONS

When the O. & M. report has been submitted and approved, it is necessary to implement the recommendations, and responsibility should be assigned for instructing in new methods, for placing orders for new machines, for re-arranging office layout (who and when); for ordering a supply of new forms, and so on.

The O. & M. officer here acts as a co-ordinating officer between personnel, supplies, line management, and among the different departments concerned. Since the changes are on his recommendation, it is his job to communicate the action required, but it is always advisable to implement recommendations through line management. This will then assure them that their responsibility has not been taken away, and that O. & M. is merely an expert advisory service. Of course, the recommendations might not be obeyed, but this is where it is essential for O. & M. to have the backing of top management.

It is often a good idea to have a pilot study before implementing in full all the recommendations. This means the use of duplicated forms before having them printed, or the testing of a new system in a small sub-section before its widespread adoption.

Equally, when recommending new machine methods, it is a good idea to have a period of running in parallel, and not to discontinue the old method until it has been proved that the new machine method can achieve the desired results. There will always be teething troubles, and the pilot run is one painless way of ironing out the practical difficulties. What seems feasible in theory, is not always so easy in practice!

It might be necessary to have a programme of implementation, by which there are numbered stages, first the use of new forms, then the training of new staff, then the installation of new machines, and so on. These stages would have to be agreed with line management. Gradual changes are much more acceptable than wholesale changes all at once.

10. FOLLOW-UP

The O. & M. department should in its operating programme set a date for a future follow-up to ensure that the system, reorganisation, forms, etc., are working successfully. It is also an opportunity for checking that the recommendations have in fact been fully implemented. This gives opportunity to discuss with management the changes that have been wrought, and if successful (as they should be), opportunity for O. & M. to receive the accolades and respect it should always be striving for.

Interviewing

In the course of the O. & M. plan outlined above, several interviews are indicated, both at the beginning and at the end, and even at the follow-up stage.

Interviewing has a very important role to play in all the stages, and although it is further dealt with in Chapters 22 and 27, attention to interviewing technique will repay itself many times over.

The O. & M. officer should be impartial, tactful, and, more positively, able to sell his ideas, and be able to persuade others of the wisdom of his proposals. This applies to the planning of the assignment, as much as to the acceptance of recommendations.

The rules of interviewing are much as for employment interviewing, and the atmosphere in which the O. & M. man is received may be remarkably chilly; often his first job is, by conversational means, to affect a "thaw" in the atmosphere.

Secondly, he must adopt his interviewing technique according to the personality of the person being interviewed. A nervous, quiet type of person has to be encouraged, but a voluble egoistic person may have to be "cut down to size."

Sometimes, the head of a department or a supervisor may insist on accompanying the O. & M. officer and then try to answer all the questions asked of the subordinates; the O. & M. officer must be quietly and firmly in control of the interview, and not allow this to happen.

Often interviews of workers have to be carried out in an open office, where others are listening, and it must be ensured that flapping ears do not hear too much. Errors of fact or misinterpretation must be admitted, but too many errors tend to put O. & M. in a bad light.

The O. & M. man should beware of any personal bias which he might have about the facts being investigated, and he must beware, even if he has no personal bias, of clinging to a quick "pat" solution.

He must have a degree of empathy, and try to put himself in the position of the person he is interviewing, bearing in mind that to many people the very fact of the appearance of O. & M. implies that they are inefficient.

To this end, the O. & M. interviewer should:

1. Prepare the interview beforehand, to the extent of knowing what information he wants, and what kind and form of questions he is going to ask.
2. Make the interview contribute to the objectives of the assignment (advisable to study them, all the time).
3. Keep it impersonal, even if an irritated worker does become personal towards him, the supervisor, or the management. Personal opinions are not facts.

It is, of course, essential that the O. & M. officers should at all times be scrupulously polite, and while being impartial, must try to heighten the interest of the interviewee. He should say that he is trying to make the system work more smoothly, or to save time and improve the service to the customer.

If necessary, he must re-phrase a question until he does get a concrete answer. He should be careful not to compliment a worker or a system which he subsequently may wish to change.

He should never criticise the staff or their ability, if anything he must try to build up the importance of their jobs, which is more likely to gain the confidence of the workers.

The balance between formality and informality is always difficult, but it is always best to start formally, and when nervousness has departed from the interview, then to become a little less formal.

1. INTERVIEW DIFFICULTIES

All O. & M. officers meet with interview difficulties some time or another, and it may be necessary to assess whether the difficulty is permanent or just temporary. A difficult interviewee might be more amenable on a return visit. But if, however many times a person is interviewed, he is still difficult, then it might be advisable to get the man's superior to interview him to get the information required. However, flattery, and the expression of respect for the person doing the job helps quite a great deal. A good desk-side manner also helps (doctors have similar difficulties with patients!).

Some of the difficulties to be encountered will be:

1. The inarticulate who cannot express himself. The interviewer must help him and suggest leading questions so that a simple "yes" or "no" answer gives the information desired.
2. The voluble who talks too much. A gentle change of the subject back to the point at issue is required.
3. The person who says "we have been doing this for twenty years and it works all right." Ask if he is completely satisfied with the results, or if he had the power, would he change anything, and does he never have any problems in the work?
4. The "automaton" who does not really know what he is doing or why. It is best to let him demonstrate his work, and then ask questions at different stages.
5. The obstinate or deceiver who does not co-operate, and may tell deliberate lies, or give exaggerated accounts of his work. His statements must be checked by other means, perhaps with the supervisor, or by records inspection.
6. The person who says "what can you find out in half an hour that has taken me ten years to learn?" They must be assured that only the main elements are being sought after, and, of course, there is often some truth in this assertion and it must be acknowledged.
7. The person whose attitude is that he is too busy to waste time on O. & M. inquiries. Remind him that he should not be so hard pressed, and it is possible that his job could be made easier.
8. The man with a grievance against the management, and who is more concerned with his security or his position. He should be gently reminded that you are not primarily concerned with his position, only with the work and its performance.
9. With the increasing use of computers and other electronic equipment, there is also more likely to be the employee who tries to conceal his replies in technical jargon. He should be asked to explain, although a good O. & M. officer will acquaint himself with the necessary amount of technical jargon relevant to the assignment before he starts. A knowledge of the person's speciality will often amaze him and help to gain his confidence. Finally:
10. Listen patiently to all a person has to say.
11. Give full attention to him, and make it clear that it is so given.
12. Never argue nor give advice (except to top management, at report time).
13. Appreciate what a person is not able to say or answer.
14. Do not divulge anything of a personal nature to anyone.

2. CONCLUDING AN INTERVIEW

It is not enough just to say "thank you" and leave after an interview. Remember that it may be necessary to return for a further interview, so leave enough time to establish a friendly relationship at the end.

E   Before the end of the interview, refer to the notes made and recapitulate on the information gathered. It gives opportunity to fill in any missing information and makes a good impression on the interviewee.

It is in the concluding stages that the interviewee often gives vent to his unofficial opinions. These should be listened to politely and carefully in case anything has a bearing on the object of the assignment. But the O. & M. officer must not comment on, nor encourage, gossiping about the management, or any particular manager. He must listen without comment.

Whoever is being interviewed, and whatever the subject of the interview, tact is the overriding quality; interviewing ability is to a degree a subjective ability, but it is hoped these hints will assist an aspiring O. & M. officer.

CASE STUDY

Edge-punched cards

MINISTRY OF AGRICULTURE AND FISHERIES

1. OBJECT

To calculate cost of Ministry of Agriculture and Fisheries stands at various shows, and to obtain facts about the impact of the exhibits on people at whom they were aimed.

2. PROBLEMS

How to get a representative section of the public attending all the shows, and to obtain the information in a most economical way. The volume of attendance would not justify machine-punched cards (there were thirty-one shows in a year).

3. COURSE OF OPERATION

A sample was taken of all shows of three days or more. The calculation of cost was based on the total cost during the calendar year, and was treated as a separate issue.

The counting of visitors actually visiting a stand was made by hand-operated counters.

A questionnaire was devised to gain the visitors' reaction to the stands. The proportion of visitors to the stands who were asked to complete the questionnaire varied from show to show, but overall 3·35 per cent were interviewed. Visitors were requested to complete the questionnaires by random sample.

It was decided to use edge-punched cards, and it would have been better for the answers to the questions to be entered direct on to such cards, but in view of the shortness of time available, the questions had to be on duplicated forms; the information was subsequently slotted into edge-punched cards (already in stock from another assignment).

The total number of cards for any one show was 1,108, and the total for outdoor shows was 7,963; to enable reference back to the questionnaires, the cards and the forms had identical numbering performed on a hand-numbering machine. The transfer of the answers from the forms to the cards was carried out at an average speed of 200 an hour. Each had nine slottings.

The analysis obtained from the edge-punched cards gave the following statistical information:

(a) Analysis of the visitors into farmers, managers, landowners, agents.

(b) The visitor's assessment of the stand.

(c) The reason for visiting the stand.

(d) Whether they had benefited from visiting the stand.

(e) Was purchase of books planned or spontaneous?

(f) Will the visitor change his methods?

[O. & M. November 1966

CHECK LIST

1. Have we established the purpose of the assignment?
2. Have we planned the stages of the assignment?
3. Have we decided (in consultation) on the terms of reference?
4. Has the problem been properly diagnosed?
5. What methods of fact-finding are to be used?
6. Has a timetable been established for the assignment?
7. Have we allocated O. & M. staff?
8. Have O. & M. staff been introduced to all staff concerned?
9. Have we verified the facts?
10. Have the facts been interpreted into simple charts?
11. Has the opinion of others on new proposals been sought?
12. Have we assessed how efficiency might be improved?
13. Have we had a pilot run of the recommendations?

14. Have we planned the interviews?
15. Have we checked on the information gained at interviews?
16. What date should the O. & M. report be ready?
17. Does the O. & M. department implement, or the line management?
18. What date is fixed for a follow-up visit?
19. What action should be taken if recommendations are not implemented?
20. Have the new proposals really achieved what was expected?

Chapter 22 Obtaining the facts

I keep six honest serving men
(they taught me all I knew),
Their names are What and Why and When,
And How and Where and Who.
(*The Elephant's Child* by Rudyard Kipling)

Investigating the organisation, the system, etc., is important, probably because it is the most time-consuming part of O. & M. It also forms the basis on which hypotheses are based and changes recommended, and if the facts are wrong, everything else is likely to be wrong also.

It is also the activity which brings the O. & M. officer into close contact with all levels of management as well as simply the working level, and therefore has a great effect on the "rapport" which ought to be in existence if an O. & M. inquiry is to be successful.

The first fact to be collected is about the objectives of the business, or of the office, and here is one of the greatest differences between management services and O. & M., for the O. & M. inquiry will accept the objectives as laid down by top management, but the management services inquiry will question and make recommendations on business objectives.

Not that management always has clearly expressed objectives; one of the dangers that has to be faced is the voicing of objectives which are no more than what is performed, and not really the proper objectives which either management wishes or should wish to make.

Difficulties

The first difficulty is therefore in getting a clear expression of objectives; very often management has to be prodded into putting into writing something which they had not really considered before.

Secondly, it is so easy to collect facts "blindly" without relevance to the purpose of the assignment, which is not only time-wasting but may even confuse the inquiry, and make it difficult to analyse accurately.

The problem here, of course, is that when making an inquiry, say, into organisation, it is obviously necessary to obtain information about the methods used as well, so that it is often important to gather information on activities related to the main purpose of the inquiry.

While it is important to obtain the right quantity of information, it is equally important that it should be of the right quality. Very general statements should be suspect from the start, for the more general a statement, the greater the misunderstanding that can ensue. A more specific statement borne out by measurements is of much greater value; thus "In Week Ended . . ., 350 file movements were recorded," is much more of a fact than a statement that "there are about 500 file movements a week!"

Another difficulty is that the facts collected might not be representative, and the facts about work flow or volume of work performed need to be measured more than once, and at different times.

Then, there may well be organisation charts, duty lists, etc., already prepared, and while not seeming to belittle such official records, they should be tested to ensure they are in keeping with the facts—which they rarely are.

It is often necessary to challenge and verify the validity of facts at the time of collection, and not wait until the fact has been recorded and maybe taken for granted.

Lastly, the O. & M. officer should be expert at rejecting unnecessary facts, so that a critical state of mind must be applied all the time when collecting them.

Principles

There is a technique in fact-finding, and while being very critical of all facts presented to him, an O. & M. officer must appear appreciative, however extraneous they may be.

Some principles to be observed:

1. Staff nearly always express themselves in general terms like— "I deal with" or "I arrange," and it is then necessary to find out exactly in specific terms what is being done.
2. Be careful of generalisations like "I often" or "frequently." Such statements must be investigated and verified in quantitative terms. It is amazing how imprecise the human memory can be, but it may well happen that something that occurs only infrequently does occupy a disproportionate amount of time, therefore it looms large in the mind of the worker.
3. Then there is the question of semantics, or the common meaning and interpretation of words. "I process these invoices" might

mean a two-minute check or a half-hour checking, and the meaning of "processing" needs to be defined.

4. Workers performing different jobs will often quote something as being Company policy, either because they have been mis-informed, or because nobody has told them and they assume it to be so. Do not accept loose statements of policy without checking at a higher level. Sometimes, of course, a policy is followed which a manager is ashamed to own, and it may be necessary to include in the O. & M. report such divergence.

5. Rather similar is the voicing of opinions instead of facts, and the O. & M. inquiry should be concerned with facts and not opinions. Opinions should be listened to politely, and noted mentally, but care should be taken not to record opinions as facts.

6. Very often a worker has been doing a job for so long in an automatic fashion that he does not really know why he is doing it, or at any rate cannot express the reasons. These should be investigated and checked elsewhere.

7. When the subject of an investigation, say a system, involves two or more people, obtain the different versions of the procedure from the various people involved, and compare the different versions (the cause of a motor accident is very often not what the eye-witnesses, or the car driver, or the pedestrian states, but is something containing elements of what they all say!).

8. While recording the facts about the main-stream work, the occasional items must not be forgotten, and there are often seasonal jobs that occur only at certain times of the month or year.

9. Look out for and record the abnormalities and exceptions, be-cause they often indicate a fault in the procedure, form design, etc., as well as being part of the picture of the total situation.

Methods

There are several methods of obtaining the facts, and each has to be used according to the nature of the assignment, according to the time available, and according to the type of persons from whom facts are being gathered. The main methods are:

1. By interview with members of management (*i.e.*, supervisors up to top management).
2. By interviews at the working level.
3. By distribution of questionnaires to be completed by staff at the working level.

4. By getting staff to maintain daily diaries.
5. By visual observation on the job.
6. By inspection of records, files, etc.

1. INTERVIEW WITH MEMBERS OF MANAGEMENT

General interviewing was dealt with in the last chapter, but here the O. & M. officer must be extremely tactful and not press for information which is clearly not known. Interviewing is not always a good method because managers are often appointed for their entrepreneurial flair, not always promoted from the working level, and as a consequence they are often grossly ignorant of what really goes on in their offices. Since it is important to gain their co-operation, it is nevertheless essential not to give the impression that managers are inadequate in this respect, but just "hope they will not mind your gathering further details from lower down the management chain?"

Such interviews are also important because the management's statement of objectives and policies may be most useful.

2. INTERVIEWS WITH THE WORKING LEVEL

These are often much more reliable than 1, particularly for obtaining detailed facts as to what is done, and who does it. Unfortunately, information gathered at such interviews is not always reliable and may need to be verified. Very often workers have "an axe to grind," and opinion becomes interspersed with fact, but the information gathered here is often a useful adjunct to that gathered in 1.

3. DISTRIBUTION OF QUESTIONNAIRES

Such a technique can be used in an organisational assignment, when it is wished to know what decisions are made, about what and how often. For such a technique to be successful, the questionnaire needs very careful construction, and questions must be strictly relevant to the work performed. Although it may save investigating time, there is the time-consuming job of subsequent analysis, but in a labour turnover investigation, it may be the only means of finding out the reasons for a high L.T.O.

4. MAINTAINING DAILY DIARIES

This method is used particularly when investigating or instituting job grading; daily or weekly diary sheets are distributed, and the nature of work performed and its quantity has to be entered under different analysis headings. Again, it saves O. & M. time, but is well known for its inaccuracies, in fact, after a few days of keeping such diaries, staff have been observed to be completing their diaries from memory. But it is probably better than merely relying on staff interviews for the facts on the volume of different kinds of work performed.

5. VISUAL OBSERVATION

Despite what is stated by top management or by supervisors, or even by the workers themselves, the only ultimate reliable method is that of direct observation, *i.e.*, by simply sitting down by the side of a worker and noting what is done, every minute of the day. Thus can be revealed the activities of personnel, the movement of forms, the methods used, and the flow of work, etc.

It has the advantage of being factual, and perhaps more reliable than any of the methods in 1–4 above, but suffers because of its artificial nature. The worker will see that he is constantly employed, and will perform as efficiently as he knows how when he is under observation.

It is the most time-consuming method, and to be reliable has to be repeated several times, perhaps on different days, and even in different weeks. To be really representative, it might even be necessary to observe at different times of the year.

Such a technique also tends to destroy confidence and "rapport" with the worker, because more than ever, he feels he is being watched, as in fact he is!

6. BY INSPECTION

This refers to the actual inspection of records and files to discover such facts as the volume of documents held, the number of documents being processed (volume of work), and even to the number of errors in the work involved. Inspection of forms which have been completed can be very revealing as to the essentiality or otherwise of the information recorded in them.

This is not to say that there is always a clear choice between one or other of these methods, and frequently all six are used, but in programming an assignment, the purpose of the assignment must be borne in mind, and the appropriate fact-finding techniques employed.

Furthermore, the facts obtained one way must be verified with those obtained another way (facts obtained in interview might be checked by inspection of the files).

It is extremely difficult to obtain the facts about organisation, systems, use of forms, etc., because of the complications (even in a small business), and it should be appreciated that a day or two in an office cannot possibly reveal all there is to know, nor the relative importance of the different facts presented. Systems are interwoven, and how they are performed may well depend on the allocation of responsibility. Emphasis must be laid on the danger of trying to improve something until as many as possible of the facts are collected.

SPECIFIC DATA

Before asking questions, it might be useful to check on which specific data should be collected, which might be classified under headings of:

1. Policies of the Company.
2. Policies of the Department and middle management.
3. Resources used (details of machines, etc.).
4. Operating data (details of work performed).
5. Quantitative data (relating to volume of work, time taken, frequency, distance travelled, etc.).
6. Qualitative data (relating to incidence of errors, general efficiency and speed, state of records, office conditions, etc.).
7. Organisation data—how the duties, authority, and responsibilities are allocated.
8. Operating costs—of staff, consumable materials, machines, and overheads.

Whether the assignment be concerned with systems, organisation, job grading, salary scales, or even just cost reduction, it is as well to analyse the constituent parts of the problem and the data to be collected under each heading. Just as the method of fact collecting needs definition at the planning stage, so does the classification of the data required also need attention.

QUESTIONING

Having collected the facts, the O. & M. officer (to repeat a thousand textbooks on work study) must ask all the questions possible:

WHY?
WHAT?
WHO?
WHERE?
WHEN?
HOW?

Fact-collecting is mainly to give answers to WHAT is being done, which is the basis of inquiry.

Then, and the most important question, is WHY? What would happen if it was not done? What is the purpose of the office, of the system, of the job? A problem here is that if a worker is asked the reason why certain things are done, he will nearly always justify the work, and it can be one of the hardest parts of an O. & M. inquiry to assess for oneself whether a particular operation really is justified. Again, even if there is a perfectly reasonable explanation about why a thing is done, it may not justify the expense of staffing or overhead administration costs involved.

WHO does the work? This question is more related to an organisation inquiry, and is connected with examining whether the right staff are performing the right duties. Should work be done by staff of a different grade? Who makes decisions about the work or its problems?

WHERE is the work performed? Should it be done centrally or locally? It is often found necessary to recommend the resiting of a whole section closer to the department that it works with. Or in a system, that it is better for an operation to be performed at the beginning, even if it does mean more work, for it often aids the system and saves work later on. Sometimes a job can be performed much more economically in one office than in another.

WHEN is the work done? A time cycle of a procedure is often required, and it is then necessary to consider the sequence of operations. Could it be performed better at some other stage in the system? Could the work be staggered (as monthly statements are in "cycle billing")?

HOW is the work performed? This includes method and motion study of bodily movements. How is work checked? How is it controlled? How much does it cost?

CASE STUDY

Obtaining the facts

NATIONAL HEALTH SERVICE

1. OBJECT

To ascertain details of a hospital management staff and to study the organisation of work and arrangement of duties at management level. To ascertain whether officers were using their efforts most effectively at a large teaching hospital group.

2. PROBLEMS

It was thought that self-recording methods would reflect subjective views too much, and random sampling would not reveal the duties without a great deal of questioning.

3. COURSE OF ACTION

A one-week continuous observation of the officers concerned. It was decided to gather facts on:

(a) The time taken by each activity.
(b) The type of activity.
(c) The sphere of activity (*i.e.*, what it was about).
(d) Whether done alone or with another person.

Record sheets were prepared showing the type of activity, the time taken, and the place it was rendered—in vertical columns.
Regarding (b), the work was categorised under:

1. reading,
2. writing (including dictating),
3. using the telephone,
4. attending formal meetings,
5. interviewing and discussing,
6. talking to observer,
7. inspecting,
8. travelling,
9. breaks (lunch, etc.),
10. lecturing to outside bodies,
11. post sessions (inspecting inwards mail), and
12. other.

Regarding (c), the main spheres of work were categorised as:

1. meetings,
2. planning,
3. public relations,
4. personnel,
5. finance,
6. buildings, plant and grounds,
7. supplies,
8. surveillance,
9. other matters.

4. RESULTS

(a) A surprising factor was the number of contacts of short duration—50 per cent were less than three minutes, and 33 per cent were one minute or less.

(b) The areas of management which were receiving insufficient attention were clearly revealed.

(c) Changes in management practice were recommended, to make more efficient use of the officers' time.

(d) It was agreed that the officers were in fact fully employed, so that in order to carry out other recommended functions, it was clear which of the work, and to what extent, needed to be delegated to other staff.

[O. & M. Bulletin November 1968

CHECK LIST

1. What is the object of the assignment?
2. What is the data needed for it?
3. What methods of fact collecting are most suitable?
4. Is time a restricting factor?
5. What are the objectives and policies of management in connection with the assignment?
6. Are they acceptable, or should they be questioned?
7. What questions need to be asked, having got the facts?
8. Have facts been separated from mere opinion?
9. Have facts been verified by reference to other sources?
10. Are the facts as recorded acceptable to management?
11. Are the facts different from management's conception of them?
12. Are the terms used generally understood and accepted?
13. Has the incidence of policy, control, and cost been remembered?
14. Are there many exceptions to the rule?
15. Have we got sufficient facts to start an investigation?
16. Have we got too many facts, so that the picture is confused?
17. Do we need more facts about related departments or systems?
18. Do we know of external requirements of law, trade associations, etc.?
19. Are the facts collected strictly relevant to the assignment?
20. Are the facts recorded intelligently for reference purposes?

Chapter 23 Charts

If a system or an organisation is described in writing, it is doubtful if it would be understood, but how much easier it is when it is reduced to the form of a chart. A chart is like a map, setting out sequential and spatial relationships, and it is a most useful adjunct of all aspects of O. & M. work.

In order to free charts from reading matter, various symbols are used so that they can be read easily and quickly without having to study them closely.

There are a number of accepted conventions in charting, which are reproduced here, although there is still a lack of standardisation, but the reader's attention is drawn to:

1. B.S. 3138: 1969—Glossary of Terms in Work Study.
2. B.S. 4059: 1966—Flow Chart Symbols.
3. Procedure Charts for Administrative Work (published by the Institute of Administrative Management, 1972).
4. Computer symbols (published by the National Computing Centre).

While it is useful to know about the conventional methods, it is often possible to devise a chart for a specific purpose, which is in fact a mixture of several charts put together, and there is nothing to be deprecated about this if it represents the circumstances more clearly than a standard chart.

Advantages of charting

1. When fact-finding, charting can be used straightaway as a kind of shorthand, for depicting the system or organisation, etc., being investigated.
2. When all the facts have been gathered, they can then be represented on various kinds of chart as an aid to analysis for improvement purposes.
3. They are a concise means of communication, perhaps from the

O. & M. officer to the line manager, or to the staff concerned with the work.

4. They can be very useful in training staff, to assist the explanation of what is done, who does it, and how.
5. Charts are particularly useful to augment an O. & M. report, for they can show more clearly facts which may be confusing to the reader.
6. In organisation and procedure charts, the relationships between different people and different operations are made clearer.
7. Graphical representation makes a much greater impact on the viewer than the written word alone.

Chart preparation

Charts should be prepared most carefully, and the use of various transfer printing devices (*e.g.*, Letraset) greatly enhances the clarity of a chart. Once it has been prepared, copies can usually be obtained easily on a copying machine, so extra effort at the preparation stage is always worthwhile. Special plastic protractors can be obtained for work symbols, for layout templates, and so on, which ensure a neat job while saving in time.

Some simple hints on charting techniques:

1. There must be a title—what kind of chart, and of what activity, boldly stated.
2. The department concerned also should be stated.
3. Persons and forms used in the chart should be identified.
4. If a number of charts are being prepared, a reference number to the chart helps to identify it correctly.
5. Also indicate a chart number and continuation number, if a chart continues on to several sheets.
6. Indicate (*e.g.*, in procedure charts) where the chart begins and where it ends.
7. Always insert a date, because sometimes circumstances change so quickly that a date is useful to identify when the situation depicted was current.
8. Use pre-printed charts whenever possible, to save time and effort of O. & M. staff.

Areas of use

As mentioned above, charts can be used in all areas of O. & M. investigation, and before looking at these in detail a survey of the areas of use is given:

1. Procedures and systems.
2. Organisation.
3. Machine use.
4. Work control.
5. Communications.
6. Decision-making.
7. Office layout.
8. Allocation of departments.
9. Information flow.

The charts under 4 and 6 are included in the relevant Chapters—35 and 36 (Work Control), and 15 (Decision-making).

Kinds of chart

1. PROCEDURE AND SYSTEM CHARTS

A summary of the charts used in connection with studying procedures and methods are:

1. Procedure chart (or Process or Work Study chart).
2. Diagnostic chart.
3. "X" chart.
4. Procedure map.
5. Flow chart.
6. Motion Study chart.
7. Multiple Activity chart.

(*a*) *Procedure Chart.* This uses standard A.S.M.E. work symbols (*see* Fig. 10), depicting the sequence of operations in a procedure, and showing the type of operation used at each step.

○ OPERATION

□ INSPECTION

▷ TRANSPORT

▽ DISPOSAL

◘ DELAY

FIG. 10.—The standard B.S. procedure chart symbols,

The five standard symbols used are shown in Fig. 10.

Some other special symbols used in depicting computer systems are shown in Fig. 11. Note that an operation is the smallest step in a procedure, and although an expert O. & M. officer can depict a system using the appropriate symbols straightaway, it may be necessary to prepare, first of all, a Procedure Record.

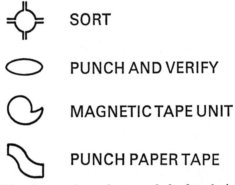

SORT

PUNCH AND VERIFY

MAGNETIC TAPE UNIT

PUNCH PAPER TAPE

FIG. 11.—Additional procedure chart symbols for depicting computer systems.

A procedure record may be necessary particularly where a complicated system is being investigated, and after appropriate coding of persons (or departments) and documents, it will appear something like Fig. 12.

POST OPENING CLERK

IN		Operation	OUT	

Person B	*Documents* 1	1. Receives mail from Registry
		2. Preliminary sort
		3. Collects empty envelopes,
		    places aside
		4. Stamps letters with date of
		    receipt
		5. Checks all enclosures
		    (and cash)
		6. Places cash aside
			Person
			
			C
				Documents
				
				Cash

FIG. 12.—A procedure record.

After this, the procedure chart can be prepared, which may be in a simple form like Fig. 13.

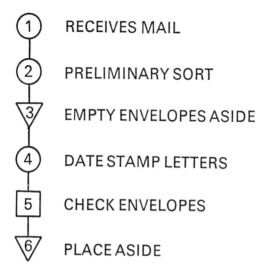

1. RECEIVES MAIL

2. PRELIMINARY SORT

3. EMPTY ENVELOPES ASIDE

4. DATE STAMP LETTERS

5. CHECK ENVELOPES

6. PLACE ASIDE

FIG. 13.—A simple procedure chart.

If a still more detailed study is required, then a standard printed form can be obtained showing the analysis of operations, and in special end columns, the distance covered and the time taken (*see* Fig. 14).

LINE NO.	STEPS IN PROCESS	OPERATIONS						OTHER STEPS			DISTANCE IN FEET	TIME	
		REF.	HAND POSTG.	TYPE OR MACH.	SORT ASSEM. COL.	FILE FIND	OTHER	TRANS	STORAGE TEMP. / PMT.	INSP.		MIN.	SEC
1													
2													
3													
4													
5													
6													
7													
8													
9													
10													
11													

FIG. 14.—An analysis of operations form.

The advantage of this last chart is that analysis, not only of the different operations, but also the type of operations is made, so that at the end, it is possible to ascertain which is the most frequent activity, the time taken by it, and the distance that documents move in the course of the procedure.

Some conventions in drawing procedure charts are shown in Fig. 15.

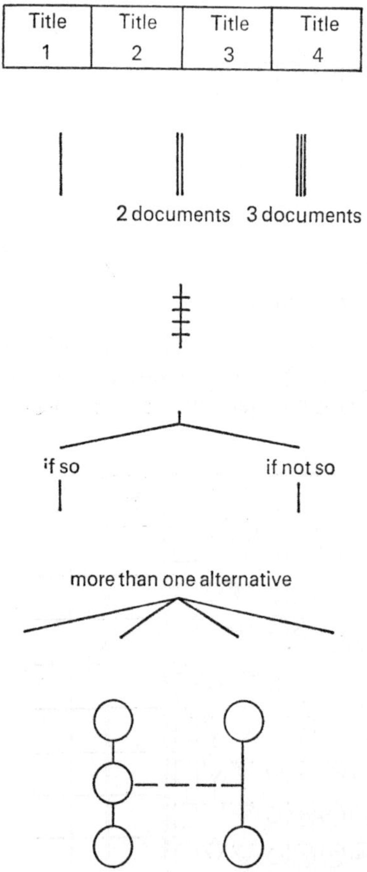

| Title 1 | Title 2 | Title 3 | Title 4 |

1. *Multiple title box*
   Used to depict a multiple set of forms.

2. *Vertical lines*
   Linking operations performed; if two or three documents move together, then the number of lines is inserted accordingly.

2 documents 3 documents

3. *Vertical barred lines*
   When more than three documents are involved.

if so   if not so

4. *Branching line*
   For alternative action.

more than one alternative

5. *Over-pass line*
   For horizontal lines crossing vertically.

6. *Horizontal link line*
   To show when an operation is performed as the result of another operation in another department.

Fig. 15.—Conventions used in drawing procedure charts.

(*b*) *Diagnostic chart.* This is a procedure record extended to a number of diagnostic columns with the basic office processes such as copying, sorting, matching, summarising, referring, movement, calculations, etc., being shown.

Opposite each operation an "X" is placed in the appropriate column. Such a chart offers a wider analysis still, and it will assist simplification and improvement of the procedure.

(c) "X" Chart. This lists all the entries made on different documents (which are listed in vertical columns), and an "X" is entered where the same information is recorded on different documents (see Fig. 16). It provides a check on the use of forms, and may suggest reduction of unnecessary writing (e.g., by the use of continuous stationery).

DATA	DOCUMENTS		
	PROOF SHEET	LEDGER CARD	STATEMENT
Date	X	X	X
Reference	X	X	X
Value	X	X	X
Invoice Number	X	X	X
Totals	4	4	4

FIG. 16.—An "X" chart, showing how the Xs can be inserted to give information common to different forms.

(d) Procedure Map. This exhibits the actual forms in use, with the number of copies, and the sequence in which they are used (see Fig. 17). Such a chart usually has coloured plastic ribbon to show the sequence between one form and another, and possibly different coloured ribbon to show the different operations.

(e) Flow Chart (or Forms Flow Chart). This is rather similar to (d), but usually the forms are drawn (for convenience of size), and the emphasis is on the number of forms and their movement from one department to another (see Fig. 18).

(f) Motion Study Chart (or Left-Hand, Right-Hand Chart). This shows the use of each hand of a worker when performing a job (see Fig. 19). The analysis columns of each hand show Operation, Transport, Hold and Delay. The object is to make the maximum use of each hand.

(g) Multiple Activity Chart. It is sometimes found that clerks are wasting time because of delays by other clerks, and an assessment of the delays can be obtained by showing the related activities on one chart (see Fig. 20). By altering the sequence, it may then be possible to eliminate the waiting time.

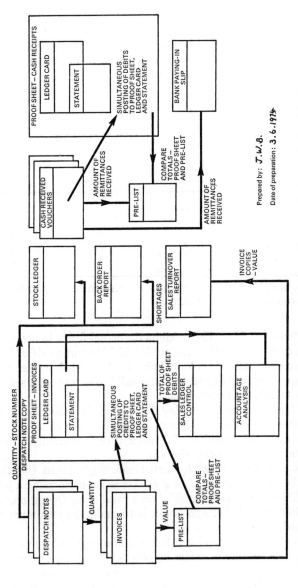

Fig. 17.—A procedure map displaying the actual forms used, and their relationship in a system.

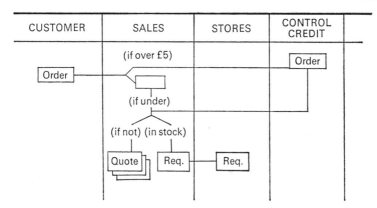

CUSTOMER	SALES	STORES	CONTROL CREDIT	

FIG. 18.—Example of a procedure flow chart, showing the types of operation and their sequence.

2. ORGANISATION CHARTS

To help analyse the organisation of an office a

    (*a*) work distribution chart, or

    (*b*) simple organisation chart

can be used.

    (*a*) *Work Distribution Chart.* This has the different categories of work listed, with the names of staff in vertical columns (*see* Fig. 21). The amount of time spent by different members of staff in different kinds of work is then entered in the vertical columns. This aids a study of how the work is distributed.

    (*b*) *Organisation Chart.* This is so well known that it does not need description here, but it is usual to show executive authority with a bold line and an advisory function with a dotted line (*see* Fig. 22). It is possible to show not only staff numbers, but gradings as well on a single departmental chart.

3. MACHINE USE CHART (or Production Chart)

Where it is wished to study the actual use of a machine compared with the occupation of the operator (who may be fully employed while the machine is idle). Such a chart will show, where by delegation of simple duties, fuller use could be made of a machine (*see* Fig. 23).

4. WORK CONTROL CHARTS

See Chapters 35 and 36.

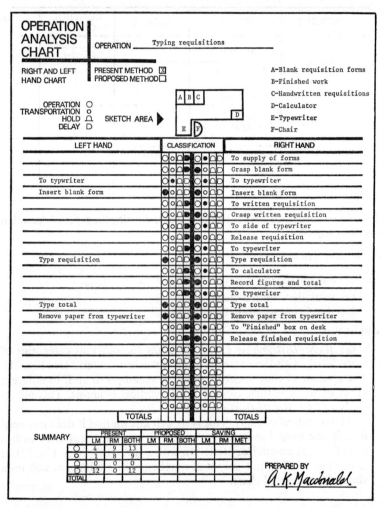

FIG. 19.—A motion study chart, showing the different kinds of operation performed by both hands.

5. COMMUNICATION MAP

This is quite simply a map of the company's offices (perhaps displayed on a map of the country), showing the types of communication available between all the different offices (*see* Fig. 24).

CLERK 1	CLERK 2	CLERK 3	TIME
Prelist			0
	Stuff invoices	Posting	15
			30
			45
			60

FIG. 20.—A multiple activity chart, showing how activities can be performed by different personnel

6. DECISION-MAKING ALGORITHMS

See Chapter 15.

7. OFFICE LAYOUT CHARTS (sometimes called String Diagrams)

These show the flow of work or documents between different work stations in an office (*see* Fig. 25). The aim, of course, is to reduce to a minimum the movement of people and of paper.

8. ALLOCATION OF DEPARTMENTS

Here a Correlation Chart shows the relative importance of different departments, measured by the volume of records moving (*see* Fig. 26).

This will require most detailed counting of the documents moving per day or per week between different departments, but it will aid in

Type of work	John Brown	Man Hours	Doreen Smith	Man Hours	Eric Green	Man Hours
Correspondence	Opens and reads letters	6	Takes shorthand Transcribes	15	Writes Post Book	9
Invoices	Drafts Invoices	3	Types Invoices	2		

FIG. 21.—A work distribution chart.

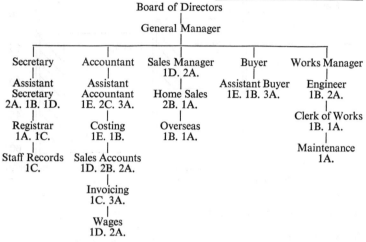

EXCEL MANUFACTURING COMPANY LIMITED

Organisation Chart
As at 1st January, 19...

Staffing

	A	B	C	D	E	Total
	24	10	5	4	3	46

Board of Directors

General Manager

Secretary
Assistant
Secretary
2A. 1B. 1D.
Registrar
1A. 1C.
Staff Records
1C.

Accountant
Assistant
Accountant
1E. 2C. 3A.
Costing
1E. 1B.
Sales Accounts
1D. 2B. 2A.
Invoicing
1C. 3A.
Wages
1D. 2A.

Sales Manager
1D. 2A.
Home Sales
2B. 1A.
Overseas
1B. 1A.

Buyer
Assistant Buyer
1E. 1B. 3A.

Works Manager
Engineer
1B. 2A.
Clerk of Works
1B. 1A.
Maintenance
1A.

FIG. 22.—An office organisation chart.

OPERATOR	Op.	TIME	Mach.	MACHINE
10 Stuff carbon in invoices 20		20		Idle
30 Typing 40				Typing
50		40		
60 Check entries 70		20		
80 Cards stamped and initialled		10		Idle
90 Idle				
		10		
100 Replace cards in pile, etc.		10		

FIG. 23.—A machine use or productivity chart.

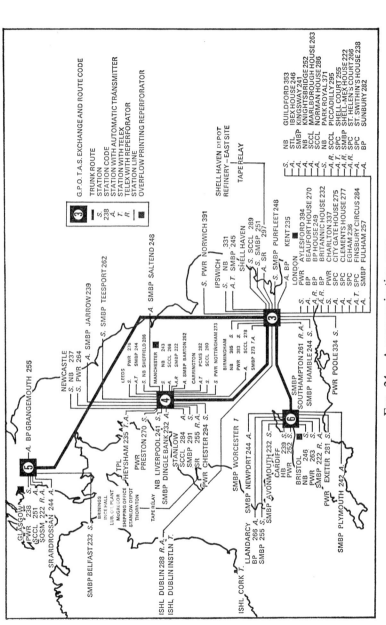

Fig. 24.—A communication map.

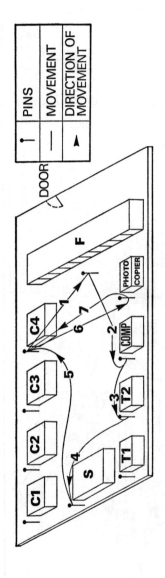

	PINS
—	MOVEMENT
▲	DIRECTION OF MOVEMENT

DOOR

F

KEY TO ABBREVIATIONS	
C1	CLERK NO.1
C2	CLERK NO.2
C3	CLERK NO.3
C4	CLERK NO.4
S	SUPERVISOR
T1	TYPIST NO.1
T2	TYPIST NO.2
COMP	COMPTOMETER OPERATOR
F	FILING CABINETS

ANALYSIS OF MOVEMENT C4
1 DESK TO FILING CABINETS
2 FILING CABINETS TO COMPTOMETER OPERATOR
3 COMPTOMETER OPERATOR TO TYPIST NO.2
4 TYPIST NO.2 TO SUPERVISOR
5 SUPERVISOR TO DESK
6 DESK TO PHOTO COPIER
7 PHOTO COPIER TO DESK

FIG. 25.—A string diagram or office layout chart.

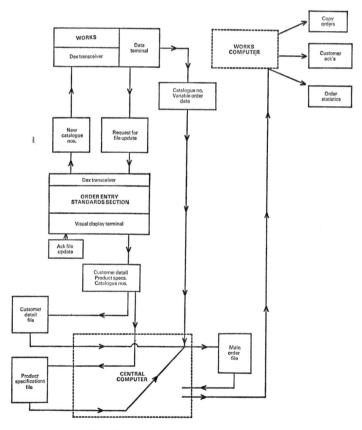

Company Secretary		
2	Personnel	
3	4	Sales
2	4	6

FIG. 26.—A correlation chart, by which different volumes of documents indicate the ideal allocation of offices

FIG. 27.—An information flow chart.

planning an office building, in helping to decide the proximity of different offices.

9. INFORMATION FLOW CHART

This is an essential when installing a computer system, and it shows how information flows from one department to another (*see* Fig. 27). There is then the problem of measuring the volume and the frequency of the different pieces of information.

Conclusion

Although this Chapter has shown several kinds of chart usable in O. & M. work, the practitioner should be able to devise his own non-conventional charts if they are more suitable to the circumstances. Thus, a simple procedure chart can be divided into vertical columns representing departments, so that it shows not only the operations, but the flow of work between departments as well. Or again, titles of forms can be displayed to show the forms, the operations, and the flow of work. But care must be taken not to make a chart too complicated; it is often better to show different aspects on different charts.

CHECK LIST

1. What is the purpose of the chart to be used?
2. What is the best form of chart?
3. Have we got all the information necessary for the chart?
4. Can a standard chart be used?
5. Is it simple and self-explanatory?
6. Would different colours be advisable?
7. Who is going to use the chart?
8. How long will it take to prepare?
9. What will it show?
10. Have we given it a title?
11. Have we put in the date of preparation?
12. Have we checked with a line manager on its accuracy?
13. How can the procedure, organisations, etc., be improved?
14. Can special protractors save time in preparation?
15. Is the proper equipment available for chart preparation?
16. Should the chart be displayed or kept secret?
17. Can the chart be used for other purposes (*e.g.*, training of staff)?
18. Is the chart based on fact?
19. Have we recorded the facts?
20. Is it the best chart for the purpose, or should we design a special one?

Chapter *24* Forms control

Forms are the basic tools of all clerical work. They are the medium for receiving, arranging, recording, and giving information, so that formal as opposed to informal methods may be practised.

If a form is badly designed it can make for inefficiency, because it can cause unnecessary inquiries, and if it does not include information that should be included, it can mean delays, as well as incorrect action based on incomplete detail being taken.

The most important reason for the control of forms is the clerical cost involved. Every additional piece of paper means more clerical work, and it has been stated in America, that for every dollar spent on forms, five dollars has to be spent on clerical labour to file them, to fill them in, and to transport them.

Printing becomes increasingly more expensive, and the smaller the number of forms in use, the smaller is the printing bill.

A common failing is for forms to be designed and printed, but to become redundant almost immediately, so that the stationery cupboard is full of out-dated, unused forms. Of course, it is better to waste paper than it is to spend on unnecessary clerical labour, but better still not to have unnecessary forms in the first place.

Forms are very much related to office systems, in fact the system can often be deduced from the forms in use. If the wrong forms or too many forms are used, it can result in total inefficiency of the whole system. Thus, however good is the enrolment system at a college, a badly-designed application form can mean delays, queries, mistakes, and faulty enrolment. It is also a principle of office systems that they should have the least number of forms.

Unless there is proper control, paperwork tends to proliferate, and there is often duplication of forms, and unnecessary forms created, *e.g.*, there being too many, and unnecessary copies being distributed.

Lastly, standardisation of forms, particularly in size and colour, can have a great effect on filing equipment and ease of handling and filing.

Essentials of control

For all these reasons, forms are important and need to be closely controlled. In a large concern, there is likely to be a separate forms controller, while in many concerns it is part of the O. & M. area of operation while investigating systems; in smaller concerns, it will be the part-time occupation of one of the under-managers. It is, unfortunately, sometimes thought to be such an unimportant aspect of efficiency, that even in some large concerns there is no specialist at all, and forms control is left to different departmental managers.

The essence of forms control is:

1. to use and retain only those forms that are really necessary;
2. having established necessity, to see that all forms are designed properly and give the greatest aid to systems, at least cost;
3. to produce forms by the most appropriate methods;
4. to distribute forms only to those who have justifiable reasons to use them;
5. to study all old forms when reprinting is required, and all proposed new forms;
6. to review periodically all forms in use, to keep them in line with current system requirements.

The storage and issue of forms is more the concern of stationery control than forms control.

Initiating forms control

Forms can be said to include every piece of printed paper in use in an enterprise, varying from printed letter-headings and compliments slips to invoices, ledgers and computer print-out. For complete forms control, every piece of paper that is used in all the offices should be included.

When there has been no central forms control, and it is wished to initiate it, then something like the following is necessary:

1. Announce to all line managers the existence of the new forms control unit, and indicate its function and authority.
2. Freeze all forms activity, so that any printing requirements for old, new, or revised forms are referred automatically to the new unit.
3. Obtain at least two copies of every form in use.
4. Make an itemised list of all the forms, and allocate form numbers.

5. Start two form files: one numerical (according to form number), and one according to function.
6. Obtain details of procedures in which forms are used, and perhaps enter such details on one of the file copies.
7. Analyse to see if any of the forms can be eliminated or combined with others. There are nearly always forms in stock which have been discontinued in practical use.
8. Start a forms register or daily log record, or both.

A difficulty of forms control is that there are so many forms used and mostly in small quantities. Thus, one concern with 750 employees had 336 forms, and of these 262 (or 78 per cent) were used in annual quantities of 1,000 a year or less. This illustrates the point that forms control means the control of a large number of low-usage items.

In a large concern, it may be useful to have a Forms Order Log Book, which provides a quick reference and printing follow-up system. Its ruling might be something like that shown in Fig. 28.

FORMS ORDER LOG

Form No. 1	Form Title	Qty. Ordered	Req. No.	Req. by	Form			To Printer				Samples		
					New	Revised	No change	Out	Proof In	Proof Out	Job Req.	Date rec'd	Num. file	Funct. file

FIG. 28.—A Forms Order Log.

The end columns constitute a check that one copy of each form is placed (*a*) in the forms (numerical) file, and (*b*) in the functional file.

In a large enterprise, it might even be necessary to have a forms register which gives specifications for reordering, although care has to be taken that this is not maintained for its own sake. Thus, when getting a form reordered, offset-litho reproduction does not need a printing specification, but a register can give brief details of use, method of reproduction, etc.

Such a forms register might be as shown in Fig. 29.

In a forms control unit of a large enterprise, there will therefore be:

1. Forms Register.
2. Forms List.
3. Forms Daily Log.
4. Forms File (numerical).
5. Forms File (functional).

FORMS REGISTER		Form No.
FORM TITLE		

HOW FILLED IN		
☐ HAND ☐ T/W ☐	DEPT. USED BY	CHECK WITH

DELIVER TO	CHARGE TO	FUNCT. FILE NO.

USED FOR	PROCEDURE USED IN

PRINTING SPECIFICATION

METHOD OF	☐ SPIRIT	NAME OF PRINTER
	☐ STENCIL	(IF EXTERNAL)
REPRO.	☐ INTERNAL	
	☐ EXTERNAL	

PAPER		COLOUR	TRIMMED SIZE

PRINT	☐ BLACK	☐ COLOUR	ONE SIDE	TWO SIDES
		(SPECIFY) ☐	☐	

MARGINS	
NUMBERING	
BINDING	
PUNCHING	
PADDING	

TYPE FONT	☐ CARBON
	☐ N.C.R.

FIG. 29.—A Forms Register.

Although forms control is dealt with here as a separate entity, many office forms cannot be considered without investigating the procedures in which they are used, and this is why it is perhaps best for forms control to be an O. & M. activity. Although systems should be reviewed at frequent intervals, partly because of the cost of printing, investigation of the procedure often is made only when new forms are required.

Methods of reproduction

It will be noticed in Fig. 29, that both spirit and stencil methods of reproduction are mentioned, and if this is suitable (*i.e.*, for less important internal matters and where the numbers are low), then either of these may be the best method. It is often found that forms having low-volume usage, which could well have been reproduced on a duplicator, have been printed and in fact the department could be advised accordingly and internal arrangements made for duplication. Copies of such duplicated forms should, however, be retained in the Forms Register and on the Form Files, because they are perhaps an integral part of departmental procedures.

More and more local authorities and businesses are, however, installing their own in-plant offset-litho machines for printing their own forms.

The advantages of such an arrangement are:

1. convenience of handling rush work (even in the best-run business, forms suddenly become out of stock);
2. a dependable and interested source to cope with printing requirements, with much better control than is possible with outside printers;
3. lower cost of printing—provided there is a sufficient volume of work;
4. assists the specialists in forms control and forms design;
5. helps to budget overall costs, instead of generating sporadic external printing costs.

The disadvantages can be stated as being that:

1. trained operators are required;
2. printing techniques, particularly of layout, take many years to acquire;
3. problems of plant maintenance;
4. expense of continuing overhead cost of labour, whether fully employed or not.

With the technical development in producing offset-litho plates on paper, plastic and thin aluminium, and with the growth of cheaper photocopying for the production of these plates, in-plant reproduction becomes increasingly more possible and economic. Already, a cheap offset-litho machine costs little more than an electric automatic duplicator, and in fact if there is insufficient printing fully to justify the purchase of such a machine, it can be used as an office duplicator, using paper plates.

CASE STUDY

Forms control

MARKS AND SPENCER LTD.

1. BACKGROUND

The Chairman of Marks and Spencer saw in the mountain of paper-work a threat to their retail prices, and so he started a paper war.

2. CAMPAIGN

For six to nine months, both headquarters staff and branch managers attacked the duplication of forms, simplification of forms, and cutting out forms wherever possible.

3. ACTION TAKEN

(a) A large volume of record was eliminated; thus instead of having separate records of goods in the stock-room and on the counter, only one stock figure is now recorded.

(b) A reduction in the detail on record was achieved, so that instead of dozens of different colours and sizes of shirts being recorded, only one stock total is inserted, and it is left to the staff and the Store Manager to indent for specific sizes and colours.

(c) Former stock-room records were abandoned and sales assistants now collect what they want from the stock-room without the need for requisitions, etc. (sales and stock headings reduced from 3,000 to 1,000).

(d) Branch Goods Received Notes were discontinued; Head Office only has to be notified when goods are not received.

(e) Sets of 500 catalogue cards were maintained at each store—now abandoned.

(f) Previously, the branches (250 of them) had received invoices from suppliers, which they checked and forwarded to H.O. Now, they are sent direct to H.O., and as in (d) above are passed for payment if there are no discrepancies reported (this saved the handling of three million invoices a year).

(g) Books for recording internal price reductions were eliminated.

(h) Customer complaint forms for sending to H.O. were discontinued.

(*i*) Pay-rolls were centralised at Baker Street H.O.

(*j*) Time clocks and clocking-in cards were abandoned (for 25,000 employees).

(*k*) 100 per cent checks were abandoned in favour of sample checks.

(*l*) The thirteen manuals issued to Branch Managers were replaced by two only.

4. RESULTS

(*a*) A saving of 26 million pieces of paper a year.

(*b*) Staff reduced by 6,000.

(*c*) A saving of £5 millions a year in administration costs.

5. COMMENTS

This is such a fantastic account of reduction of paperwork as to be almost a classical example.

(*a*) De-centralisation of responsibility and control to Branch Managers.

(*b*) Centralisation of wages and salaries preparation.

(*c*) Changes in policy, *e.g.*, getting rid of time clocks and substituting supervisory checks.

(*d*) It demonstrates how forms are closely related to systems, which in turn are often based on policies.

(*e*) The success of the campaign undoubtedly was due in no small part to it being initiated by the Chairman of the Company.

Marks and Spencer is a fairly centralised concern, and seems to have been in need of such a paper purge, for among the records discontinued were 150,000 inwards-mail records.

[*Business Equipment News* February 1962

CHECK LIST

1. Is there one central forms control in the enterprise?
2. Are all forms included in the control?
3. Has a form numbering system been introduced?
4. Is there periodic review of forms?
5. What are the methods of reproduction?
6. Is volume of annual usage taken into account?
7. Have we in-plant printing facilities?
8. Will it be economical to install?
9. Do we maintain a Forms Register?

10. Do we know how the forms are used?
11. Has the total cost of forms been obtained?
12. Has forms control reduced this cost?
13. Or improved efficiency in other ways?
14. Could new forms be duplicated?
15. What proportion of forms are used less than 1,000 a year?
16. Do we know the procedural use of forms?
17. Have we reduced the number of forms in use?
18. Can some be eliminated?
19. Or combined?
20. Have we really got control of all office forms in use?

Chapter 25 Forms design

As mentioned in the last Chapter, forms design is a part of overall forms control, but while many writers have given prominence to forms design, there is comparatively little attention given to forms control, which should really be the starting-point of forms design. Unless there is some kind of forms control, there is not much point in giving attention to forms design, because each department of a concern will have the forms it thinks fit—and in the style it thinks fit.

There are many authors, but few designers, of forms, and forms design is concerned not only with *what* information is contained in a form, but with *how* it is displayed.

Forms design is important for all the reasons listed in the last chapter, *i.e.*, it is concerned with efficiency, with the extraction of data, with the avoidance of errors, and with economy. Forms are an essential part of systems and unless designed in the right way, with the right quality paper, and of the right size, they can be an impediment to the correct functioning of an office system.

Forms design is a very diverse subject because it covers every bit of printed paper used in an enterprise, and it requires not merely a knowledge of printing, paper and layout, but also of machines and systems.

Whole books have been written on forms design, and outstanding are those published by the Management Services Division of the Treasury, as well as by the Institute of Administrative Management, so only an outline of the salient features is given here.

Principles of forms design

If there are guiding principles of forms design, they can be summarised as follows:

    1. The first and most important question to ask is whether a form is really necessary at all, and a good guide can be obtained by asking "What would happen if it was discontinued?"

2. Having established its *raison d'être*, ask "Can it be combined with some other form?"
3. Look at its function and purpose in the procedure. The form should always assist the purposes, and have in mind control and costs.
4. Information on a form should be reduced to a minimum. An unfortunate habit of many form authors is to include even exceptional items which may not be required in ninety-nine out of a hundred cases, thus requiring a great deal of unnecessary writing. So not only the function of the form, but the numerical frequency of the items of information on the form should be assessed.
5. Design should be such as to reduce clerical error to a minimum.
6. Forms design should be assessed in terms of simplicity of entering as well as simplicity of extracting data; whichever is more important should be given emphasis, and if it is about equal, then a compromise must be effected. For what is convenient when entering a form is not always convenient for extraction of data; it depends on the purpose.
7. Amount of space left for entering of data should allow for the maximum of data to be entered. This involves investigation of what is actually entered in the relevant spaces.
8. A form should always have a title so that it is clear what it is. This is particularly useful for reference purposes and for identification in procedure analysis.
9. A good form should be mainly self-explanatory, and any instructions necessary should be clear and as brief as possible. Where too many instructions are required, then it is likely that it is a badly designed form.
10. Important data for filing and routing purposes should be displayed prominently.
11. Costs should be considered, not merely of a form, but of its entering, handling and filing. Sometimes an expensive form can save money in other ways, and conversely a cheaply produced form can cause all manner of mistakes and inefficiencies.

Factors of form design

The Management Services Division of the Treasury has issued a Forms Design Check List containing eighty-five questions, and there have been many classifications of the numerous factors. No matter what kind of classification is adopted, there will always be overlapping, but it is suggested that a convenient classification of the main factors is:

1. Entry of data.
2. Use (on extraction) of data.
3. Use of form (how entered and how used in the system).
4. Reduction of errors.
5. Economy (overall costs).
6. Identification for filing, handling, etc.

These are now examined in detail:

1. ENTRY OF DATA

Appearance—does it encourage its use?
Layout—probably sequence of data.
Type fount(s)—do the headings overshadow the variable information?
Spacing—should be relevant to method of entry and volume of data to be entered in the majority of cases (standard typewriter characters are ten to the inch).
Information boxes—not only to improve appearance, but to guide the filling in of the form.
Check boxes—to save time in writing.

2. USE OF DATA

The factors for the use of data on the form are very much the same as in 1 above, but it must be remembered that sequence and layout suitable for entering is not always most convenient for extraction of data. If for computer input, then the method of use (*e.g.*, for punched cards) will have a distinct influence on the way information is displayed.

3. USE OF FORM

Here, pre-eminently, it must be considered how the form is entered, *e.g.*, by hand, typewriter, computer, etc.
Size of form must be related to handling and filing.
Form title is important so that users can identify it.
Colour of paper may help in routing.
Colour of print is also related to 1 and 2 above, as well as being relevant to the colour of the paper.
Quality of paper (this is dealt with in greater detail below).
Make-up—*e.g.*, padded, etc.
Number of copies is related to the use in the procedure concerned.
Handling and filing is relevant to thickness of paper and size.

4. REDUCTION OF ERRORS

Guide lines for entering (say a bold line every five lines—or even lines for writing where entered by hand).
Vertical columns to ensure entry in the correct place.
Clarity is concerned with captions and type fount.
Instructions should be as brief as possible, but should be inserted if this will help prevent errors.

5. ECONOMY

Cost of forms is related to the number of copies, the number of different colours used in the printing, etc.
Annual usage should be assessed, and depending on importance, a form with low distribution should not be an expensive one.
Method of reproduction (*see* previous Chapter).
Cost of a form should be related to the cost of clerical work required to enter, handle and file it. So an expensive form might save more expensive labour, and a cheap form might be expensive in overall costs.
Paper quality and size is relevant, bearing in mind standard filing sizes and printers' standard cutting sizes.

6. IDENTIFICATION

Form title is important.
Form numbers should always be printed.
Each should be clearly differentiated from any other similar forms (*e.g.*, credit note from invoice) by using different coloured paper, in different coloured inks, etc.

Size

While the old conventional sizes of foolscap and quarto, etc., still remain (and much filing equipment is still based on these old sizes), there has been a gradual change over to the International Paper Sizes, which has the advantage of replacing over thirty sizes of paper by seven, and for practical purposes by four.
These I.P.S. are:

A0   841 mm × 1189 mm (a square metre)
A1   594 „   × 841 „   (half of A0)
A2   420 „   × 594 „   („ „ A1)

A3   297 mm ×   420 mm (half of A2)
A4   210 „   ×   297 „ („   „ A3)
A5   148 „   ×   210 „ („   „ A4)
A6   105 „   ×   148 „ („   „ A5)
A7   74 „   ×   105 „ („   „ A6)

For all practical purposes, only sizes A3–A7 are likely to be considered for office forms.

The size of a form must be chosen giving consideration to:

1. amount of information to be entered;
2. size and style of type fount desired;
3. method of entry;
4. convenience of handling and filing;
5. economy, for a form should be as small as possible, but bearing in mind 1–4 above.

Some business concerns have standardised all their letter headings on A4, without taking account of short letters for which A5 would be quite suitable, and a study of the length of letters and their volume would show whether it would be worth a separate printing. The cost of a separating printing should be compared with the saving in paper costs.

Eleven different-sized envelopes are also obtainable in I.P.S. classification, and where forms are sent through the post the appropriate-sized envelope should be chosen.

Thus:

A4 forms can be suitably folded for C4, C5, C6 or C7/6 envelope sizes.

A5   „   „   „   „   „   „ C6 or C5/6.

depending on the number of folds required in the forms.

The Post Office announced its intention in 1967 of including a lower postage rate for letters sent in P.O.P. sizes (Post Office Preferred), but its implementation has been continuously deferred. It was then announced that to comply with the P.O.P. range, envelopes should be at least 90 mm × 140 mm and not larger than 120 mm × 235 mm, and be oblong in size with the longer side at least 1·414 times the shorter side, and made from paper at least to 39 g.s.m. (grammes per square metre).

Paper

The factors in choosing paper to be used will include:

1. *Use*—related to the amount of handling, method of printing, etc.
2. *Entries*—a matt surface is best for ball-pen entry, used mostly in offices.
3. *Erasing*—the ability to erase may be important.

4. *Economy*—some paper is twice the cost of other similar papers.
5. *Appearance*—an expensive bond paper is often chosen for letter-headings, because it has an impressive appearance.
6. *Security*—how much proof does it offer against fraudulent alteration?
7. *Colour and surface*—the colour of the paper will be related to clarity and the density of the surface and the appearance of printing made on it.

Rag paper can be used for very expensive and important forms, although most paper is chemically constituted and called sulphite; but there are substantial variations in quality, and it is therefore advisable to call for samples when buying paper or getting printing performed. Tests can then be carried out:

1. Test for visibility on both sides (if entry is required on both sides). All machine-made papers have a top side and a wire side. The worse the quality of paper, the greater is the difference between the sides.
2. Thickness of paper is measured now in the standardised "grammes per square metre" (*e.g.*, 19 g.s.m.); and the thickness should be chosen bearing in mind the usage, method of entry, and economy.
3. Grain of the paper is very important when buying paper for offset-litho reproduction, and this can be established by holding two identical strips together, one from a horizontal and one from a vertical cut of the paper. If the grain is the wrong way (it is wanted lengthwise), the paper will not feed well in an offset-litho machine.
4. Strength of paper can be tested by crumpling and by tearing, and in fact special tensile testing machines can be purchased for this purpose.
5. When mechanical wood is present in paper, it will tend to discolour and detection after exposure to light. This can be detected either by a light test or by looking at the colour and listening to its sound when crumpled. Wood-free paper stock has a snap not present in mechanical wood paper. Chemical testing with phloroglucine to see if it retains its yellow colour or whether it turns brown or red is another possibility.

Forms design in practice

Some prefer to give a rough design of a form to the printer, and leave it to him to set it out and use appropriate type founts, etc. just contenting themselves with content, colour, size and paper. But while a good printer will produce what is required, many others will not be so assiduous, and if the wrong style print is used, if the spacing is all wrong, and if captions are too weak or too bold, then the forms designer is to blame. Furthermore, it matters little how beautiful a form may appear if it is not suitable to its purpose. If a printer's proof is not acceptable and has to be amended, it can add quite considerably to the final printing bill.

When submitting a draft form for printing, it should leave little doubt in the printer's mind about the customer's requirements, and the only sure way is to present a visual impression of the printed form, corroborated if necessary by written detail.

There should be a specification, stating whether the forms are single- or double-sided, snap carbon set, continuous stationery, etc. Also, there should be instructions about any special treatment such as numbering, colour of paper, colour of printing, pre-punching, etc.

Then, the forms designer should use an actual-size piece of paper (but specifying the type of paper required), with, if possible, actual-size printing founts. The Varityper, and the use of dry-adhesive lettering like "Letraset" is very useful here, although time-consuming. If the information is typed on a form, its type fount should be specified, together with spacing, but typewritten preparation leaves a lot to be desired in actual spacing on a form, even if elite or mini-elite type style is used.

The aim should always be to make the draft resemble the finished product as closely as possible in order to help the printer avoid mistakes.

Before ordering a printed form, it is a good idea to:

1. check with users;
2. check with previously filled-in copies of the form;
3. make practical tests by actually filling in a form, and;
4. for essentiality of information, have a test-run by using a duplicated form for a short period.

When giving instructions to the printer, the form designer should be familiar with printer's "language," such as single and double lead spacing, and when making corrections to a proof, proper printer's correction symbols should always be used.

Finally, printing should always be ordered well in advance to allow time for proofs, corrections, and any delays in printing (a common occurrence).

A standard Printing Specification can be adopted which not only helps the printer, but reminds the forms designer of all the information which should be specified. Such a form should accompany the draft to the printer, and might appear as in Fig. 30.

FORM PRINTING SPECIFICATION TO: Date

Form No.	Title	Size: Deep Wide
		Tolerance: Depth
		Width

Paper	Kind	Weight	Colour
Grain:			

Printing	Colours and Face	One side	Two-sided Head to Head	Two-sided Tumbler
		☐	☐	☐

Register	Form must register exactly with

Line spacing	☐ Vertical	☐ Horizontal

Punching	☐ No. of Holes	Diameter............	Shape......................

Perforating	all ☐ as indicated	Other: specify
	Slotted ☐	Round ☐

Pad ☐	Gum at head ☐

Bind	top/left	sheets to a pad/book

Fold	No. of times	horizontally or vertically as indicated

Corners	Round ☐	Square ☐

Special instructions

FIG. 30.—A form printing specification, to give printers exact information on form design requirements.

CASE STUDY

Forms design

CIVIL SERVICE DEPT.

1. Previously, a reminder form "Driving Licence Reminder" was sent out in an envelope (six million a year).
2. By redesigning the form, so that it could be posted when folded, it saved the equivalent of £2,700 per annum.
3. As a postal folder, it showed the following economies:

   (*a*) saving of six million envelopes a year;
   (*b*) time saved in inter-departmental accounting;
   (*c*) folding of the form to send out to motorists can be performed by industrial staff instead of office staff;

(*d*) folding machines and spare labour capacity were utilised, thus saving the Local Taxation Offices.

Comments

While not a very extensive case study, it emphasises the importance of
forms design, in its effect on staffing, on postage, and overall costs.

[*O. & M. Bulletin* April 1956

CHECK LIST

1. Is the form really necessary?
2. Can it be combined with another?
3. Have we examined all the factors of forms design?
4. What are the overall costs of a form?
5. What method of reproduction is used?
6. What is the annual usage of different forms?
7. Have we evaluated cost in terms of clerical usage?
8. What is the best size for a form?
9. What is the best paper for the purpose?
10. Have we examined the form in its procedure content?
11. Have we checked with the user on a new form design?
12. Are different coloured inks justified in view of the cost?
13. Has the form a title and a form number?
14. Have we really obtained control of forms?
15. Do we know how many forms in use?
16. Have we a forms register and a forms file?
17. Have we discarded discontinued forms?
18. Do we send to the printer a facsimile proof, or a rough proof?
19. How much are the printing bills increased by revisions to proof?
20. Have we actually used a new/revised form to test its efficiency?

Chapter 26 O. & M. reporting

Submitting the O. & M. report to management is the culmination of the whole assignment, but it should be remembered that the recommendations are advisory only, and it is not a question of telling management what should be done. Furthermore, and it is an important attribute of an O. & M. officer, there should be an ability to sell the ideas involved in the recommendations. It is one thing telling an ailing patient what is wrong, but it is quite another matter persuading him of the efficacy of your remedies!

Before the report

Although reporting is communicating in writing, communication can also be by word of mouth, and it is often advisable to do both. Thus, before the official report is submitted it may be advisable to communicate orally with the line managers, to let them know what is going to appear in the report.

It is often advisable to have a meeting of managers, outlining the recommendations, this presents the opportunity of gauging their reaction and acceptance of the proposals; it may (although it should not) give ideas for final revision of some of the recommendations.

When a new machine is being introduced it might be part of the selling of the recommendations to arrange a demonstration of the new machine, so that reactions of staff might be included in the report. This gives opportunity of discussing alternatives, and emphasising the benefits of the new proposed method.

It might even be necessary to have a series of conferences, perhaps at different management levels, before the report is submitted.

If it can be said to top management that your supervisors or departmental managers have agreed to the recommendations, it removes some of top management's fears straightaway.

When introducing a computer for the first time, a two-day conference has even been known to have been held, explaining the machine, and the effect it would have on the work of the concern.

Writing a report

The essentials of writing *any* report in business are:

1. Address it to a definite reader (Managing Director, etc.).
2. Have a salutation (for courtesy).
3. Have a simple title.
4. Introduce the report by quoting terms of reference.
5. Make the report have sections with headings for each section.
6. Recommendations are important, so they should either all be at the end of the report, or at the end of each section, and should begin boldly in block capitals RECOMMENDED.
7. The report should be signed (with designation of post).
8. Be dated.

Style of writing

1. The most important aspect of style is that the report should be so written that it is easily understood by the reader for whom it is intended. Even if it is about a technical subject, technical language should not be used if it can be avoided. It is often difficult to avoid technicalities, but there are often different interpretations of what is meant by them, and it is better to over-simplify than to mislead.
2. A good report should be scientific in style, *i.e.*, avoiding exaggerations, and being positive, based on fact; a report should not be an essay consisting of personal opinions. It should be in plain English, and simply written.
3. It should not be too long, for a manager is much more interested in the recommendations than in all the ramifications of argument leading up to them. But there must, of course, be reasons adduced for the changes proposed.
4. While there must be criticism, if only implied, of existing systems, organisation, etc., it is not advisable to criticise any past management nor members of management.
5. It should be impartial, and set out the main differences between the old systems/methods/organisation, etc., and the proposed one.
6. It might be advisable to give credit to staff who have been particularly helpful in the investigations, particularly if their ideas have been incorporated in the final proposals.
7. In a lengthy report, there should be a summary of the main

recommendations, so that the main proposals can be grasped easily.

8. The report should be illustrated by the inclusion of flow charts, organisation charts, specimen forms, etc., from which the new proposals can be seen more easily.

Contents of the O. & M. report

The actual contents of an O. & M. report will vary with the nature and size of the assignment, but generally speaking the logical sequence of different sections of such a report will be:

1. Terms of reference.
2. Reasons for the assignment.
3. Investigations made.
4. Faults and problems.
5. Their causes.
6. Conclusions.
7. Alternative remedies.
8. Those recommended.
9. Benefits arising therefrom.
10. Comparisons in costs of the old and the new.
11. Suggestions for implementing recommendations (and time-table).
12. Appendixes.

1. TERMS OF REFERENCE

This is important, to establish what the O. & M. assignment was about, when requested, and by whom. The reader can then compare the investigations and recommendations with the terms of reference.

2. REASONS FOR THE ASSIGNMENT

The reasons might be included in the terms of reference, but if not, then it is advisable to state why the assignment was made.

3. INVESTIGATIONS MADE

The methods of investigations, the duration, and the personnel consulted should all be included, for they give a measure of the thoroughness with which the investigations have been made.

4. FAULTS AND PROBLEMS

The faults in the system, organisation, etc., should then be set out. This is the diagnosis and should be very plainly stated. It may be that management policies are at fault, and this is possibly where a Management Services assignment is superior to a mere O. & M. report where policies may have to be accepted. Management policies are often a cause of inefficiency, and they should be assessed and recommendations made accordingly.

5. THEIR CAUSES

There may be historical causes of the faults discovered. There may be nothing wrong with a system, only faulty personnel, and the cause of faults and the problems in dealing with them should be presented.

6. CONCLUSIONS

Then follow the conclusions based on what is wrong and the causes, and the suggestions derived from them.

7. ALTERNATIVE REMEDIES

There is often more than one way of tackling a problem, and management may prefer a course of action different from that proposed; it is therefore advisable to include all the different possible approaches to solving a problem.

8. THOSE RECOMMENDED

Out of the alternatives, the ones chosen should be stated. It is of great assistance if after outlining the changes recommended, a summary is included showing what effect there would be on:

- (*a*) organisation,
- (*b*) system,
- (*c*) forms,
- (*d*) machines, and
- (*e*) layout, and so on.

9. BENEFITS ACCRUING

In this section (although it might be combined with 8) are the reasons for the course of action recommended. The need to sell the recommended proposals should be remembered, although this does not mean over-selling or exaggerating the benefits. Thus the benefits might be fewer errors, reduction of fatigue, increased productivity, reduced paperwork, reduced movement of personnel, low operating costs, or even less overtime. Nothing should be omitted, but the benefits should be fairly certain before being committed to paper. These, after all, will be the standards on which the O. & M. assignment will be judged.

10. COMPARISON OF COSTS

Although, as previously explained, the aim of an O. & M. inquiry is to improve efficiency, this does not necessarily mean saving in money, but

ANNUAL COSTS (£)

	Labour £	Machines £	Paper £	Total £
Before investigation	15,000	200	500	15,700
After assignment	10,000	600	400	11,000
Savings	5,000	400 (increase)	100	4,700

FIG. 31.—A comparative costs statement.

this is still important to management. A comparison statement something like that in Fig. 31 should therefore be included.

11. SUGGESTIONS FOR IMPLEMENTATION

A great advantage of employing internal O. & M. departments is that they have the job of implementing the recommendations that are adopted, and it is therefore a good thing to state how any changes should be made, in logical sequence, together with a suggested timetable of implementation.

12. APPENDIXES

Flow charts, movement diagrams, new forms, etc., relevant to the text of the report should be included as an Appendix. Reference to these should be made in the report, and they should be clearly numbered for reference purposes.

Finally, the report should have a good appearance and look attractive, and perhaps be contained in a special definitive cover. However good the contents, if it is presented in a slapdash style, it does not inspire confidence.

Implementation and follow-through

Having obtained management sanction for all or some of the O. & M. recommendations, it is then necessary to see they are implemented. Here, again, a methodical approach, and communication with the right people is essential.

Implementation must be by the line manager, but acting on the advice and guidance of the O. & M. officer.

The file on the particular assignment should thus contain a summary of the action needed, so that an action chart can be prepared, something like that in Fig. 32.

		INFORM	DATE PERFORMED
1. Forms:	Revise CF 99	Dept'l Head	
	Revise CF 101	Dept'l Head	
	Revise CF 105	Dept'l Head	
2. Machines:	Replacement of spirit by stencil duplicator (Model X recommended)	Buying Dept.	
3. Staffing:	Change in duties (see Report)	H.O.D. (and Personnel)	

FIG. 32.—An action chart.

Having taken action on the proposals, there should be entered in the O. & M. diary, a date (agreed with the Head of Department) for the inception of the new system or organisation. It may be dependent on the printing of new forms, or the obtaining of a new machine. However, there will always be a degree of informal consultation over the implementation, to decide on the best timing.

Then, the O. & M. diary should contain dates for follow-up (again by prior arrangement with the department), so that visits can be made to assess the working of the new system, etc., and to assist with any problems which may be occurring.

It is an unfortunate fact that what seems feasible in theory does not always work in practice, and it is little use bludgeoning staff (although there may be a certain resistance to the change) and the follow-up visits give opportunity to modify or adapt the procedures, organisation, etc., previously recommended.

Sometimes a lack of improvement is due to the staff not fully understanding a change in emphasis or priorities, and further discussions may improve understanding and make for better working.

CHECK LIST

1. What are the particular terms of reference?
2. What investigations have been made?
3. What faults diagnosed?
4. What are the best solutions?
5. What are the alternatives?
6. Have we communicated with line managers sufficiently?
7. Would it be advisable to have a conference beforehand?
8. To whom is the report addressed?
9. Will he understand the technical terms of O. & M.?
10. Have we summarised the proposed changes?
11. Have we prepared all necessary charts as required by the report?
12. Have we fixed a date for implementation?
13. Have we drafted new forms?
14. Have staff been inducted in the proposed changes?
15. Have we fixed a date for implementation?
16. What problems are likely to occur?
17. What dates for follow-up visiting?
18. Is the report lucid in its presentation?
19. Does it meet the terms of reference?
20. Have we compared costs both before and after the changes?

Chapter 27 Resistance to change

Introduction

O. & M. and Management Services usually recommend desirable changes in systems, organisation, etc., and a most difficult thing to overcome is resistance to change. It is an aspect not mentioned in many treatises on O. & M., but it is suggested that it is really a most important one.

It is important because, if O. & M. is to be successful, it must not be imposed, but its findings must be acceptable and even sought for. Very rarely is this the case.

Psychologists say that we are all naturally resistant to change. We like to perform our toilet in the same order each morning, even sit in the same seats in trains and buses, because we do not have to think about it. We are creatures of habit, and do not like our habits disturbed. To this extent, it is the job of O. & M. to overcome resistance to change, and to encourage acceptance of change.

Not that change in itself is always desirable, because there are some managers who seem to be fond of change for the sake of change. It is true that there is "nothing so permanent as change," but it is suggested that change to be acceptable must be for the better. This is one of the stumbling-blocks of O. & M., for it is *hoped* that a new system will be better (from management's point of view), but it does not mean that it will be better from the worker's point of view!

O. & M. is often a matter of faith, and what seems to be an improvement in theory, does not always result in practical improvement. The reasons for this may be:

1. resistance of staff to changes in the system;
2. fact-gathering (whichever method is used) is rarely completely accurate;
3. changes in circumstances subsequent to the investigation;
4. difficulty of assessing the practical consequences of theoretical improvements;
5. interaction of procedures in one office with those of another office (might be the same as 2);

241

6. failure to have full consultation with staff during the investigation.

The foundation for building change is particularly difficult to create when there have already been many and frequent changes, because there is an attitude of "What, another change?", and it is the job of O. & M. to try to convince that this one really is different, and really is an improvement.

Some resistance to change must be expected, it must be viewed as natural, and the O. & M. investigator must have techniques for dealing with the standard objections.

General approach

It is likely that the resistance will take different forms, and be expressed in different ways, and there will therefore be different techniques to overcome it, according to whether it is from a top manager, a supervisor, or a member of the working staff.

Whatever the levels of management being approached, it is important that an ability at selling ideas should be present, *i.e.*, persuading and convincing people of the value of the product being sold.

In general, it can be said that it is advisable to *stress the advantages* of a new idea to management (if speaking to members of management, *e.g.*, supervisors upwards), whereas the advantages to the staff themselves (rather than to management) should be stressed if selling to working levels. People are much readier to accept something if it is to their own benefit. The difficulty here, of course, is that there is often no benefit at all to the worker (he might even be redundant), in which case it is almost impossible to stress benefits to him. Although it is a good opening gambit to express a hope that the person addressed is equally interested in obtaining efficiency in the concern!

Stressing of benefits is the first strategy, and perhaps next comes the *invitation to participate*. If an individual is asked for his ideas, and if he gets the feeling that his ideas are important, and might even be used, he will be much more ready to accept changes which he has suggested himself. In the last Chapter, it was also suggested that acknowledgment of staff contributions might even be made in the report.

Thirdly, the O. & M. man should always endeavour to *give reasons* for suggested changes, because people are much more ready to accept such changes, than where there are no reasons given, or insufficient reasons. This is not exactly the same as stressing benefits, because often the benefits are indirect and might even be outside the department, whereas reasons explain the need for change.

Different reactions

There will undoubtedly be different kinds of reaction from different levels of management, and while top management might be enthusiastic (perhaps at the prospect of reducing costs), lower levels might be less enthusiastic (perhaps at the prospect of losing their jobs). Or, very often, it is the reverse, with top management resenting any intrusion into their authority, and lower levels welcoming O. & M. because they know of working methods that could be improved.

So, when dealing with top management (as any functional specialist should), stress the help which is being given, and the advantages to management generally. Emphasise monetary savings, for those working on tight budgets will welcome this.

Proposals are best presented in narrative as well as in simple diagrammatic form. Top managers are apt to become rather impatient with a series of technical and what to them are complicated diagrams.

With top managers, it is also essential that the findings should be based on fact. If there is constant liaison with top management at different stages of an assignment, the facts can be verified at each stage, and even proposals agreed at each stage as well, so that the final report is also likely to be accepted.

With departmental managers, selling of O. & M. ideas is very important because they are more concerned with how the work is done in their departments. If O. & M. not only suggests improvements, but offers assistance in implementation, departmental managers will not be left "holding the baby," and are more likely to co-operate. There may be violent opposition from such managers, and it may be necessary to compromise and concede minor points which do not affect the main issues of the recommendations.

It must be remembered that a departmental manager may be losing staff (and implied status) from O. & M. recommendations. If there is consistent opposition and non-co-operation, it may even be necessary to report this to the chief executive, but any appearance of having improvements *imposed* on a department is likely to destroy the confidence and climate of working. It is essential to successful O. & M. that there should be a good working atmosphere, and it is not obtained by the use of force from above.

With supervisors, the approach should be different, because although supervisors are a part of management, their job is also to safeguard their subordinates. To this extent, it might be desirable to stress the advantages to management and to workers—as well as to themselves, who have the job of controlling work and workers.

With the working level, it is, as already stated, advisable to stress the

REACTION	TECHNIQUE
1. "Our work is so different from anybody else's"	Agree with the point of view, and try to get the speaker to identify the supposed differences. It may be in fact different, and it is well to find out whether it is or not. You may still not agree in your own mind, however.
2. "Your suggestions might work in a big firm (or a small one)"	Agree that a system (or whatever) has to be related to the size of a concern (which it does), and that it would be foolish to use large- (or (small-) scale methods in the wrong context.
3. "We've been doing it this way for the last twenty years, and we've never had any trouble"	This is probably difficult to counter, because the speaker thinks the office operation is efficient (and it may be so), but on the other hand, the speaker may be unaware of how uneconomic of staffing or stationery it may be. If deficiencies are known, attention can be drawn to them, but management problems, of, say, rising cost are not likely to appeal to the average worker as a reason for inefficiency.
4. "We've never done it that way before"	This is a straightforward resistance to change, and an implied unwillingness to change, so the advantages of a suggested change should be emphasised.
5. "We've tried that method before, and it was unsuccessful"	This may be true, and it serves as a warning that a proposal may not be as good as it seems. Or it may well be that a different version of the proposal was tried before, or half-heartedly. It is best not to argue the point, but to verify with senior staff the correctness of the statement.
6. "I know of another concern which tried that once, and it failed"	This may be true, but what fails in one set of circumstances, might be successful in another. Point out the difference that circumstances make, while agreeing with the statement. If possible, a successful application of the proposed method should be quoted. Hearsay is not the best guide to action.
7. "Why change it when it's working all right?"	This is rather similar to 3 above, and changing circumstances may indicate a need to change. Concentrate on the reasons why change might be beneficial and try to obtain agreement. This is part of the process of "selling."
8. "The management (or the workers, or unions, or customers) will never accept that"	There is often an in-built prejudice about what some other party will accept without really testing it. It might be as well to note this reaction, and to test it. It might even be right, but it is generally a bias borne of prejudice against change.

Fig. 33.—Standard reactions to envisaged changes, and suggested O. & M. attitudes.

benefits, and the reasons for the proposed changes. Of course, with the larger number of workers at this level, there are more likely to be individual differences in personality and in reaction to change. Opposition is likely to be more violent (particularly if staff are being made redundant) or less violent (if they know of the need for improvements). Gaining participation is also a very useful weapon at the working level. A summary of individual reactions is given in Fig. 33, and although there are no universal panaceas, some suggested techniques to employ might help the situation. Figure 33 shows a list of standard reactions to O. & M. changes, and some suggested courses of action which might meet them.

O. & M. behaviour

As stated at the beginning of this Chapter, a great deal will rest on the personality of the O. & M. officer, for he must be firm, patient, impartial, persuasive, and yet acceptable, and have an aura of conviction.

Thus it would not be advisable to take offence at whatever inflammatory statement is made, and he is sometimes subjected to sarcastic and even abusive remarks. He must weather the storm and command respect.

The O. & M. man must not only be superior, but seen to be superior to ordinary mortals, while he should not be provocative, nor invite arguments, nor take part in arguments by argumentative types.

He should not become involved in things irrelevant to the line of investigation, neither should he cut short an interview, although with a voluble person he may need to take command of the situation and not merely be a negative personality.

He should at all times have good manners and if he endeavours to discover the working background of the person he is interviewing, it may help in his assessment.

It is always advisable, although often difficult, to talk with an employee in private, for other staff are always keen on eavesdropping and may hear things not intended for their ears.

All O. & M. proposals should be based on fact, because these are more acceptable, and moreover, should wherever possible be quantified.

If proposals are rejected

If, arising from resistance to change, all the O. & M. proposals are rejected, as they sometimes are, then it may be as well to refer to top management for arbitration. The difficulty here is that if change is imposed on workers or management, it is not likely to be as successful as when it is agreed to.

If there is downright non-co-operation, then, of course, such circumstances should be reported, and the chief executive may have to "persuade" the line manager of his folly, and lack of concern for increasing efficiency. Diplomacy and tact by the chief executive are greatly needed in this situation.

If a company has adopted a liberal policy regarding redundancy, it may assist in creating a good working climate, and help to meet objections of managers (who may lose staff and supposedly prestige), and of staff (who may lose their jobs).

CHECK LIST

1. What is the nature of resistance to change?
2. Is it different at different working levels?
3. Is there a good working climate?
4. Has management a policy on possible redundancy?
5. Has it been communicated?
6. What are the possible reactions to change?
7. What are the possible techniques to employ to meet them?
8. Is resistance based on poor morale?
9. Is it based on lack of faith in management?
10. Is it based on experience?
11. Has line management been involved in the assignment at every stage?
12. What are the benefits of the proposed changes?
13. Is cost the only criterion?
14. Is there likely to be serious resentment?
15. Would it be bad for the image of the concern (say, with customers)?
16. Have we assured line managers of O. & M. assistance in implementation?
17. Is there total lack of co-operation?
18. Is it the fault of the O. & M. approach?
19. Is it the fault of management's failure to communicate?
20. Do we include staff in deliberations and invite their participation?

Part Five: Operational Research 23/2/81

Chapter 28 Operational research techniques

Operational research has been defined as "a scientific method of providing management with a quantitative basis for decision-making regarding operations under their control" (O.R. Society). This definition is not comprehensive, because as well as decision-making, operational research helps with management problems of control, and even of organisation.

In simple English, O.R. is the application of the two sciences of mathematics and statistics to problems of management, and it is obvious from the definition that it can only deal with the precise measurable aspects, and not with any other.

Further, it can be said that since the findings of O.R. depend on the accuracy of its premises, the findings will only be as good as the premises. In other words, the precise measurable aspects are not always so precise, nor up to date. The consequence is that O.R. solutions often only provide management with a guide to decision-making, which therefore has to be applied with caution. As with market research, it can be said to be the navigational aid to solving management problems. It should be put in perspective.

O.R. is a management tool (or rather a box of tools), which like any other tool needs to be used intelligently. The right tool must be chosen for the job. Whole books have been written on O.R., so only an outline is given here.

It is suggested that the application of the findings of O.R. requires as much policy-making ability as the application of the findings of industrial research. It does not replace art in management, but assists it. It has been said that "art begins where science leaves off."

Importance

O.R. is, of course, an aspect of scientific management, and should replace a great deal of "hunch" and intuition; as mentioned above, it assists in decision-making, control, and even in organisation and

247

systems. It should reduce the number of decisions required of top management, and should save their having to decide on minor detailed matters.

O.R. should help in making for financial savings in the most efficient use of resources, and in making sound management decisions.

Method

If any general approach can be stated to using O.R., it is:

1. Define the problem.
2. Collect all relevant facts.
3. Analyse the information and construct models.
4. Report the results of the research.
5. Follow-up to check on the success of the findings.

Techniques

In many books, Critical Path Analysis (or Network Analysis) is viewed as a separate technique from the main body of O.R., but for convenience, it is included here as a technique of O.R.

The main techniques which can be used are:

1. Critical Path Analysis.
2. Linear Programming.
3. Model Making.
4. Regression Analysis.
5. Queueing Theory.
6. Exponential Smoothing.

These are specific O.R. techniques, but it is not the total of quantitative aspects of management, because work measurement in O. & M. and Work Study, T. Grids in staff assessment, aptitude testing in staff selection, can all be expressed in measurable terms, as can Discounted Cash Flow techniques in assessing the purchase of assets.

The outstanding value of O.R. techniques is that they are universally applicable to any area of management, i.e., to broad management problems, as well as to O. & M. problems of office management.

Uses of O.R.   OR THE SCOPE OF OR

A survey made in recent years has listed the uses of O.R. in order of importance as being:

1. production planning;
2. planning of sales and marketing;
3. stock (especially re-ordering levels);
4. transport (alternative routes);
5. industrial research;
6. accounting;
7. purchasing;
8. personnel.

Techniques in detail

1. CRITICAL PATH ANALYSIS

This is a method of discovering the best sequence of jobs in order to achieve a total project in the shortest time. It is a technique which concentrates on forecasting and planning and assists in deciding what is the critical path or, in other words, what is crucial to the project time, and what activities are most important to it.

Analyse the project into separate steps or activities, and represent them on a chart by arrows showing how they are interrelated. Each activity is then given a time value, and by totalling the activities on different parallel chains, discover which is the longest time (or the critical path) which is then the shortest possible project time (*see* Fig. 34).

The importance of this technique is that it imposes a degree of planning of all the activities, and having established the Critical Path, it means that if there are any delays on it, it will affect the total project time.

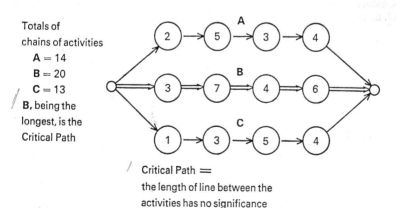

Totals of
chains of activities
A = 14
B = 20
C = 13
B, being the
longest, is the
Critical Path

Critical Path =
the length of line between the
activities has no significance

FIG. 34.—Critical path activities.

By cumulative addition of the time values of each activity, it is then possible to discover the E.E.T. (Earliest Event Time), as well as the L.E.T. (Latest Event Time). This gives an indication of when an activity should be started and when is the latest time for starting it. The difference represents SLACK time, or time in hand. The L.E.T. is calculated by working back from the end of total project time (*see* Fig. 35).

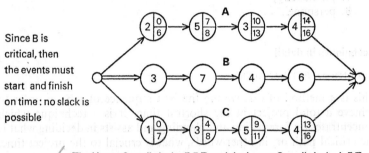

Since B is critical, then the events must start and finish on time: no slack is possible

The Upper Quartile is the E.E.T. and the Lower Quartile is the L.E.T.

FIG. 35.—Finding E.E.T. and L.E.T.

This technique can be used for anything from installing a computer or moving an office, to the preparation of final accounts. It is particularly useful when there are many parallel chains of activity. As well as concentrating management attention on the need of forecasting and planning in great detail, it gives data on which subsequent control can be exercised. Thus, if there is a delay in an activity in the critical path, it will affect the total project time, so it may be possible to switch resources and labour to the critical path activities to prevent it. Alternatively, delays in other activities may be accepted, provided the delays do not exceed the periods of slack.

2. LINEAR PROGRAMMING

This is sometimes known as resource allocation, and there is more than one method available.

    (*a*) *Allocation method.* This is a method of ascertaining the best combination of a number of variables (*see* Fig. 36), and thus finding

Machine	Ann	Betty	Celia	Jane	Average
Elec. T/W	198	208	210	224	210
Calculator	164	192	200	220	194
Ord. T/W	156	182	196	202	184
Tape Punch	154	182	182	192	178
Average	168	191	197	210	191

FIG. 36.—The allocation method.

how to make the best use of resources (*e.g.*, of machines in a factory or office). "Linear" means a line or direct relationship.

Jane is obviously more productive on all machines, but what is the best arrangement to obtain maximum productivity from the staff? The allocation method of Linear Programming is to re-write the table in Fig. 36 to show cost per girl, allocating to each girl other than her optimum.

Thus, "zeroing" for the Electric Typewriter produces the situation in Fig. 37.

Machine	Ann	Betty	Celia	Jane
Elec. T/W	0	0	0	0
Calc.	34	16	10	4
Ord. T/W	42	26	14	22
Tape Punch	44	26	28	30

FIG. 37.—Zeroing for the electric Typewriter.

Then "zeroing" *along* the rows successively (*e.g.*, 4 from 10, 4 from 16, etc.) produces the situation in Fig. 38.

Machine	Ann	Betty	Celia	Jane
Elec. T/W	0	0	0	0
Calc.	30	12	6	0
Ord. T/W	28	12	0	8
Tape Punch	18	0	2	4

FIG. 38.—Zeroing along the rows successively.

The minimum loss is therefore achieved by placing Ann on the Electric Typewriter, Jane on the Calculator, Celia on the Ordinary Typewriter, and Betty on the Tape Punch.

(*b*) *Simulation or algebraic method.*
Problem: A factory has

2 machines called Process A
3   ,,   ,,   ,,   B

It makes two *Products*:

C—which requires 1 hour on Process A and
2   ,,   ,,   ,,   B
D—which requires 5   ,,   ,,   ,,   A and
3   ,,   ,,   ,,   B

But the *profit* on the two products C and D is £15 and £30 respectively.

If the factory works a 40-hour week, what is the best combination of the products to manufacture, to give maximum profits?
Solution:
Maximum *machine hours* must be:

Process A—2 machines at 40 hours = 80

„   B—3   „   „ „   „   = 120

If x = machine hours, then

(a) $x + 5y = 80$
(b) $2x + 3y = 120$
(c) $15x + 30y = P$ (profit)

We seek to maximise P subject to the *constraints* implied by the equations in (a) and (b).

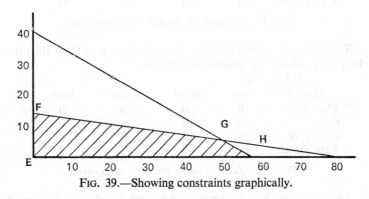

FIG. 39.—Showing constraints graphically.

These constraints can be shown graphically as in Fig. 39.

$$\text{if } x + 5y = 80, \text{ and } x + 1\tfrac{1}{2}y = 60$$

The shaded portion then represents the area satisfying the problem (EFGH), and the proportion of each product is shown by drawing horizontal and vertical lines from G, as in Fig. 40.

These two figures obtained by inspection of the graph represent the proportions of each product necessary to give maximum profit.

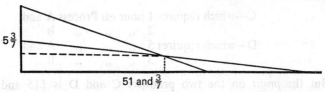

FIG. 40.—Graphing proportions of each product to give maximum profit.

To illustrate the difference in profits, between production of products in these proportions, and making production consist entirely of x or y:

	All y	All x	
x	0	$51^{3/7}$	60
y	16	$5^{5/7}$	0
Profit	£480	£942	£900

$(51^{3/7} \times £15 + 5^{5/7} \times £30 = £942)$

The solution to the problem then becomes:

Hours employed	Product C	Product D	Total
Process A	$51^{3/7}(x)$	$28^{4/7}(5y)$	80
„ B	$102^{6/7}(2x)$	$17^{1/7}(3y)$	120

Should the profit on x be reduced to 6 instead of £15, then the table would be:

x—$51^{3/7}$ (as above)
y— $5^{5/7}$ (as above)
Profit £48 $(6 \times £51^{3/7} = 30 \times 5^{5/7})$

Thus, linear programming helps in making management decisions where there is a direct linear relationship between the different constraints of the problem, as illustrated above, such as different machines with different production capacities, with different products with different profit margins, and so on.

3. MODEL MAKING

A main concern in a basic O.R. technique is first discovering the nature of the problem and then representing it in various forms (graphical, algebraic equations, etc.), so that a solution to the problem can be obtained.

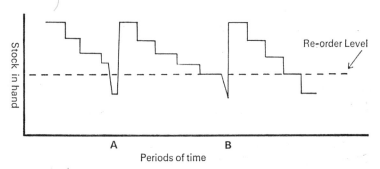

Points A and B   Fresh supplies received

FIG. 41.—A stock re-order chart.

Thus, in stock level problems, a model (or chart) of the ordering and stock processing can be represented, as in Fig. 41.

But the constraints to the stock problem can be quantified, and the amount to re-order each time can be discovered by using the formula:

$$\text{E.O.Q. (Economic Order Quantity)} = \sqrt{\frac{2dc}{k}}$$

where d = average daily demand
        c = cost of ordering
        k = cost of stock in hand.

This can be represented graphically as in Fig. 42.

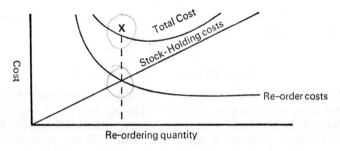

X — Minimum re-order quantity

FIG. 42.—A stock re-order graph.

4. REGRESSION ANALYSIS

This is a statistical device for helping to forecast what might be probable in the next item in a series of items. Thus, where X is the value of the time series, $\bar{X}$ is the average, and Y = figures in the series, and $\bar{Y}$ is the average, then the formula for ascertaining the trend is:

$$b = \frac{(Y - \bar{Y})(X - \bar{X})}{(X - \bar{X})^2}$$

and by applying the trend factor, the next item in the series will then be $Y = b(X - \bar{X})$.

R.A. is a method of establishing a trend from a series of statistics, from which it is then possible, by using the appropriate formulae, to forecast any value at a future point in the series.

It is thus a tool of assistance in forecasting and planning.

    1. If the series is charted in graph form, and the line drawn is a regular straight line or a regular curve, it can be continued and

drawn into the future (*i.e.*, by extrapolation) so that future points on the line can be plotted.

2. If this is not possible, a regular trend line might appear if the chart is drawn on logarithmic paper or log. log. paper.

3. If there is still no regular trend line, then regression analysis can be performed by calculation.

Month	Usage (000 units)
Jan.	20
Feb.	18
Mar.	16
Apr.	12
May	10
June	10
July	10
Aug.	10
Sept.	10
Oct.	12
Nov.	16
Dec.	18
Jan.	20

FIG. 43.—Chart showing the calculations involved in regression analysis problem.

When a chart appears as in Fig. 43, and the problem is to forecast the consumption for February, the calculations are as follows.

Let Y = figures in the series 20, 18, 16, etc. ($\bar{Y}$ = average).
Let X = values of time series (months 1, 2, etc.) ($\bar{X}$ = average).
Tabulate Y, total and calculate average = $\bar{Y}$.
Tabulate X, „   „   „   „   = $\bar{X}$.
Calculate $Y - \bar{Y}$ for each value of Y.
Calculate $X - \bar{X}$ „   „   „   „ X.
Calculate $(Y - \bar{Y})(X - \bar{X})$ for each successive value of Y and X.
Calculate $(X - \bar{X})^2$ for each value of X.

These steps are shown on the table in Fig. 44.

Formulae

$$b \text{ (rate of trend)} = \frac{(Y - \bar{Y})(X - \bar{X})}{(X - \bar{X})^2} \text{ which equals } \frac{0}{182} = 0$$

Y (next term in the series)
$$= Y + b(X - \bar{X}) \text{ which equals } 14 + 0(X - \bar{X}) = 14$$

So that the next term in the series (*i.e.*, the 13th month) will be 14.

Y	X	$Y - \bar{Y}$	$X - \bar{X}$	$(Y-\bar{Y})(X-\bar{X})$	$(X - \bar{X})^2$
20	0	+6	−6	−36	+36
18	1	+4	−5	−20	+25
16	2	+2	−4	−8	+16
12	3	−2	−3	+6	+9
10	4	−4	−2	+8	+4
10	5	−4	−1	+4	+1
10	6	−4	0	0	0
10	7	−4	+1	−4	+1
10	8	−4	+2	−8	+4
11	9	−2	+3	−6	+9
16	10	+2	+4	+8	+16
18	11	+4	+5	+20	+25
20	12	+6	+6	+36	+36

$Y = 14$ $X = 6$ —   —   Sum = 0   Sum = 182

Fig. 44.—A regression analysis table.

5. QUEUEING THEORY

This is a technique for discovering what intervals of time would be the optimum for issuing stores, for turn-round of vehicles, and so on. The average waiting time can be obtained by adding the products of the intervals (or service time) and the frequency with which it occurs.

Thus, where production managers are unable to meet the manufacturing requirements despite having adequate machinery, etc., it is possible by mathematical means to work out the average length of a queue in terms of the average interval between random arrivals, and the average service time.

The average waiting time will be

$$\frac{S^2}{A - S}$$

where A = average interval, and
       S = the average time of service.

6. EXPONENTIAL SMOOTHING

This is a statistical device, whereby a smoothing factor is applied to a series of items which on a graph look absolutely chaotic, with no definite trend discernible, so that when the items are redrawn on a graph, it shows a distinct and easily discernible trend. By extrapolation, it is then possible to extend the trend into the future, thus helping to forecast a future item in the series.

Only an outline of the main techniques involved in operational research has been given here, and the reader is referred to the various treatises written entirely on the subject, but suffice it to say that with O.R., local authorities have been able to route their school buses more effectively and even to determine the relative values of buying flower seed or seedlings. In business, it can be used to assess the productivity of machines, the calculation of the best stock levels, and even the best siting of a whole factory, taking into account transport costs and market demand.

It will be apparent that the techniques are valuable in O. & M. and in Management Services, *i.e.*, in matters of office efficiency and in improving the offices of the whole business. The techniques aid forecasting and planning, decision-making, and assist in control.

CHECK LIST

1. What is the nature of the problem?
2. What is the best technique to use?
3. Have we got all the necessary data?
4. If not, how long will it take to gather?
5. Will it be worth the time and effort involved?
6. Will the solution be reliable?
7. How reliable are the premises used?
8. Are there other considerations to take into account?
9. Are there policy or political pressures, and are they acceptable?
10. Is the problem really quantifiable?
11. Have we obtained all the constraints to the problem?
12. Are some more important than others?
13. Should we concentrate only on the important ones?
14. Is a theoretical solution likely to be practical?
15. Can the solution be presented in ordinary English?
16. Are we bending the problem to suit a particular technique?
17. What are the purposes of the situation being reviewed?
18. Are we bearing them in mind?
19. Do we consider cost as well as time in the problem?
20. What are the important factors to increased efficiency?

Chapter 29 Office applications of O.R.

In the last Chapter, the basic theories of operational research were outlined, together with some examples, most of which appertain to management generally. For the benefit of O. & M., it is useful to see to what extent these same techniques are applicable to problems in the office.

But, as has been mentioned previously, the areas of O. & M. and Management Services do overlap, and since an office is concerned with exercising control, the calculation of stock levels, for example, and the re-ordering points, can be viewed as coming within the area of O. & M.

However, there are still businesses where O. & M. would be viewed as exceeding its authority if it dared venture into the realm of management decision-making. Where this occurs, to what extent can O.R. assist a purely O. & M. investigator?

Those techniques of greatest use are probably:

    1. Critical Path Analysis.
    2. Model making.
    3. Queueing Theory.

Critical path analysis (or network analysis)

As previously mentioned, this is a technique of universal application, for it can be applied to any project where there are parallel chains of activities.

Thus, C.P.A. can be used for:

    1. Installation of a computer.
    2. Launching an advertising campaign.
    3. Moving an office to another location.
    4. Arranging a conference or dinner.
    5. Preparation of Final Accounts, and so on.

Figure 45 is an example of the activities involved in the preparation of a sales conference. It will be noted that the activities are serially numbered, and that the two figures to the right of each activity number

PLANNING A SALES CONFERENCE   Activity times in weeks

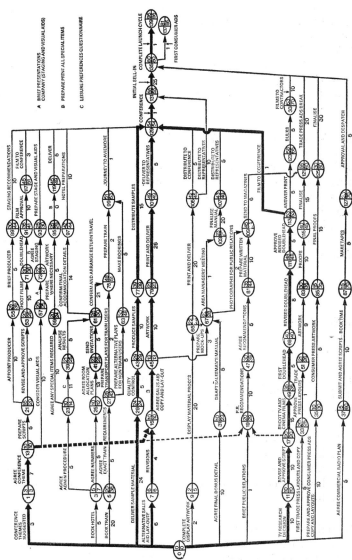

Fig. 45.—Critical path diagrams for planning a sales conference.

are the Earliest Event Time, and the Latest Event Time, the difference being the amount of "slack" or delay possible without upsetting the total project time. The Critical Path is in heavy type, and activities on this line must not be allowed to get behind, for they are vital to the total project time. It will be noticed that dotted lines (or dummy arrows) connect up activities on the different chains of activity, which indicate a linking of different activity on different paths. Usually it means that one activity cannot be completed before the other (at the end of the dotted line) is also completed.

Before such a chart is prepared, it can be seen that it is first necessary to list all the activities concerned, and then to give estimates of their individual duration.

The drawing of the chart is the control document, and since control involves *regular comparisons*, it is then necessary to identify the date for completion of each activity, and further regularly (perhaps every day) to check on the actual completion of the activities concerned. Then tick or mark the chart that an activity has been completed, with the dates of completion (or on a separate list). It can then be ensured that the total project is completed in the time forecast, and if there are delays on any activity, action can be concentrated on trying to compensate for the lost time.

Model-making

In the last Chapter, an example was shown of the use of an algebraic equation for arriving at the Economic Order Quantity and the right time for re-ordering. A similar example of building a model for office work is the checking of purchase invoices.

In a certain local authority, the following facts were elicited:

1. Invoices sent to the wrong authority   = 0·25 per cent
2. Invoices for which no goods received   = 0·05 per cent
3. Invoices where there was defective delivery = 0·80 per cent
4. Invoices incorrectly paid   = 0·29 per cent
5. Invoices with critical errors   = 0·139 per cent

It could be deduced that the percentage of invoices on which there were no queries or correspondence arising was 98·47 per cent. So instead of sending all copy orders to the Supplies Department indicating whether delivery was satisfactory or not, it was arranged that only those with defective delivery (using the principle of exception) should be sent.

Further, it was wished to find out which was the best level of checking to justify the checking process at all. If a graph is drawn comparing the expected losses with different degrees of checking, it would appear something like that in Fig. 46. From Fig. 46 it can be seen that the checking of 50 per cent of invoices, would avoid all but trivial loss.

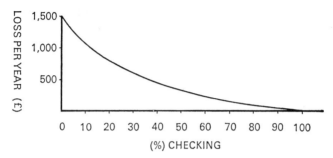

FIG. 46.—Graph showing expected losses occasioned by different degrees of checking.

But this must be compared with the cost of checking, so that the above graph line can then be charted comparing it with checking costs, as in Fig. 47.

So where the two lines intersect, *i.e.* 20 per cent, is the best level to check, bearing in mind the loss likely to occur and the cost of checking.

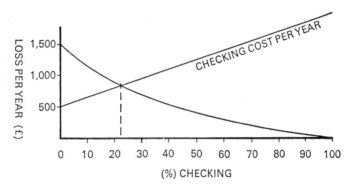

FIG. 47.—Graph comparing different costs of different degrees of checking.

Queueing theory

This concept can be applied to any situation where there are a number of applicants waiting to be served, and only one or a few servers. It applies to patients waiting in Out Patients' Department at a hospital, to issues of stores, issues of stationery, and even to the review of telephone calls (indicating the most suitable switchboard) in an office.

It requires patient logging of

1. arrival times of the applicants;
2. their individual waiting times;
3. the time taken in serving each applicant; and
4. the idle time of the server.

Ideally, there should be no waiting of the applicants, so that they do not waste their time, and no idling on the part of the server, so that he does not waste his time either. It is rarely possible to achieve this ideal situation, where waiting time of both is reduced to nil, but it is possible to reduce it to the optimum.

It is possible to work out mathematically, what the *average length of the queue* is in terms of the average interval between serving the applicants. The formula for calculation of the average waiting time is

$$\frac{S^2}{A - S}$$

where A is the average time between arrivals (appointment times), and S is the average serving time.

Thus, a chart relating to a queueing problem might read as in Fig. 48.

Applicant No.	Arrival Interval	Arrival Time	Service Time	Time In	Time Out	Waiting Time	Idle Time of Server
1	30	30	40	30	70	0	30
2	65	95	50	95	145	0	25
3	50	145	30	145	175	0	0

FIG. 48.—A queueing problem chart.

At the end of such recording, it might be found that the *Average Waiting Time* for 40 *applicants* is, say,

$$\frac{2,700}{40} = 67 \text{ minutes}$$

Total Idle Time of *Server* over first 40 applicants = 160 minutes

i.e. employment of server $= \dfrac{2,240 - 160}{2,280} = 91$ per cent

So, in this example, the server is fairly well occupied, but the applicants are kept waiting.

It is obvious that if the interval of serving is increased, it will reduce the waiting time of applicants, and this is where the formula shown above can be applied. If the Average Serving Time is 51 minutes (S), and the Average Arrival Time (A) is

$$\frac{(2,700)}{40} = 67 \text{ minutes,}$$

then the Average Waiting Time is

$$\frac{S^2}{A - S} = \frac{51^2}{67 - 51} = 163 \text{ minutes.}$$

CHECK LIST

1. Is the problem capable of being expressed in numerical terms?
2. What is the nature of the problem?
3. Which technique will be of most use?
4. Are we bending the problem to the technique or searching for the best one?
5. Is there really a suitable O.R. technique for the problem?
6. Can a mathematical model be created?
7. Do we have all relevant facts?
8. Is the O.R. answer the perfect one?
9. Are there other circumstances which make the answer doubtful?
10. Is the purpose of using O.R. one of control or of decision-making?
11. Do we recognise the disadvantages of a mathematical solution?
12. What is the clerical cost of devising an O.R. solution?
13. Are there likely to be human problems involved?
14. Have we explored the use of all O.R. techniques?
15. Are there internal political factors which work against O.R. solutions?
16. Can O.R. help management make better decisions?
17. Does O.R. really add to efficiency?
18. Have we considered all the parameters of the problem?
19. How much time is there to apply the O.R. techniques?
20. Have we sufficient knowledge of all the techniques?

Part Six: E.D.P.

Chapter 30 Electronic computers

One definition of a computer is "an expensive machine capable of making mistakes faster than one would imagine possible," and if the dictionary is consulted, a computer would seem to be synonymous with a calculator. Of course, the word has a special meaning today, but does it always have the same meaning? A visible record computer is vastly different from a £2 million computer complex, a typesetting computer is different from an audio-response computer and an analog computer is different from a digital computer.

All that they have in common is:

1. they operate electronically;
2. they all have a memory store;
3. they operate by a programme of instructions; and
4. they perform calculations at prodigious speeds.

In fact, programmable calculators are obtainable, which can be said to be mini-computers.

Computers and management information systems

An enterprise can have (and usually does have) a management information system—without having a computer. Because of its great abilities in providing information, the two seem to have become merged, and no doubt a great deal of a computer's value lies in providing management with information.

However, an accountant who gives monthly control figures to his board of directors is operating a management information system. The method by which he produces the information may be by electric calculator, electronic accounting machine, or punched cards without even using a computer.

In the same way, the term "data processing" has become linked with the computer image, partly because of the use of the term E.D.P. (Electronic Data Processing). But data is only another word for information or facts, and "processing" only means doing things with figures, such as analysing and classifying them for management purposes. In other words, data processing can be performed without computers.

But computers are an aid to the provision of management information, because they can produce data which otherwise would be unobtainable, and because data can be produced ten times quicker than bv other means.

Computer installations

It is not intended here to describe a large-scale computer, because it is assumed that the reader will already have such knowledge. But it is desirable to assess what kinds of installation come under the term of "computer," and it is suggested that the following are possible:

1. Buying a computer outright.
2. Renting a computer.
3. Buying or renting a computer, and buying different compatible terminals.
4. Using a computer on a time-sharing basis.
5. Using a computer bureau.
6. Buying or renting a mini-computer.
7. Buying a visible record computer.

The main factors to consider when considering the use of one of these are:

1. What is the purpose of the work?
2. What is the volume of work?
3. What is the capital outlay?
4. What are the running costs?
5. What is the length of time before it can be operational?
6. What are the likely effects on staff?
7. What are the likely effects on management?

These factors are examined in more detail in a later Chapter, but it does show that use can be made of computer technology in many ways.

Kinds of computer

Apart from the kinds of machine and methods of installation mentioned above, there are two basic divisions in computers:

1. Analog and digital computers.
2. Batch processing and real-time computers.

Computers were developed in the 1940s and 1950s, and the first areas of use were in the scientific field; the kind of computer developed was the analog computer which was (and still is) mainly used for scientific purposes, and is concerned with problems of spatial relationships, vibration, etc. But analog computers are also used in the commercial field. Tesco Stores (Holdings) Ltd. called in management consultants to improve the stock-holding facilities, which used to be three-and-a-half weeks' average usage. The consultants recommended the use of statistical forecasting and planning technique using exponential smoothing (*see* Chapters 28 and 29). Since Tesco's handle 1,500 lines of goods, the constant calculation for each stock line would require formidable clerical effort, and as a result an analog computer was purchased, which was developed for just this problem. The computer (the "Oracle") cost only £1,500, and it can easily be operated by a member of the clerical staff—hence saving months of expensive programming time. Using the new system, Tesco find that it needs to keep only two weeks' stock, and furthermore claims a higher standard of availability of goods.

However, the kind of computer mostly in use in business is a digital one, which means that it deals with figures usually in thousands of small arithmetical calculations, which is the normal occurrence in office work.

Most computers are batch processors, which mean that they deal with one thing at a time, in accordance with the programme fed into it and the file information provided. Thus, a computer is switched from creating sales invoices to compiling the pay-roll, and the machine is not used until a relevant batch of customers' orders or workers' time sheets is prepared for the input.

On the other hand, there has been a growth in real-time (or "on-line") computing, which means that the computer accepts information fed into it sporadically, and compares it with what is in its memory, and gives out information then and there, immediately following the feeding of information.

The outstanding example of real-time computing is the complex installed for B.E.A. (before it became part of British Airways), where two large-scale computers were connected to 416 Unisets—combined input and output devices. A booking clerk receives an air transport booking on the telephone, and by fitting the appropriate "flight plate" on the console of the machine, the computer gives back information on the availability of seats; if seats are available, the operator presses a "BOOK" button, and the computer automatically makes the booking and up-dates the computer flight records with the new information.

It will be seen that such a computer is different in function from the more normal batch processing machine, because it is instantaneous, it gives management instant control, and helps in day-to-day decision-making. It does more than just give management information at intervals.

Function of a computer

A computer can be installed for many purposes, which will have a bearing on the type of installation used.

It is sometimes stated that its main job is to produce management information, but in fact its first job is usually to automate an office system, say, wages or dividend preparation, which was previously performed electro-mechanically. This is not to say that the provision of information is not important, because the whole basic function of an office can be said to be to arrange and give information to management, to customers, to staff, etc.

While a computer can be said to be acquired for one particular main purpose, it is often used for other purposes as well, and with such an expensive machine it is only right that spare capacity on the machine should be fully utilised.

The main function for which a computer is acquired should be considered very carefully; it may be one of the following:

1. To automate existing office systems, such as wages and salaries and stock control, and to produce sales invoices—*operational.*
2. To provide management information quicker than ever before, and perhaps more information than previously—*management information service.*
3. To give day-to-day controls over certain areas of work (as with a real-time computer—*see above*).
4. To assist the centralisation and greater management control over a widespread enterprise.
5. To store large volumes of information and to gain selected extracts from it as required—commonly referred to as *data storage and retrieval.*

Impact on management

The effect of computers on management will depend on which kind of installation is preferred (*see above*), as well as on how efficiently any of the methods are installed and operated. Some large-scale concerns have large-scale computers, when they would probably have been better off with visible record computers. Some are struggling with visible record computers, when the need is really for large capacity machines, or the position would be improved by using a computer bureau, and so on.

As already mentioned, the computer can and does provide more management control information, and quicker than ever before, thus giving management tighter control.

Because of its enormous calculating capacity, a computer (usually by using O.R. techniques) can give information to aid decision-making (e.g., on the siting of a factory, on product profitability, and so on).

Computers usually have quite an effect on the organisation of an enterprise, if only because they usually create a greater degree of centralisation. Not that the use of a computer necessarily means greater central control, but the fact that all data processing is dealt with centrally usually means that centralisation is aided. It could be argued that in so far as it provides decentralised managers with control information, it may even assist decentralisation, but the company ethos will have some influence here.

The computer, at least to those employed in the concern, seems to exercise increasing control on what is done and how it is done. It can affect systems and procedures throughout the concern.

A large-scale computer usually causes some staffing difficulties, in that it can be upsetting to working staff (causing fear of redundancy and higher labour turnover), upsetting to line managers (who fear loss of prestige), and, not least, creates a personnel problem relating to the need for computer staff themselves (high labour turnover, training problems, etc.).

With a large-scale computer, management may have a problem of making maximum use of its capacity before it becomes economic, and often a twenty-four-hour shift is operated in an endeavour to compensate for the expensive installation costs. Then there are the language barriers between members of the management, who do not always grasp what computer programming, etc., involves, and the computer staff who do not always understand management requirements.

A much-repeated stricture is that over half the computers are failures in so far as they do not achieve the hoped-for objectives. Both in Government and O.E.E.C. reports, it is revealed that there is rarely the expected savings in staff. But in large-scale operation with a preponderance of routine work, computers are eminently suitable, e.g., in large insurance companies, in electricity and gas corporation operations, with literally millions of customers.

The future

It is always difficult to forecast future developments, but the indications are that the following will increase in popularity:

1. The use of visible record computers and mini-computers, not needing large specialised computer staffs.
2. The development of input systems which will automatically feed information into the machine without the need for punched cards, punched tape, etc.
3. The greater use of computer bureaux.
4. The installation of large multi-access computers (as installed at Edinburgh University, where as many as 200 scientists can make use of the computer at the same time).
5. With the development of ever-smaller storage devices, the reduction in computer size.
6. The simplification of programme languages, and even the setting up of programmes by non-skilled programmers.
7. The development of data transmission systems (*e.g.*, the Datel services of the Post Office, which will facilitate the siting of a computer anywhere in the country).

Conclusion

This is by way of being an introduction to some of the main "facts of life" about computers, and in the following Chapters there is closer examination of aspects of installing computers, of their impact, of software, and of assessing efficiency when computers have been installed.

CASE STUDY

Installing a computer

SCAFFOLDING (G.B.) LTD.

1. The computer, an I.C.L. 1301, took just under two and a half years to install from the date it was ordered; it was working three weeks after it was installed; it cost £150,000.
2. The change-over to a computer was facilitated by the fact that the Company had been using punched-card machines during the previous ten years.
3. The reason for the installation of a computer was mainly to handle a greatly increased volume of work caused by the rapid expansion of the Company.

4. No employees became redundant, although some were worried about their prospects in the Company, but it was explained to them that the computer would perform the routine work, leaving them to do the more interesting jobs. The Company gave a guarantee to the staff that no staff would be made redundant as a result of installing the computer. Special meetings were held in all sections of the business to explain how the computer would affect the work.

5. Most of the major forms in use could continue to be used. The punched-card operators had to learn to operate 80-column cards instead of the former 40-column variety.

6. S.G.B. arranged with I.C.L. for aptitude testing of their staff to see if they were suitable for computer programming, etc. The Company have one Data Processing Manager, two systems analysts, and four programmers. There are now altogether about 40 staff concerned with the operation of the computer, including 20 punched-card operators; a permanent computer engineer is also employed.

7. The computer operators work a regular two-shift system, and for two weeks a month a three-shift system.

8. During the two and a half years waiting for the computer to be delivered, the staff were recruited and trained, with the result that some 50 different programmes could be operated shortly after it was installed.

9. One of the important jobs of the computer is the monthly statements for each of the Company's 20,000 customers, involving some 250,000 entries every month—an almost impossible task without the computer.

10. It is also used for sales ledger work, purchase ledger, monthly profit and loss statements for each of the depots, wages and salaries, job costing, stock records of equipment on hire and contract. It does many jobs not possible with the mere punched-card system.

11. The computer manager prefers to recruit staff from inside the Company whenever possible.

12. Decisions on what work the computer should do are made jointly with the line managers; they tell the D.P. Manager what results and information they want from the computer.

13. The computer has been so successful that a second one has been installed even after only three years of operation of the first one, but with the technological advances happening every year, it is realised that a new computer will have to be purchased—perhaps inside ten years from the original date of purchase.

[*Norwood News* February 1966

CHECK LIST

1. What is the purpose of buying a computer?
2. Which computer method would be most suitable?
3. What would be the advantages?
4. What are the likely difficulties?
5. What will be the impact on management?
6. Should we have real-time or batch processing?
7. Would an analog computer be useful?
8. How much capital is available?
9. How quickly do we want the installation?
10. Is there some technical development taking place shortly?
11. Do we expect to save staff?
12. Or just to automate existing systems and gain in speed?
13. Do we aim at more information and quicker than before?
14. Have we considered the impact on organisation?
15. Have we considered the impact on systems and paperwork?
16. Have we a large-scale business?
17. Are the clerical procedures of a routine nature?
18. Would we need constant revision of programmes?
19. What effect is likely on existing staff, can we use them?
20. Is it really worthwhile?

Chapter 31 Installing a computer

Preparation

The first question to ask about any machine to be installed in an office is "What is its purpose?" Then, to ask if there is in fact a suitable machine on the market. The same applies to installing a computer.

The well-known consultants, McKinsey and Co. have indicated in a survey that half of Britain's computer users believe that their machines are not even paying their way, and a large proportion of the others are unable to quantify the benefits computers have brought to them. Perhaps the main fault in a computer installation has been bad assessment of suitability in the first place. But even with a good assessment of suitability, very often the wrong computer is chosen. Many firms have discovered the lack of capacity in the machine for their needs after its purchase, and have had to start thinking of buying a larger one almost immediately.

The preparatory stage—*before* a computer is installed—is therefore most important, because it will have a great bearing on the success or failure of the machines used.

Perhaps the main questions to be asked are:

What are the reasons for installing a computer?
What are the purposes for using a computer?
Is there a suitable machine available?
What are the advantages and disadvantages of even the most suitable machine?

1. Too few managements ever think of defining the objectives of their computer installation, the purchase of a computer is thought of as the fashionable thing to do, the step which will restore the Company's fortunes, or a means of reducing administrative costs—all in a vague kind of way. This is examined in more detail below.

2. The assessment of the purposes for which a machine is to be used, will of course have a great effect on the kind of machine selected. Thus, a machine for processing the pay-roll only, might be different from one on which all the data processing of

273

a business is to be performed. It is a question of capabilities, and of not buying unwanted capacities. Thus, for example, it is silly buying an expensive calculating machine if a much cheaper adding machine will be sufficient, and it is equally foolish buying a cheap adding machine when the work requires a more sophisticated calculating machine.

3. The establishment of whether there is a suitable machine is more difficult with a computer, because manufacturers always say they have a model which is suitable—or which can be adapted. It is up to the user (and here he needs expert technical assistance), to assess real suitability.

4. To assess what are the probable advantages and disadvantages requires assessment of one's own circumstances, assessment by the computer manufacturers, and experience of other users. A difficulty is that rarely will other users admit they have made a mistake in their choice of machine; also what might be suitable to their circumstances is not necessarily suitable to one's own.

Objectives

As with any other office machine, it is then advisable to define what the objectives are of using a particular machine.

1. Is it *to reduce costs*? This is a very doubtful objective, because, in practice, costs often prove to be double the estimated ones. A computer feasibility team can always produce estimates of how savings can be made in other departments (which usually do not materialise), and the computer costs are nearly always underestimated. This is examined in greater detail below.

2. Is it *to produce more* (*or better*) *management information*? The problem here is that management is not always sure what information it really requires, and sometimes (in effect) says give us "the lot," and then complains that it is submerged beneath mountains of paper which it cannot understand and does not use. It must be precisely stated by management what information it requires and in doing so it must assess whether this will aid control or forecasting and planning, and in which areas of the business operation. A fundamental problem with a computer is that it can produce with lightning speed a mass of information, but this is pointless if such information is meaningless.

3. Is it *to produce control information more quickly*? One large chain store has stated that with a computer it obtains its total stock position in three days instead of the previous two to three

weeks, and the tightness of control meant that it could save in stocks by 10 per cent—which easily paid for the capital outlay on the computer.

4. Is it *to increase productivity*? Is the aim better production planning by which better use can be made of machines, so that productivity and profitability can be increased. This can also show an indirect savings in costs.

5. Is it *to improve customer service*? Thus, a computer may not save any money, but it may mean the production of sales invoices quicker than ever before.

The problem is that management itself is not always sure of the objectives, although it may know of areas in which its management could be improved; then it is a question of assessing whether and to what extent a computer can assist such improvement.

Feasibility study team

The usual approach is to set up a feasibility study team of investigators, and Denys Field, whose feasibility studies led to Shell-Mex B.P. installing their LEO III computer, has stated the following:

1. The investigating team must be full-time and not part-time.
2. It is wrong to lay down any limited investigating time.
3. Members of the team must undergo computer training courses.
4. Computer manufacturers should be frequently consulted.
5. It is advisable to keep in touch with other enterprises using computers.
6. Do not concentrate attention on one computer only.
7. Do not hesitate to say if a computer is thought *not* to be feasible.

A main problem is that the investigating team needs to have as members, staff with a knowledge of the business, but who perhaps have little knowledge of computer working, and must also have computer experts, who usually have little experience of the business concerned. It is, however, advisable to have a senior staff member of every department on the team so that they are involved, and can say how it is likely to affect their departments.

Such a team must obviously have the Accountant, the Company Secretary, the O. & M. Officer (or Management Services Manager), and the Personnel Officer, as well as some computer experts.

Feasibility study

Having decided on the objectives of using a computer, the feasibility
team has then to assess what is being done and how, and how (and if)
it can be adapted to electronic data processing, and then assess whether
it is worthwhile. The latter is its main *raison d'être*, but, of course, if it
recommends the installation of a computer, it is expected to say how,
when, how long it will take, what actions must be taken in preparation,
and in short, to see that it works. As many an O. & M. investigator
knows, it is one thing to assess theoretical advantages and make
recommendations, but it may be altogether a different thing to put the
recommendations into practice, and seeing that they work. What is
possible and advisable in theory, does not always work in practice, even
with the simplest of things!

This critical examination will require investigation of:

1. the organisation;
2. the management information produced;
3. the procedures;
4. the staffing;
5. the machines in use at present;
6. the forms in use.

A number of charts must be prepared on each of these aspects, so that
it is known what is done, how it is done, when it is done, and where,
and above all, *why* it is done at all.

With regard to 1, it must be remembered that an organisation chart
does not reveal all there is to know about an organisation. It only
reveals the type of organisation, its divisions, and the number of levels
of management. It does not reveal individual responsibilities or
authorities, which must be obtained from job descriptions.

Regarding 2, it should be borne in mind that the management
information obtained previously may not be what should be obtained.
While management information is nearly always an aspect of computer
application, it may not be the sole reason for having a computer (*see*
objectives stated above).

Since the different charts depict organisation, procedures, forms, etc.,
they will need to be correlated, and it may be advisable to draw up one
composite chart with extended diagnostic columns showing Departments, Forms, Machines, Methods, with a final column showing
Automation changes, and a Remarks column.

It might also be necessary to draw up a management information
chart showing how information flows from one department to another.

An extract from such a chart might be something like that (*see also* Chapter 23) shown in Fig. 49.

The information flow between departments can be established, then the kinds of information and their volume and frequency must be assessed.

From this assessment of existing systems, it should be possible to assess the most profitable areas for computer application, bearing in mind the objectives of installing a computer. If a company is spending hundreds of thousands of pounds on a large-scale computer, it will most

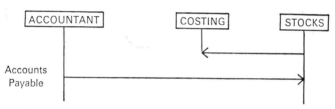

Fig. 49.—A section of a management information chart.

likely want maximum use of the machine, and therefore want I.D.P. (Integrated Data Processing) whereby when one routine is being performed it automatically produces information for another department. Thus, sales invoicing can be performed and integrated with stock control and credit control.

But if I.D.P. is attempted straightaway, then the concern is heading for likely chaos, and it is best to choose one particular area—the most profitable areas—for initial application. In this case, the head of the department concerned should be told of the decision, as well as the reasons why.

The decision

The word "computer" has been used in this Chapter as though there was just one type of machine which can be used, but it is also part of the job of the feasibility team to investigate and recommend a choice between buying a large-scale computer (or renting it), a mini-computer, a visible record computer, or again, using a computer on a time-sharing basis or using a computer bureau.

The decision to install electronic data processing by whatever method must involve an investigation and report on the likely effect on:

1. costs (*see below*);
2. systems;
3. forms;

    4. organisation;
    5. staffing.

The E.D.P. decision must then be made, taking account of:

1. the total volume of work;
2. the volume of input data;
3. the volume of output data;
4. the speed of processing;
5. the computer storage needed;
6. the likely growth of the business and need for expanded capacity in the future.

It is the writer's opinion that many large business concerns with large-scale computers would have been better off if they had just installed visible record computers. A shipping agent in London who went into liquidation eighteen months after installing a computer owed over £500,000, and would have been better off if it had not installed a computer at all.

Feasibility problems

One of the feasibility problems is convincing managers that while a computer can perform calculations in literally millionths of a second, the preparatory work necessary for feeding the information to the machine can take many months, or even years, of preparation. Generally speaking, therefore, a computer is not suitable for *ad hoc* jobs, which may take longer on a computer than by any other method.

Secondly, a feasibility survey can take several years to complete, and there might be a degree of cynicism about its working, so the cost of the survey must be included as part of the cost of installation if it is decided to install a computer.

Thirdly, it is important to bear in mind the human relations aspect of computer installation, because there will be fears that staff will be made redundant, and fears that heads of department will lose responsibility and prestige. Management should have a policy on all these matters, and see that their policies are communicated and known. Close co-operation with top management all the time is essential.

The feasibility team usually finds that it is exploring areas not previously looked at, and for future success of a computer installation it may be necessary to have a Management Services Department, if one has not existed previously to give continuous and close surveillance of the working of a computer—it should not be left to the Computer Manager, who after all is mainly in charge of the practical working of the machine.

Computer installation

Assuming that all the difficulties have been surmounted and a choice (or not) of computer has been made, it is then a matter of drawing up a contract with the computer manufacturers and agreement on a date of delivery.

This delivery date is a key factor in the plan for installation, even though it may be a year after the signing of the contract. However long it is, it never seems long enough for all the preparatory work which has to be done!

Planning the installation of a computer will include:

1. Appointment of a computer manager.
2. Selection and training of special computer staff (especially systems analysts and programmers).
3. Training of other staff in charge of systems and forms.
4. Spreading information to management (at all levels) about the computer and its future operation.
5. Allocating staff for the purpose of changing the system.
6. Deciding on form changes and ensuring their availability.
7. Deciding with management on any changes in organisation, and drawing up job specifications.
8. Ordering necessary auxiliary equipment (collators, sorters, files, etc.).
9. Planning and designing accommodation required (with perhaps air-conditioning).
10. Preparing a time-table for implementation.
11. Deciding on the period of parallel running with existing systems to discover if the computer system really works.
12. Preparing office layout of computer department and of input and output sections.
13. Preparing schedules of furniture and fittings.
14. Arranging for maintenance of the computer, and for input and output devices, and air-conditioning.
15. Seeing to current stabilising equipment, and possibly generating plant (in case of power failure).

Costs

Management will be very much concerned with costs, and, of course, precise costs can be obtained (apart from factors of inflation) of all machines, equipment and furniture, while staff salaries will have to be estimated depending on the market rates.

The *Office Machine Guide*, an international publication, a few years ago made comparable cost estimates of preparing insurance policies, which gave:

	per policy
By hand	= 30 cents
By typewriter	= 25 cents
Accounting machine and addressing machine	= 5 cents
Punched-card machines	= 7 cents
Punched-card Computer	= 9 cents
Magnetic Tape Computer	= 4 cents

These figures are, of course, greatly dependent on the correct choice of machine, successful operation, and so on.

If the installation of a computer is proposed only on the ground of saving in costs, it will be seen that using an accounting machine and addressing machine creates little difference in costs compared with a magnetic tape computer. There are no details in this survey as to the constituent parts of each cost, and some of the costs of each will doubtless vary from one concern to another, but it is nevertheless an interesting comparison.

In an American report, it was stated that frequent causes of under-estimation of costs were:

1. The period during which it is necessary to run the old and the new systems in parallel (the ironing out of "bugs" in the computer system often takes longer than expected).
2. The number of magnetic tapes required is often under-estimated, particularly when large quantities of data have to be stored for long periods.
3. Salary costs are often under-estimated, often through the failure to take account of the need to continue programming and re-programming after the initial period of installation.
4. The viewing of punched cards and stationery as insignificant items of expenditure—it sometimes amounts to 15–20 per cent of the annual running costs.
5. Expected savings in staff are often not achieved.

In addition, there are usually special machines required, such as decollators, for handling the continuous stationery, as well as collators, guillotines—and the staff to operate them. The computer usually needs air-conditioning, dust control, a false floor, a power supply room, and engineers' room. In fact, the computer is usually housed in greater luxury than the chairman of the company, but its luxury is essential though expensive.

A few years ago (figures need to be adjusted according to the percentage inflation since then), the following costs were quoted for a typical magnetic tape installation:

Hire of computer	£18,000
Staffing	12,000
Input preparation	5,000
Output handling	1,500
Computer suite	1,250
Electricity	500
Paper tape and cards	250
Magnetic disc pack	2,500
TOTAL	£41,000 per annum

It should be noted that the final costs were more than double the original estimates for the computer alone, and this estimate is supposed to include depreciation costs over four years.

The benefits of computer installation, whatever they are, have then to be measured against this estimated cost, and presented to management. It may not be any service to management to show an estimated saving on previous methods which subsequently proves to be more expensive.

This is not the whole story, however, because in preparing any cost/benefit analysis, there are probably indirect savings which cannot be quantified. But careful investigation at an early stage can avoid a lot of disappointment and recrimination two or three years later.

CHECK LIST

1. What are the objectives of having a computer?
2. Is there a suitable machine available?
3. What are the possible advantages and disadvantages?
4. Who should compose the feasibility team?
5. Have we got the views of other organisations?
6. Have we made a thorough investigation of systems?
7. Have we made a thorough investigation of information flow?
8. Have we made a thorough investigation of the organisation?
9. Have we made a thorough investigation of forms?
10. Have we examined the various ways of using E.D.P.?
11. Do we want full I.D.P.—or in one department at a time?
12. Have we suitable staff, or can they be trained?
13. Have we sufficient office space?
14. Have we carried out a cost/benefit analysis?
15. Have we included all possible costs?
16. Have we taken account of future expansion?
17. Have we under-estimated costs of stationery, staffing, etc.?
18. Are our systems suitable for E.D.P.?
19. Have we got expert, impartial computer advisers?
20. When decided on, have we planned the installation fully?

Chapter 32 Hardware and software

It is assumed that the reader knows what a computer is, although in the previous Chapters it has been already stated that a visible record computer is vastly different from a large-scale digital computer. Further, it is possible to buy computer time, *i.e.*, to have computer time-sharing of large-scale computers.

However, whatever the size of installation, there are two main aspects worthy of attention, which are also very relevant to a computer feasibility survey, and they are:

1. the hardware, or the actual machines used; and
2. the software, or basically, the systems analysis and the programming.

These are very important to the success of the use of a computer, *i.e.*, that the right machines be chosen, that the correct systems analysis be performed preparatory to correct programming.

Hardware

The heart of a computer is its calculating section and storage, which is usually termed the "central data processor." Linked to the C.D.P. are peripheral units for the purpose of feeding information to the C.D.P., and for obtaining output after calculations have been performed. The choice of input and output devices is very important and is discussed in greater detail in the next Chapter.

However, the typical hardware installation will consist of:

1. the central data processor (with monitoring and control console);
2. a buffer store (*see below*);
3. peripheral equipment which may consist of one or more of the following:
   (*a*) teleprinter tape reader;
   (*b*) punched card input;
   (*c*) teleprinter tape output;

282

(*d*) electric typewriter input and/or output;
(*e*) magnetic tape input and/or output;
(*f*) V.D.U. (visual display unit input);
(*g*) M.I.C.R. (magnetic ink character reader);
(*h*) mark senser—sensing graphite markings in appropriate positions.

One outstanding problem of computers has always been that the C.D.P. can work literally in millionths of a second (a nanosecond equals 1/1,000,000,000 of a second) while the machines for input and output are so much slower, and cannot keep pace with the C.D.P. As a consequence, buffer stores have developed by means of which comparatively slow input can be fed into a fast random access storage in the machine, for (relatively) fast feeding to the C.D.P. These devices include magnetic core store, magnetic discs, and so on.

Of course, the peripheral units chosen must be both compatible to the C.D.P. and suitable to the system in use.

Even though both these aspects might have been fully considered, there is then a problem of verification and amending mistakes. Thus, although there is a magnetic tape input machine, it is probably not so easy to check its accuracy as, say, punched cards or punched tape. But no matter what peripheral units and methods of input/output are chosen, the machine will produce wrong information if it is fed wrong information. The Americans have a saying "Trash in, means trash out," and if mistakes are made either in the programming or in the information fed to the computer, then it will print wrong information.

Without going into too much detail, some of the major developments in hardware can be outlined. The Post Office provides a Datel service, enabling information to be fed from anywhere (*i.e.*, not necessarily at Head Office), because it is accessible over the telephone. In keeping with this development, there have been many peripheral units developed to give faster and simpler computer access and output.

One American machine on the U.K. market is an electric terminal which is compatible with existing I.B.M. and teletype mechanical printing terminals, providing silent selectronic printing speeds of up to 300 words per minute (30 c.p.s.). This means less computer-connect time, less telephone charges, and is much faster than many 10 c.p.s. terminals on the market. This also means that wherever a telephone and a power unit is available, a user can communicate with a remote computer simply by plugging into the power point.

There are many who deride the efficiency of the telephone service in the U.K., and it might be questioned whether telephone communication is to be desired, but it seems to be developing nevertheless.

In choosing hardware, there is the possibility of being "dazzled" by manufacturers' statements about processing speeds, and input and output speeds. This is not to say that these are not important, but perhaps the most crucial factors are:

1. Size of memory, measured by not only the number of addresses, but by the individual word length of each address. Many computer users, after installing a machine, wish they had chosen a machine with greater storage capacity. The word length must be the maximum required by the system, and can only be assessed and established by systems and computer experts.
2. Speed of input and output to the buffer store and transfer from that store to the C.D.P.
3. Capital costs (or rental costs) of the machine.
4. Maintenance service and costs.

In practice, it is fairly common to find that the most expensive part of a computer is the C.D.P. unit, which is operational for only 20 to 30 per cent of the time. There can be two approaches to this problem: to use a slower, cheaper C.D.P. which would cope equally well, or to take steps to try to use the machine to its fullest extent. The trouble here is that statistics and figures may then be produced without viable management value, just to make full use of the machine's potential.

Another problem here is to decide how much additional work can be accommodated before extra computer capacity is needed. For example, an extra 20 per cent improvement in a computer output on a fully loaded system rented at £6,000 per month, will release computer time to the value of £1,000 per month; by making greater use of an existing computer, a proposed increase in size of computer might defer a bigger rental of, say, £6,000–£8,000 per month, and show a saving of £24,000 a year at least for the next year or two.

Computer performance analysis is very important, since a computer is the most expensive machine a business buys, and is further discussed in Chapter 34.

C.O.M. (computer output on microfilm)

There are three methods of achieving C.O.M.:

1. straightforward microfilming of computer printout, *i.e.*, of the continuous stationery;
2. a computer peripheral which generates graphical material on to a video screen which is then microcopied; or
3. E.B.R. (Electronic Beam Recording), which uses an electronic gun to write characters direct from magnetic tape to microfilm.

The last method is developing fast, and one C.O. Microfilmer translates data from magnetic tape into readable language and microfilms it at speeds of up to 120,000 c.p.s.

To give some idea of the further development of C.O.M., the British National Bibliography is the first to be published by C.O.M.; it was produced on to microfiche, and the reduction ratio was such that 2,380 pages were accommodated on one 4 in. × 6 in. microfiche. The reader then enlarges each of these pages to a screen size of 11 in. square (magnification factor of 150 ×).

Software

As previously stated, the term "software" basically comprises systems analysis and programming.

Systems analysis is quite simply the investigation of business systems and their adaptation to suit the programming and subsequent processing by a computer. It is a very difficult part of using a computer, and it is also one of the reasons for the failure of a computer installation.

It is a difficult area because for good systems analysis it requires a knowledge of:

1. O. & M. and management services;
2. programming and computer technology;
3. the business, its objectives and policies and its technical background.

It is difficult to obtain good systems analysts, because an expert O. & M. officer may have a knowledge of 1 and 3 above, but not 2, and a computer-trained expert will have 2 and probably not 1 or 3.

The term "systems analysis" is more than its name implies, for it should be an analysis of the organisation, of the information flow, of the systems, of the forms, of data production, and so on. It is a very lengthy job requiring extensive knowledge, and as a consequence some authorities hold that it is a waste of time analysing existing systems for the purpose of adapting them to the computer, and that the better policy is to ignore all old systems, to start afresh from objectives, examining data requirements, etc., and then design the systems to suit the computer.

The advantages of analysing the existing systems are that the purposes are revealed; the controls are highlighted; how systems interlock is shown; and a study of existing forms which may be re-usable is involved.

If it is agreed that the application of a computer should not be merely to automate old-fashioned systems, then the system should not be the starting-point—system is the method of achieving the aims of the office work and old system analysis wastes a great deal of time.

While it may be rewarding to examine what is being done already, it should not be forgotten that a great deal of this may be extraneous when a computer is installed.

Further, it should be stressed that a procedure chart depicting a system is not sufficient in itself, and the various charts mentioned in Chapter 23 should all be used in examination and assessment of systems, forms, information flow, etc.

Computer work symbols

The systems analyst has to record and then chart the system and in re-charting for computer application, there are various computer operations for which ordinary work symbols are unsuitable. Thus, in charting the use of punched card, punched tape and magnetic tape (and some computers use all three) special symbols are required.

In 1966, a British Standard was issued on the symbols for these special operations (*see* Fig. 50) but this no doubt could be amplified in the light of computer developments since that date.

Programming

Programming is the conversion of the systems analysis into detailed working instructions for the computer, so that there is a complete set of instructions for each computer application—for wages preparation, for sales invoicing, and so on.

An outstanding difficulty of programming is that it requires such extensive work, for the computer programme is written in the microscopic detail necessary for the application (there are over 9,000 steps in the wages programme at Ford's at Dagenham). Because of this, it takes a great deal of preparation time. Managers unaware of the limitations of computers, but knowing that they perform calculations at lightning speed, are apt to ask E.D.P. managers for a particular job to be completed in a day or two! A lengthy programme often takes several man-years to write, and to reduce this time a team of programmers can be employed. If written in a hurry, the programme may contain mistakes and after testing and "de-bugging," has to be re-written many times!

In large concerns where there are constant changes in sales policy, the re-writing of a programme is often required at very short notice, meanwhile the computer continues to work in accordance with the old programme, making the inevitable mistakes.

It must be stressed that a computer will only understand its own programme language, and just as it has been a dream that mankind's problems could be solved by the common language "Esperanto," so it has been hoped that a common computer language would be found that was completely interchangeable. But as the United Nations has five

Symbol
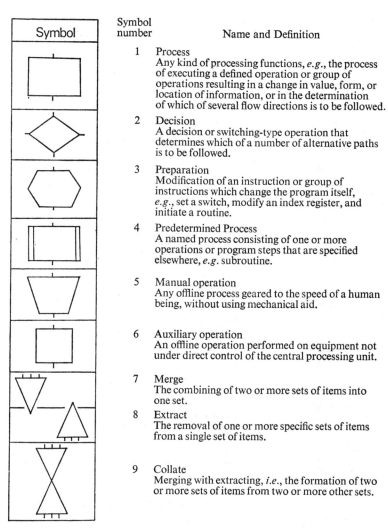

Symbol number	Name and Definition
1	**Process** Any kind of processing functions, *e.g.*, the process of executing a defined operation or group of operations resulting in a change in value, form, or location of information, or in the determination of which of several flow directions is to be followed.
2	**Decision** A decision or switching-type operation that determines which of a number of alternative paths is to be followed.
3	**Preparation** Modification of an instruction or group of instructions which change the program itself, *e.g.*, set a switch, modify an index register, and initiate a routine.
4	**Predetermined Process** A named process consisting of one or more operations or program steps that are specified elsewhere, *e.g.* subroutine.
5	**Manual operation** Any offline process geared to the speed of a human being, without using mechanical aid.
6	**Auxiliary operation** An offline operation performed on equipment not under direct control of the central processing unit.
7	**Merge** The combining of two or more sets of items into one set.
8	**Extract** The removal of one or more specific sets of items from a single set of items.
9	**Collate** Merging with extracting, *i.e.*, the formation of two or more sets of items from two or more other sets.

FIG. 50.—Standard computer work symbols. (Continued on next two pages.)

Symbol	Symbol number	Name and Definition
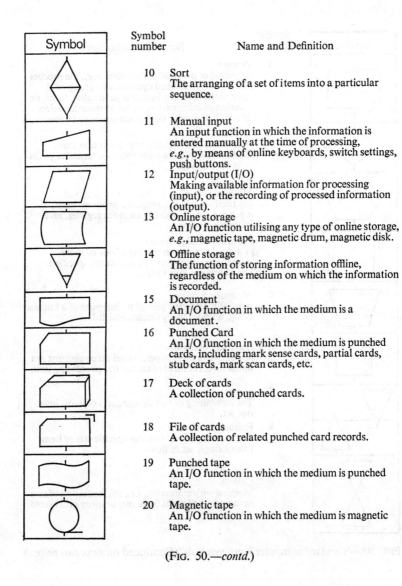	10	**Sort** The arranging of a set of items into a particular sequence.
	11	**Manual input** An input function in which the information is entered manually at the time of processing, *e.g.*, by means of online keyboards, switch settings, push buttons.
	12	**Input/output (I/O)** Making available information for processing (input), or the recording of processed information (output).
	13	**Online storage** An I/O function utilising any type of online storage, *e.g.*, magnetic tape, magnetic drum, magnetic disk.
	14	**Offline storage** The function of storing information offline, regardless of the medium on which the information is recorded.
	15	**Document** An I/O function in which the medium is a document.
	16	**Punched Card** An I/O function in which the medium is punched cards, including mark sense cards, partial cards, stub cards, mark scan cards, etc.
	17	**Deck of cards** A collection of punched cards.
	18	**File of cards** A collection of related punched card records.
	19	**Punched tape** An I/O function in which the medium is punched tape.
	20	**Magnetic tape** An I/O function in which the medium is magnetic tape.

(FIG. 50.—*contd.*)

Symbol	Symbol number	Name and Definition
	21	Magnetic drum An I/O function at which the medium is magnetic drum.
	22	Magnetic disk An I/O function in which the medium is a magnetic disk.
	23	Core An I/O function in which the medium is magnetic core.
	24	Display An I/O function in which the information is displayed for human use at the time of processing, by means of online indicators, video devices, console printers, plotters, etc.
	25	Flow line The function of linking symbols crossing of flow lines junction of flow lines
	26	Parallel mode (no flow lines are shown) The beginning or end of two or more simultaneous operations.
	27	Communication link A function in which information is transmitted by a telecommunication link.
	28	Connector An exit to, or an entry from another part of the flowchart.
	29	Terminal, interrupt A terminal point in a flowchart, *e.g.*, start, halt, delay or interrupt.
	30	Comment, annotation The addition of descriptive comments or explanatory notes as clarification.

(FIG. 50.—*concluded.*)

basic languages so in the computer world there are several languages which have more or less official standing (with some other languages on the sidelines).

To start with, computers had coded programmes which required quite a large degree of translation, but the last decade or so has seen a development in high-level languages whereby a single English word or phrase can signify a whole series of instructions to the computer.

Four of the main high-level languages are:

ALGOL—Algorithmic language—which is an international language used for *scientific* problems
FORTRAN—Formula Translation—also a *scientific* language
COBOL—Common Business Language—now recognised as an international *commercial* programming language
PL-1—Programming Language 1, developed by I.B.M.—a fairly new language for scientific and commercial work.

Some comparisons between the different languages can be gauged from Fig. 51.

Although the computer languages are much easier to understand than the machine code, they still have rather irksome grammatical rules, and limitations, which take some time for the user to master.

INSTRUCTION LANGUAGE	COMPUTER INSTRUCTIONS
1. Machine language	21 0100 02000
2. Fortran	YTDE = YTDE + EARN
3. Cobol	ADD − EARN to YTDE

FIG. 51.—Comparison between computer languages.

Programming time

While the aim has been to simplify programming, and so reduce the time required to do it, it is still impossible to estimate accurately the work involved in writing a programme. On the other hand, it is a good thing to recognise the factors which can so easily lead to under-estimation of the time involved. These include the following:

1. The efficiency of the systems analysis, and the extent to which it has to be modified in the course of programming.
2. The programming experience with the computer, especially of the particular make and model of computer being used.
3. The capacity of the particular computer. Thus, if there is limited storage capacity for the programme, then it has to be

condensed in order to fit the computer. This may mean re-writing and so takes more time.

4. Availability of machine time for testing and de-bugging. This is a time-consuming task, and unless computer time is available, it means further delays.

5. Programming requires lengthy spells of concentrated work, and if the programmers are subject to many interruptions in their work, it can easily double the time spent in doing the job.

6. Economy in running time. Thus, with most commercial jobs, there is a vast amount of data which is required quickly, and the faster the run required, the more work it throws on the programmer.

While the actual programme is important, it is equally important that the programmer should record his workings in constructing the programme, because when it comes to re-writing, there must be guide-lines to assist the process. Unless working notes are kept with the programme records, it is often like trying to solve an abstract puzzle to explain why it was written in the way that was chosen at the time. Nearly all programmes have to be re-written, first in the testing immediately after writing, and secondly in the future when changed circumstances or policy changes require it.

CHECK LIST

1. What are the purposes of the work?
2. Is there a computer capable of its performance?
3. What would be the most suitable peripherals?
4. Is speed an important factor?
5. Have we taken care of checking accuracy?
6. Do we always need hard copy?
7. Do we always need great speed, and at what cost?
8. What is the storage capacity of the computer?
9. What special operator training is required?
10. What is the cost of auxiliary equipment?
11. What is the most suitable programming language?
12. What is recommended by the manufacturer?
13. Are good programmers obtainable—in that language?
14. Have we taken care of all the factors in writing a programme?
15. Are there work records to support the programmes written?
16. Have the programmes been tested and de-bugged?
17. Is the programme written in a way which is economical of computer time?
18. Have we fully estimated the time required for programming?
19. Have we allowed for labour turnover in programmers?
20. Have we taken account of programming costs as well as of machine costs?

Chapter 33 Input and output

One of the greatest problems when installing electronic data processing is deciding on the best methods of input and output. This is difficult because of increasing numbers of methods available, and because of the many factors which have to be considered in choosing one.

It is a very important aspect of computer operation and the success or failure of a computer can hinge on choosing the best methods. The following methods of input/output are currently available:

> Electric typewriter
> Teleprinter
> Punched cards
> Punched paper tape
> Magnetic tape

Modern developments
INPUT   M.I.C.R. (Magnetic Ink Character Recognition)
         Optical scanning
         Mark sensing
         V.D.U.s (Visual Display Units)
         Datel (over the telephone)
OUTPUT Line printer
         C.O.M. (Computer Output on Microfilm)

The choice is bewildering, and most large-scale computers offer various methods. The main factors in choosing are:

1. Speed.
2. Economy.
3. Staffing.
4. Office space.
5. Convenience and use.
6. Geographical spread of units.
7. Accuracy.

There are probably some others, but it is suggested that these are the main factors, and making a decision is often a very difficult task in which invariably some compromise has to be made.

Speed

Although the central processing unit can calculate in literally millionths of a second, no existing means of input or output can match that speed, so that computer users are continually searching for ever faster means of input/output to make the best use of their machines.

It is even difficult to make a comparison, because different manufacturers use different standards and even different terminology in describing their products. Thus, while one manufacturer quotes an input speed of 340 cards a minute, the question then arises how much information is recorded on a card. In an eighty-column card with only denary punching, this means in practice forty or fifty characters per card, or even less. Then, it is possible to have binary punching, so that if the holes represent binary digits horizontally, it is possible to have eight digits per line, or $12 \times 8 = 96$ denary digits, or double the number, although it is relatively complicated to punch a card in this fashion.

Punched paper tape is faster than punched cards, and standard five-channel tape can be fed at speeds as fast as 1,000 c.p.s., although on slow-speed computers, it is often as low as 100/300 c.p.s., although this is even then three to four times faster than punched cards.

Magnetic tape is faster still, and even on low-priced computers, speeds of up to 2,000 c.p.s. are common (ten times faster than average punched tape) and with more expensive machines using high-speed tape speeds of up to 680,000 c.p.s. are quoted.

Manual input by electric typewriter or teleprinter is of course relatively slow, and although 10 c.p.s. is quoted by some manufacturers, this means over 100 w.p.m., and is unlikely to be achieved in practice.

M.I.C.R. and optical scanning (and mark sensing) are two of the more modern developments and 9,150 documents per minute are claimed for M.I.C.R., while optical scanning is even faster.

Visual display units are relatively slow, although faster than punching cards or tape, but V.D.U. has other advantages in terms of accuracy, staffing, etc.

Economy

The initial cost of input/output machines (or their rental) is only part of the total cost, and operator costs, materials, and breakdown costs for different machines must be considered.

It is also difficult to make comparisons between the different methods because of the great diversity of models. Thus, while a 110 c.p.s. tape punch can be obtained for, say, £500, a larger higher-speed combined tape punch and reader can be bought for £4,000 or even £8,000.

The cost of materials is easily obtained. At the time of writing (1973), a 1,000 ft (300 m) reel of paper tape could be bought for a mere 50p, and 2,000 punched cards containing about the same amount of information for about £3, but a factor to be considered here is that verifying paper tape doubles the quantity in use, whereas only incorrect cards are replaced when verifying punched cards.

The cost of magnetic tape depends on its width as well as on its quality, so that high-speed tapes are more expensive than those of lower speeds. But in view of the higher density of data on magnetic tape (200 or even 800 bits per inch (25 mm)), it is likely to be the most economic. The American machines for putting data direct on to magnetic tape are, however, still in the testing stages in this country.

Speed of reading magnetic tape can be many times the speed of punched tape, but the machine costs about £4,000–£5,000.

When it comes to staffing costs, it is a question of cost/benefit analysis; trained operators on magnetic tape machines might have a greater output than punched-card operators—although the labour cost of these is not low these days. Whichever method is chosen, the direct staffing costs have to be compared with labour turnover and re-training costs.

When it comes to maintenance and breakdown costs, some punched-card machines always seem to need maintenance and users of punched-tape machines say they experience frequent breaking of tapes. Probably the electronic input/output machines are more reliable, and where M.I.C.R. or optical scanning is used, the intermediary staffing costs are reduced to nil.

Some interesting cost comparisons were compiled in America, which for making out 1,000 insurance policies showed the following:

	Cost per policy	% machine cost to total cost
1. By hand	30 cents	0
2. Typewriter	25 cents	2·3
3. Typewriter and calculator	24 cents	1·7
4. Book-keeping machine	24 cents	8·6
5. Book-keeping and address m/c	5 cents	21·9
6. Ordinary punched card m/c	7 cents	69·8
7. Punched card computer	9 cents	96·8
8. Magnetic tape computer	4 cents	97·4

It would be interesting to see an updated cost comparison in view of modern developments of M.I.C.R., optical scanning, V.D.U.s, etc.

On the output side, there is little doubt that C.O.M. is most economical (if hard copy is required) for vast quantities of data, for although there is the extra cost of microfilming, the saving in paper, and in office floor-space, soon makes it a worthwhile proposition. But the requirement of hard copy needs to be studied before C.O.M. is installed.

Costs can be further reduced if punched tape, say, is produced as a by-product of some other machine operation, e.g., for cash registers in retail stores which produce magnetic tape automatically. This will probably develop more in the future, as all intermediary staffing costs of data preparation are eliminated.

Staffing

With staffing, it is not merely the comparative costs of wages and the comparison with productivity, but the training needed, the labour turnover, and the cost of errors also have to be taken into consideration.

One company is known to have preferred electric typewriter input, so that it could use its typing staff, wishing to uphold staff morale by not making them redundant.

There is also the question of availability of suitable staff, because if availability is low, then training costs will be high. An advantage of punched card peripherals is that the machine companies will provide training. But, equally, any typist can soon master a punched-tape machine or teleprinter. The trend, of course, with optical scanning, etc., is to dispense with intermediary input preparation staff altogether.

Office space

When as much as £20 a year per square ft (0·09 m²) is payable for office space, this is also a cost factor, and here not merely the dimensions of individual machines, but their number relevant to their output, has to be compared and special conditions of use—magnetic-tape machines will probably require dust-free air-conditioning.

It is also not only a question of space taken by the machines, but also by the auxiliary equipment necessary to use them. Thus, the punched-card files will take much more space than magnetic tape, while punched tape will take less space than punched cards, and so on.

A main advantage of C.O.M. output is, of course, the saving of as much as 95 per cent of space taken by hard copy, but, as mentioned above, the incidence of hard-copy requirements have to be studied.

Convenience and use

The use of a machine is always the first factor for consideration when buying it, and this applies just as much to input/output machines. Thus, is C.O.M. output convenient? Are punched cards, while being used as input, also used (after interpretation, or automatically with it) as readable records? This is one outstanding advantage of using punched cards. But a stack of punched cards can be upset and some mislaid, which cannot happen with punched tape. Equally, a wrongly punched card can be altered or replaced, which is not so easy with punched tape or magnetic tape.

V.D.U.s are certainly simple in operation, and M.I.C.R. and optical scanning involve certain complications in the forms used in the system, which are probably not so simple or convenient in preparation.

The purpose for which a computer is to be used must be considered in deciding on convenience of use in the particular system being computerised.

Geographical spread of units

When the input and output of data concerns business units which are geographically spread out, then consideration must be given to the speed, cost and efficiency of the peripherals chosen.

A few years ago, billions of punched cards were conveyed from various districts back to the computer centre by special delivery vans, but faster and more direct means are now being used.

The use of the Post Office Datel services are obviously a great advantage in such circumstances. So also is the teleprinter, but staffing and machine costs have to be considered as well as relative speeds of input/output.

Accuracy

No means of input is any more accurate than the operators or the source data, but apart from this, there must be means of checking the input as well as output. Punched cards and punched tape provide fairly easy methods of verification, but magnetic tape is not so easy.

M.I.C.R. is accurate, but optical scanning requires lengthy visual checking, while V.D.U.s provide simple instant visual checking which is also quick.

Conclusion

While some of the main features in choosing input and output peripherals have now been examined, many of them may overlap, and must be considered simultaneously. Thus, while magnetic tape input might be faster, if it requires special air-conditioning, its overall cost might be greater in running costs. While V.D.U.s might be simple and more convenient, and require less staff training, the rental costs might be much greater than with other methods.

Cost, staffing, convenience, speed, etc. are all ultimately subservient to what is suitable to the use in the particular system, and physical factors such as geographical spread must have an effect on the equipment chosen.

Manufacturers of equipment are apt to emphasise speed, but is speed always so important? It depends on the use being made of the equipment, and while faster speeds of input/output will make greater use of the central processor, the question of costs and the use of a bigger processor will also have to be considered.

Only by considering the work situation and the machines available is it possible to make the decision on input/output devices.

CHECK LIST

1. Have we considered all the factors in choosing methods of input?
2. Have we considered all the factors in choosing methods of output?
3. Is speed really the most important factor?
4. How expensive is the media?
5. What are the likely labour costs?
6. How much space is likely to be taken by the media?
7. Is distance between the terminal and the computer important?
8. What is the possible incidence of errors?
9. Are the terminals compatible with our particular computer?
10. What is the effect on staffing likely to be?
11. Are there special conditions required for magnetic recording?
12. Have we considered C.O.M. in the interests of economy?
13. What is the capital outlay likely to be?
14. What is the cost of maintenance?
15. How much training of staff is required?
16. Is office noise a factor?
17. Can staff be obtained?
18. Is hard copy required?
19. Is the output clear and understandable?
20. Are the source documents properly designed for input?

Chapter 34 Checking E.D.P. efficiency

We have already quoted Sir Frederick Hooper's maxim that "specialists should be on tap and not on top." The meaning of this statement is quite clear—specialists should be advisory and not executive. Further, unless management knows enough of the specialisation to ask the right questions, then it is in the hands of the specialist. The trouble with specialists, generally speaking, is that their views tend to be very narrow, and not a broad management view.

It has been stated that computer professionals are not trained to direct a company's computer effort. It is for the management to direct the computer towards the best interests of the business.

Too many managers view the computer as just another office machine for mechanising existing systems, instead of realising that it offers fresh capabilities. Given a free hand, the computer specialist will create complex solutions to business problems, and in doing so often obscures the management viewpoint.

Management participation

If management is to gain maximum benefit from the use of a computer, then it must become closely involved in the planning of the computerisation programme. It must be prepared to set the goals and direct efforts to areas yielding maximum benefits. It must then assume responsibility for evaluation of proposed programmes and must assign priorities.

This does not mean that managers must become technological experts, but it means that they must have more than a nodding acquaintance with the computer, its capabilities, and its shortcomings. Only with this knowledge can they evaluate the costs in time, staffing, and equipment, and compare these with the benefits derived.

Thus, instead of assessing the benefits of a computer in possible savings of clerical staffs in providing order documentation, the manager should be more concerned with the statistical analysis of the order pattern, and the credit position, which the computer can produce very quickly—thereby giving indirect savings in making better management

298

decisions. Close information control (provided the computer installation is not itself too expensive), should help to give information to prevent ever-spiralling costs.

Programme, Planning and Budgeting (P.P.B.) is one method of comparing the cost of individual sectional programmes with objectives. This technique assists the selection of programmes of activity to be undertaken, and in highlighting not only those with most importance, but also their suitability to computer operation.

Computer staffing faults

Computer staff are often more concerned with creating an inflexible mechanical system than with giving attention to the base of data information and accessibility. To be fair, when managers are asked what information is required, they are not always sure of what *is* essential management information, nor of the capabilities of the computer to give it.

The central origination of data is called in computer jargon the "Common Data Base," and the computer staff must accept that this comes before all else.

Again, few computer experts have had training in the so-called behavioural sciences, and there is often little awareness that there are social problems to be considered.

It is on record that when a company called in computer experts on a feasibility study, the management gave no guide-lines on the proposed use of a computer, and *neither did the experts ask for objectives* [*sic*].

Cost/benefit analysis

In attempting a cost/benefit analysis, it is very difficult to obtain precise figures. Thus, the cost of a computer may be much more than just the outlay entailed with hardware and the software. There are social costs in causing frustration to the staff, there may be the cost of lowered morale, and a high labour turnover. This, of course, is apart from the numerous meetings of highly-paid executives at frequent intervals. Even if the actual recorded costs are totalled, the incidence of fresh expensive stationery, of auxiliary filing equipment, of microfilm, etc., are not always taken into account.

As for the benefits, most companies are still wondering what the benefits are! A computer may save in clerical staff costs, but too often it does not, or it may involve a reduction in numbers of staff but an increase in costs!

But, as mentioned above, the benefits are often intangible, and therefore very difficult to quantify. Thus, if a computer provides information for stock control in three days instead of the previous three weeks, does it really mean that the level of stocks can be reduced, thus giving indirect savings? If there is more buying and no excessive usage, it may not produce any savings at all. But if tighter stock control means that "stock-outs" can be avoided, and sales are increased, then a computer can easily pay for itself inside one year.

Computer objectives

To assess whether any installation is successful, it is necessary to compare its performance with its stated objectives. This, of course, relates back to Chapter 31, and to the importance of having objectives when installing a computer. Too often, the objectives are hazy, imprecise and incapable of achievement—if the management and the computer experts are honest about it.

Objectives can include one or more of the following:

1. To reduce costs of staffing (rarely obtained), of office accommodation, and systems, etc.
2. To improve the volume of management information, and to produce information not previously capable of production because of the expensive methods employed.
3. To produce not merely more, but better quality and more appropriate, management information.
4. To improve the speed of production of management information.
5. To overcome problems posed by a high labour turnover.
6. To improve management control by production of more or better information.
7. To produce information which will help management make better decisions either in, say, capital expenditure or in general planning for the future.

Of course, it may well be that a computer increases costs, and that the achievement of one or more of these objectives is worth the costs involved. But it may be extremely difficult to quantify and compare the full costs and the full benefits which are so often intangible. It may take years before it is possible accurately to assess whether in fact better planning and forecasting has resulted. The difficulty also is that the intangible benefits are usually more important than the tangible ones.

It is, moreover, important to introduce a time scale. Thus, it is not uncommon for between one and two years to elapse before benefits are discernible. Even after implementation, realisation of tangible benefits can be delayed by costs of running in parallel, programming faults and various other operational teething troubles. A projection should be prepared showing when the cost of a project is likely to be recouped, and setting out the return over each year.

A project justification should include:

1. a timetable of the project phases;
2. a schedule of computer and human resources required;
3. cost comparisons between new and old systems;
4. an assessment of tangible and intangible benefits—compared with the declared objectives of the system;
5. a cost/benefit analysis, which then becomes the document for future assessment.

It is the job of the data-processing manager to ensure that the computer department is run as efficiently as possible, and that the hardware and software meets the management's needs at the lowest cost. One of the problems is that most users find it difficult to realise more than 80 per cent of the potential of the computer.

There is very often a lack of factual information about the detailed usage of each functional component of a computer. As a result, there is difficulty in assessing how efficiently computer equipment is in fact utilised. In practice, it is fairly common to find that the most expensive part of a computer system, the central data processor, is operational for only 20 to 30 per cent of its time, and often a slower, cheaper unit would have been able to cope equally well.

American rules

What rules then can be applied to obtain maximum efficiency from a computer? The Mortgage Bankers Association in America has suggested the following:

1. Do not delegate computer planning to programmers.
2. Continue to educate users of computer output and create a climate of acceptance.
3. The computer should be a tool of management analysis, so what demands do you make of it?
4. Insist on complete documentation of programmes, and do not be totally dependent on one man for programming.
5. The further down the organisation chart the computer department is placed, the less effective does it become.
6. Do not let technicians design systems they know nothing about, this should be done by a systems analyst who knows the business.

7. Do not change computers just to do the same job faster—unless systems are improved, such conversion can be uneconomical.

8. Do not let departmental heads abdicate to the computer, so that they stand by as non-too-friendly onlookers.

9. Do not allow a computer system to be installed and operated without full documentation. There should be records available which a layman can understand.

10. Have a disaster plan, and ensure that flow-charts, etc., are properly prepared.

11. Rotate staff frequently to prevent fraud; do not be in the hands of the programmers.

Accuracy

Too many newspaper stories of computer mistakes have been published to need repeating here, but no computer is any better than the information fed into it, nor better than its programme (or its electricity supply).

With punched cards and punched tape there are methods of verification, but even then, a bad figure 3 can be read as an 8 and verified in the same way. So there must be systems of control on source data entry and the forms used need to be very carefully designed to help prevent errors. One problem is that where information is received on documents from outside the business (such as purchase invoices) there can be little control over the systems or forms design.

All the possible steps to prevent error should be taken, and with internal codings, check-digit validation can be installed as part of the programme, so that coding errors can—and should—be prevented. Punching equipment can be used which incorporates an adding machine, so that the totals at the end of punching runs can then be compared with a pre-listing on an adding machine. Such checking may mean more work, but is often worthwhile.

With any system of doing office work, there is always the chance of error, but the field of errors being committed should be made as small as possible.

Conclusion

In the history of management, there has probably never been a machine costing more in capital investment, yet it is often not regularly assessed as to its operational efficiency. The task is not easy, but when several hundred thousand pounds is involved, surely it should be attempted?

An American computer consultant has given the following advice on controlling computers (and remember that it is the initial installation which is often to blame for its subsequent failure to live up to expectations):

1. Prepare a careful long-term plan.
2. Always compare tenders of different manufacturers.
3. Allow at least two years for the implementation of a total computer project.
4. It is better to select a computer manager from among managers than from among technicians.
5. Always expect costs to be 200 per cent more than the estimates of computer staff, and 500 per cent more than those of the computer manufacturer.
6. Make sure that all line managers have attended courses on computer systems and analysis and are always involved in the preparatory stages.
7. Avoid dependence on individuals, and change staff round at least once a year.
8. Audit the computer performance against the forecast.
9. Continually educate staff and managers.
10. Promote data processing management out of data processing at least once every three years.

Some of the precautions are more possible of adoption than others. Thus, it may be ideal (to prevent possible fraud and over-reliance on specialists) to rotate staff at regular intervals, but in how many concerns is it feasible or practical? However, it can be seen that checking efficiency of a computer is concerned with its installation, with its working and with subsequent comparison with its objectives. Checking efficiency may be difficult but it should be attempted.

CHECK LIST

1. Are the objectives of computer installation clear at the outset?
2. Are line managers involved at the start?
3. Do we use P.P.B. in checking with objectives?
4. Is there regular contact of management with computer staff?
5. Do we have a time scale for cost comparison?
6. Have we assessed all the real costs of installation?
7. Have we assessed all the benefits tangible and intangible?
8. Have we just tried to mechanise the old system?
9. Are we realising the true potential of the computer?
10. Does management know enough of computer technology?
11. Are computer staff informed of the Company objectives?
12. Do we have full documentation of programmes, etc.?

13. Is the system analysis carried out by experts with knowledge of the business?
14. Have we got systems of check digits as well as verification?
15. Are the forms properly designed to meet computer requirements?
16. Have we got a computer with greater capacity than required?
17. Is the central data processor fully used?
18. Have we obtained utilisation data of all hardware?
19. Have we explored the relation of the computer to better planning and decision-making?
20. How can the efficiency of the computer be increased?

Part Seven: Control of Work

Chapter 35 Work control: quantity

Introduction

It has been stated that office workers work only at 50–60 per cent efficiency, and statistics in recent years have shown that by the 1980s clerical and administrative staff will comprise over half of the total work force. In many offices, staff are waiting for work, waiting for the supervisor to be free to deal with a query, or carrying out work duplicated elsewhere in the enterprise.

While a business manager will readily see the need for production control in the factory, and indeed it is relatively easy to control work performed by machines in the factory, he cannot always see a corresponding need in the office, that is until his overhead expenses rise phenomenally.

Again, it is reiterated, that the essence of control is:

1. the setting up of measurable standards;
2. the regular comparison of events with such standards; and
3. the taking of corrective action.

The difficulty with controlling office work is that it is not easy to measure, and therefore it is even more difficult to take the first step, that of setting up standards.

It has to be faced that there are inherent difficulties with measuring clerical work:

1. it is not always performed on a machine, as in the factory;
2. it is not of identical units, *e.g.*, the work required in writing orders or invoices varies enormously;
3. it is subject to interruptions and telephone calls, etc.;
4. it is subject to numerous queries which upset the smooth flow of work;
5. office staff are not necessarily idling when they have nothing to do, and there are often great fluctuations in work flow;
6. office staff do not like their work being measured and checked (a psychological dislike, which they feel puts them in the same class as factory operatives).

However, it can be argued that:

1. clerical work could be measured (which management does not attempt to do);
2. more and more office work is performed on machines, which is comparable to the factory situation;
3. with increasing clerical costs, some control of work and of staff numbers is essential;
4. without some control, management is in the hands of the workers.

The Work Study approach involves Method Study, and Work Measurement, and while the first is always applicable, there is little doubt that the second is not always so. In fact, where method study is undertaken, it is often sufficient in itself in improving productivity, so that work measurement is unnecessary.

Thus, an office manager was thinking of installing a new expensive machine, and after studying the methods used and eliminating some unnecessary work, he found it unnecessary to buy the machine at all. Or, again, an office manager with fifteen staff discovered when assessing the office organisation that many senior staff were doing junior work, and by reallocating the duties, double the amount of work could be performed by simply employing two new juniors to the junior work.

Without any form of work measurement, an office manager nevertheless must have some idea in his mind of what is a fair day's work, which is the standard he applies to any new employee. This standard will result from his experience with previous staff in doing different jobs, but it also means that the standard used is that set by the worker, and may be below what it should be.

Advantages of work control

The most obvious advantage of work control is that of reducing costs of clerical staff or of containing increasing costs.

Secondly, it may be of advantage to the employees who may benefit from increased pay, especially if there is a productivity deal.

Thirdly, work control can help smooth out peak loads of work, and draw attention to problem areas.

Fourthly, it can, if presented properly, involve the participation of workers, and thereby improve their morale. Most workers prefer to be gainfully employed than sitting round idle.

Fifthly, it is an essential of good management to have control, and as the volume of clerical work increases, it needs increasingly to be controlled.

Lastly, it can help management in planning and budgeting for the future, because work standards and costs are available.

Kinds of work control

It is suggested that there are basically three kinds of work control:

1. over quantity;
2. over quality;
3. time scheduling.

It is proposed to deal with 1 in this Chapter, and with 2 and 3 in the next.

Quantity control

As mentioned above, the prime requisite is to establish standards to be used for comparison purposes. From an American source, here are some suggested standards for some office work:

	Average	Good	Excellent
Typing address labels	125	141	159 per hour
Writing envelopes by hand	98	111	124 per hour
Filing 5 in. × 3 in. index cards	187	211	237 per hour
Filing correspondence	115	130	146 per hour
Posting accounts on posting machine	214	242	271 per hour

It will be seen, however, that these standards can be criticised (the author does not vouchsafe them), on the grounds that it all depends on the machines and methods in use. Thus, to take 1, if performed on an electric typewriter with block address (straight left-hand margin), the work would be much faster than on a manual machine with staggered address lines. Or, again, to take 4, a great deal will depend on the method of filing: is it by slipping the papers loosely in a folder? by punching one hole and threading on to tags? or by punching two holes and inserting on prongs and closing the fasteners? To take 5, what kind of posting machine is used?—an electronic machine will probably post ten times as much as an old-fashioned electro-mechanical machine.

In short, it can be said that it is advisable, and perhaps fairer, for a concern to establish its own standards relative to its own work, methods, and machines, although it should be mentioned that with clerical work synthetic times (P.M.T.S.) of universal application can be used.

But if quantity control is to be exercised, work must be measured (*a*) to set measurable standards, and (*b*) to make subsequent comparisons. Various techniques can be used according to the nature of the work, its importance, and the time available. The techniques vary from the imprecise estimating (or guesstimating as it has been called), down to the precision of P.M.T.S.

The methods available, in order of increasing precision, are as follows:

1. Estimating.
2. Records inspection.
3. Work Diaries.
4. Activity Sampling.
5. Batch Timing.
6. Time Study.
7. P.M.T.S.

1. ESTIMATING

When the volume of a particular aspect of work is not very great, estimates can be obtained from the workers concerned, and from the supervisor. It is advisable to obtain more than one estimate, and people sometimes prove to give most fantastic exaggerations of the real volume of work performed; estimating should be checked with 2.

2. RECORDS INSPECTION

This is where an inspection is made of actual past records, and precise numbers can be obtained and related to the times in which they were performed. Usually, workers will qualify such information by pointing out how circumstances have changed in recent times, and therefore, why such inspections cannot be trusted.

3. WORK DIARIES

This involves each worker being supplied with a self-recording diary sheet (*see* Fig. 52), to be maintained over a specific period of, say, two or three weeks. Such a technique will give more information, *e.g.*, about the work problems, and disturbance than 1 or 2 above, but it suffers from the disadvantage that the worker tires of filling in the diary precisely, and tends to enter it up from memory—very often after only a few days of its use.

4. ACTIVITY SAMPLING

This is dealt with separately in Chapter 37.

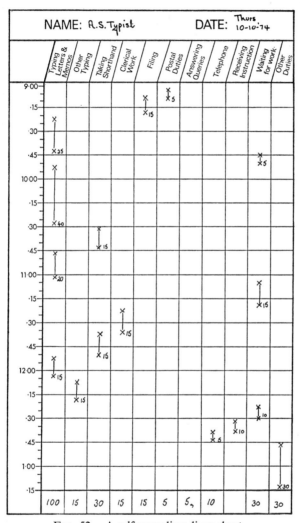

FIG. 52.—A self-recording diary sheet.

5. BATCH TIMING

This is a technique which can be applied either to a group of workers, where individual times would be difficult, or to a batch of work, when individual work items vary quite considerably. Quite simply, it means the comparison of the batch total with the time taken. Where documents are numbered, then it is quite simple to take the first and last numbers of the documents, say, each day.

6. TIME STUDY

This is the familiar technique of timing with a stop-watch the time taken to perform a specific job for the purpose of establishing standard times.

To be a fair standard, it should (*a*) be taken from a number of workers, (*b*) the employees themselves should be rated, and (*c*) allowances in the timings should be made for relaxation, contingencies, etc.

Office workers do not like being timed in this way, but many large concerns both in industry and in the Civil Service have used the straightforward work study approach for the establishment of standards for typists (*see* case history at end of Chapter).

Factory operatives are not keen on being timed, and when this technique is used in the office, it needs double the normal tact, and ability to sell the idea to the workers. Of course, if it means (as it has done), say a 20 per cent increase in pay, then many employees will be quite willing to co-operate.

7. P.M.T.S. (PRE-DETERMINED MOTION TIME SYSTEMS)

These are based on the use of synthetic times, sometimes referred to as Mulligan standards, after the originator, who introduced them in the 1950s.

The objective of P.M.T.S. is the provision of basic standard time data for all basic elements of clerical work, so as to assist its measurement. Each unit is expressed in man-hours and contains an element (say, one-sixth) to cover personal needs, fatigue, etc. An example of the use of P.M.T.S. is shown in Fig. 53.

CLERICAL WORK ELEMENT	TIME STANDARD
1. Pick up forms from a pile, not more than 50·8cm away	0·00048 hours
2. Read 3 word part description and 4 digit cost code and decide if correct	0·00073 hours
3. Multiply 4 digit price by a 2 digit quantity on printing calculator	0·00208 hours
4. Post a 5 digit number to box on form	0·00113 hours
5. Turn over form and put aside	0·00023 hours

FIG. 53.—Use of P.M.T.S.

The total standard time for the whole clerical operation is 16·75 seconds.

Such P.M.T.S. standards are obtainable for all clerical activities, whether they be manual, mental, or performed on a machine; much office work is a mixture of all three.

The great advantage of this technique is, of course, that the standards are already obtainable and waiting to be used, and it is then only a matter of comparing them with the physical events of the office. There may be difficulties in application of such standards, however, not least through the incidence of queries, telephone calls, etc., and either:

1. a re-organisation must be attempted, *e.g.*, so that the supervisor deals with the queries; or
2. a telephone answering machine is used to reduce such interruptions; or
3. the queries and interruptions have to be assessed and included in the work standards; sometimes this cannot be avoided.

Incentive bonus schemes

Many examples have been published not only of clerical work measurement, but also of the use of an incentive bonus scheme, in fact in one (Shannon Ltd.), the increase in productivity was not obtained until an incentive scheme had been introduced, and new typists were also recruited.

The advantage of such schemes is, of course, that they are a method of obtaining greater productivity for management, as well as extra pay for the workers, and that if the staff have to work harder with better control (as they usually do), why should not they share in the benefits? Furthermore, a worker who is fast can reap the benefit of increased rewards.

But the disadvantages should also be considered:

1. The need to have a continuous flow of work, so that bonus can be earned.
2. The trouble that can result when work is retimed (usually because of extra-large pay packets)—this has caused many a strike in the factory.
3. The psychological feeling of pressure on the staff, and the lowering of morale.
4. The increased incidence of absenteeism and even higher labour turnover.
5. The cost of implementing the scheme and of maintaining the necessary work records (although in the case study on p. 313, the system was to a great extent self-recording).

The author has contact with a punched-card department working on an incentive bonus system, and staff usually start looking for other jobs as soon as they are told that their week's work is below standard. The intangible disadvantages may well outweigh any solid advantages of increased productivity.

The usual technique is to set up standards (*e.g.*, by P.M.T.S. methods) for the work being performed, multiplying these by the number of pieces of work, and then comparing with the actual times taken.

Example:

255 letters* @ 2·25 minutes (standard time)   =   573·75
1,003 circulars @ 1·45 minutes (standard time) = 1,454·35
Other work   =   75·00
                                              2,103·10 standard mins.
Actual time taken   = 1,200·00
                                            903·10 minutes saved
rewarded at, say, 25p per 100 minutes = £1·25 bonus.

* The letters in this example were standard lithographed letters.

That such incentive bonus systems can increase output is undoubtedly true, but the introduction of such a scheme needs much careful preparation. Explanation to the workers, inviting them to participate, selling of the advantages of the scheme are most important, and should be used at all times.

Even then, money is not the sole object of working, and to compensate for the likely work pressure, the best physical conditions should be provided, so that at least the office is a pleasant place to work in.

Probably the best compromise between the flexibility of time rates and the pressures of incentive bonus schemes is what was instituted at a Philips factory in recent years. This was called the Premium Planning system, whereby the workers were told of the minimum standard expected after training, subject to which the workers could raise the standard (and earn extra pay) according to their individual capacities and willingness. This system reduces the feeling of pressure, gives the workers a greater degree of participation, and allows the worker to go at his own speed.

But it will be noticed that there is a minimum or threshold standard of work, and this should always be in existence whatever system of payment is used—it is the essence of control.

CASE STUDY

Work measurement

UNEMPLOYMENT INSURANCE COMMISSIONERS

1. BACKGROUND

A typing pool of twelve typists in the Civil Service.

2. OBJECT

To obtain good-quality typing by the least number of employees.

3. COURSE OF OPERATION

1. Time studies were made of all the work performed by the typists and work standards were set up, such as:
   letterheading, salutation, etc.   2·8 minutes
   subject-matter of letter   0·26 minutes per line
   addressing envelope   1·60 minutes per envelope
   (with 60 rating, with Rest Allowance 12½ per cent and Contingency Allowance about 10 per cent)
2. These standards covered 92 per cent of the work performed.
3. Each typist measures her own production, which is entered three times a day on a record sheet (the body of a letter is measured with a ruler, and each inch is six lines single spacing).
4. As a result of the scheme, a group bonus is payable at the end of each month, making allowance for absences.
5. To compensate for the effect on typist-beginners, an allowance for them is made, so that of 372 standard minutes in a day, a typist with:
   Nil experience is given allowance of 240 minutes per day
   1 month experience is given allowance of 180 minutes per day
   2 months experience is given allowance of 120 minutes per day
   3 months experience is given allowance of 60 minutes per day
   4 months experience is given allowance of Nil minutes per day
6. To ensure that work of the highest quality is obtained, an officer carries out spot checks of the work, and if necessary, a penalty is imposed for bad-quality work.

7. Since the typists record their own work, to deter fraud any recorded excess lines of typing are multiplied by five and debited against the total.

4. RESULTS

1. The scheme has been in operation for over five years and has fulfilled all expectations.
2. A team of four typists (instead of twelve) can now cope with the work load, with the occasional help of a relief typist.
3. The typists now receive considerably more pay than previously.
4. The work is also of better quality.

5. COMMENTS

This is an interesting account of work measurement applied to typing, providing a simple means of measurement (lines of typing).

Also it overcomes one of the objections to incentive bonus schemes—the clerical work involved in recording—for the typists do it themselves.

[*O. & M. Bulletin* August 1965

CHECK LIST

1. Have we any real control over clerical work at all?
2. Have we quantity control?
3. Have we any work standards?
4. What is the best method of establishing standards?
5. What is the nature of the work?
6. What is the volume of the work?
7. Would it be advisable to use two methods?
8. Is there any relationship of staff numbers to volume of work?
9. Has the work ever been measured?
10. Can methods be improved?
11. Can reorganisation improve chances of work measurement?
12. Is work measurement really the answer?
13. Is the volume of work performed satisfactory?
14. Is the staff at fault?
15. Would an incentive bonus scheme improve output?
16. Can P.M.T.S. be used?
17. Is group assessment applicable?
18. Has the amount of work increased?
19. Can we obtain the acceptance and participation of staff?
20. What is the best method of control?

Chapter 36 Quality control

Introduction

If it is difficult to control the quantity of work in the office, it may be even more difficult to control the quality of work performed. Generally, we refer to quality of work being concerned with the number of errors committed, but there can be sins of omission as well as commission, which might be more serious still in their consequences. Thus, although a customer of a business may complain if he is given the wrong information, he will complain even more if his enquiry is seemingly ignored for weeks on end.

When things are forgotten or delayed, it is usually because the worker has too much work to do, lacks a follow-up system, lacks a methodical approach to his work, or has insufficient authority to deal with the work problems (or the supervisor is too busy to deal with them for him). These are connected with recruitment and training of staff and with organisation.

The O. & M. cost/benefit approach should be to compare the cost of checking, etc., with the costs of the probable mistakes which will occur without any checking at all.

The reasons for office checking are:

1. mistakes affect goodwill of the public;
2. control of errors can reduce subsequent expense in putting them right;
3. it acts as a check on staff abilities;
4. it ensures that reliable information is produced;
5. thus avoiding management displeasure;
6. to prevent fraud;
7. to uphold the prestige of the department or company.

An error in itself might not be serious, but if (as it often does) it involves an exchange of correspondence before it is put right, the cost of such error in terms of staff time can be quite large.

315

Checking need

Of course, one of the disadvantages of increasing productivity of work is that it often leads to corresponding increases in errors committed. While quantity of work is certainly required, management also wants good quality.

If experienced workers are employed, it should not be necessary to check their work, but it must be remembered that since the delegator is ultimately responsible, he should always exercise some control over the work performed by his subordinates.

If reliable staff are recruited and properly trained, there should be a need for only minimal checking, but however good the staff, it should be remembered that they are only human. The degree of checking necessary will not only relate to the quality of staff employed, but also to the importance of the work, and to the cost of the checking.

Investigating errors

When investigating errors, many questions should be asked in addition to the basic WHO was responsible? WHY were the errors made deserves equal attention, as well as HOW they were committed.

It is also necessary to assess the type and importance of different errors, and to look at WHEN they occur, and WHERE they occur. It is likely that they occur at certain times each month or each year, and in this department rather than that one.

If errors are really frequent, it may indicate some basic fault—usually on the part of management.

Causes of error

A large business in America reduced its number of errors by 50 per cent in the course of one year, by the simple expedient of:

1. keeping records of errors committed;
2. having error conferences with staff committing them;
3. investigating the causes and reporting on the correction of errors.

As a result of the investigations, it was found that there was often bad organisation (lack of definition of responsibilities); that very often there was lack of proper training; and that many procedures needed changing.

Furthermore, it was reported that dull and monotonous jobs were more prone to error unless some more responsibility was added to their content. Equally, persons performing more responsible jobs had not really the time to make important decisions.

Where there was 100 per cent checking, the staff were deliberately careless, knowing that such checking was taking place. Many errors are caused by bad staff selection. Thus it has been discovered that a clerk who does not like detailed work is likely to commit more errors, as will an intelligent person given a boring routine job to perform.

Errors can be classified as attributable:

1. to management generally: bad recruitment, lack of training, bad organisation, lack of information, etc.;
2. to office management: bad forms design, faulty systems, bad physical conditions causing distraction, poor supervision, and lack of checking;
3. to the worker: too hasty, lack of method, lack of experience, bad figures or writing, laziness, tiredness or gossiping.

In practice, many of these causes overlap and are related. Thus, if a worker makes mistakes because of excessive gossiping, it might be the fault of the supervisor, or again the fault of management in not training its supervisors properly.

Methods of checking

There are three basic methods of checking on the quality of work:

1. *Spot check*, where a check of items of work is made occasionally (*e.g.*, every tenth item in a series).
2. 100 *per cent check* of all the work performed.
3. *Partial check*, whereby a part only (usually the most important part) of the information is checked, thus reducing the amount of checking work required.

to which can be added:

4. *Random check* made in accordance with statistical tables, being really a more scientific version of 1.
5. *Principle of exception*, whereby a standard is fixed, and only the exceptions are reported. This still requires a great deal of checking, but reduces the paperwork (*e.g.*, a list of operations that *should* be performed in connection with a particular work activity).
6. *Statistical quality control*, which is a graphical percentage method of recording the errors and comparing the percentage with upper and lower limits of acceptability.

7. *System check, e.g.*, having control accounts in the sales ledger and bought ledgers, and using check parity digits with a computer.

Method 1 is the easiest and cheapest method, and provided good experienced staff are employed, should be sufficient.

Method 2 should be reserved only for work which is very important, such as the preparation of statistics for the board of directors, or printer's proofs of matter intended for printing.

Method 3 should always be used where it is suitable. The O. & M. Department of Stewarts and Lloyds Ltd. discovered years ago that if they checked only the purchase invoices valued over £100 or more (*i.e.*, for arithmetical accuracy), they would save 80 per cent of the checking. Furthermore, in the O. & M. report that was published at the time it was stated that if the full 100 per cent checking had been continued, not only would it cost the salaries of clerical staff to do it, but it would have meant discovering on balance that the firm had been *undercharged* (this may have been a coincidence)! But the principle of partial checking can be applied in different circumstances in all companies—checking to the nearest pound, or that the right account number is used, or the right name and address only, and so on. The area of checking should, of course, be discovered by investigation of the errors and their relative importance to the results.

Steps to reduce errors

Investigation of errors should reveal where and when they occur, although the reasons why are often quite mystifying. Some of the main steps that can be taken are:

1. simplify procedures, so that there are no complications or complicated instructions;
2. simplify forms design, so that it is quite clear what is wanted, and that there is adequate space for entry of the information required;
3. ensure that staff are properly trained, and fully understand the work they are doing;
4. ensure that all staff are performing the work they are best fitted for;
5. install simple internal check systems whereby one person checks on the work of another;
6. install various methods of checking as mentioned above, and report to the individuals concerned who make mistakes;
7. consider distraction caused by bad lighting, heating, ventilation, etc.

CASE STUDY

Quality control

SPIEGEL INC.

Spiegel Incorporated is the third largest mail-order business in America, with 5,000–6,000 employees and £130 million annual turnover. Over half the employees are employed in clerical work. The Company exercises quality control by having a system of random sampling of all clerical work, and where errors are discovered, by the issue to the employees of printed error slips, detailing the errors, which the employees must sign.

Errors are classified according to three types and their relative importance, and every week, each employee is given his/her summary of errors, showing the units of work checked, the errors found, and these are compared with the standards.

For the purpose of error analysis, all clerical jobs were placed into one of three categories:

	EFFECT	EXAMPLES
Group A	Affects customers	Order addresser
		Payment—mail reader
Group B	House records	Accounts clerk
		Mail classifier
Group C	Negligible	Sorter
		Draft attacher

The same jobs were then classified into four numbered categories according to the relative opportunity for error:

	DEGREE OF DIFFICULTY	EXAMPLES
Class 1	very easy	Sorter
		Ledger poster
Class 2	easy	Order advisor
		Bill lister
Class 3	difficult	Stencil
		Distribution balancing
Class 4	very difficult	Accounts clerk
		Mail reader

A range of accuracy standards was then devised for each job. The standards were lower or the allowable percentage differed, as the jobs were designated A–C and then 1–4 within each grade.

An example of the standards for a particular classified job reads as follows:

The job of Typing Cheques is classified as A2, which was
A = Effect of error on customers
2 = Degree of difficulty = easy

ACCURACY STANDARDS	ERROR (%)
Excellent	0 to 0·2
Noticeably satisfactory	0·3 to 0·4
Acceptable	0·5 to 0·8
Probationary	0·9 to 1·2
Unsatisfactory	1·3 to 100

For top management, a weekly Quality Report is presented with the various aspects of clerical work tested, and with the percentage errors recorded, compared with last month's average, and even the percentage of employees deemed to be below "acceptable" in each group of work.

On a personal level, each employee may also be given a Poor Quality Caution Slip, as well as a Weekly Quality Certificate.

This is a broad outline of all the forms and methods used in this fascinating case history. It shows how in a large business with a great deal of routine clerical work, it is possible to have a detailed control of the quality of office work.

CHECK LIST

1. Do we have any checks on quality of work at all?
2. Does everyone know why errors affect the business?
3. Have the real costs of errors been assessed?
4. Is it worth checking work?
5. What method of checking would be least costly?
6. Are the errors recorded?
7. Have the causes of errors been investigated?
8. Are errors due to bad training?
9. Do supervisors follow up errors with employees?
10. Have systems been simplified?
11. Is the main cause bad forms design?
12. Are intelligent staff given routine jobs?
13. Do staff know the theoretical background to their work?
14. Is there a scheme for giving recognition to good work?
15. What is the cost of checking and is it justified?
16. Do staff learn from their mistakes?
17. Do staff of one department realise how their work affects the work of other departments?
18. Is there a standard of acceptable errors?
19. Is there some work where errors are not acceptable at all?
20. How much is due to the faults of management/supervisor/employees?

Chapter 37 Activity sampling

Activity sampling has been a standard technique for many years, but (as with other work study techniques) only fairly recently applied to office work. It is a simple technique to use, although often requiring extensive work in its application.

In B.S. 3138 (A Glossary of Terms in Work Study), it is described as:

"A technique in which a large number of instantaneous observations are made over a period of time of a group of machines, processes, or workers. Each observation records what is happening at that instant, and the percentage of observations recorded for a particular activity or delay is a measure of the percentage of time during which that activity or delay occurs."

It is variously referred to as the "random observation method," as "work sampling," "ratio delay method," and even "snap reading method."

In simple English, it is a method of taking a number of random samples of work in an office; from the information revealed can be gained:

1. Percentage use made of machines.
2. Percentage work activity of staff.
3. Distribution of various work activities among staff.

Activity sampling is particularly useful:

1. where, because of the multiplicity of kinds of work, it would be uneconomic to attempt its assessment in any other way;
2. in circumstances where there may be a changing content of different kinds of work; and
3. where a complete detailed record is not especially required, but only a cross-section or representation.

So it is a technique especially suited to office operations, because they are often diffuse, and changeable, and staff often have a mixture of duties to perform.

28 89 65 87 08	13 50 63 04 23	25 47 57 91 13	52 62 24 19 94	91 67 48 57 10
30 29 43 65 42	78 66 28 55 80	47 46 41 90 08	55 98 78 10 70	49 92 05 12 07
95 74 62 60 53	51 57 32 22 27	12 72 72 27 77	44 67 32 23 13	67 95 07 76 30
01 85 54 96 72	66 86 65 64 60	56 59 75 36 75	46 44 33 63 71	54 50 06 44 75
10 91 46 96 86	19 83 52 47 53	65 00 51 93 51	30 80 05 19 29	56 23 27 19 03
05 33 18 08 51	51 78 57 26 17	34 87 96 23 93	89 99 93 39 79	11 28 94 15 52
04 43 13 37 00	79 68 96 26 60	70 39 83 66 56	62 03 55 86 57	77 55 33 62 02
05 85 40 25 24	73 52 93 70 50	48 21 47 74 63	17 27 27 51 26	39 96 29 00 45
84 90 90 65 77	63 99 25 69 02	09 04 03 35 78	19 79 95 07 21	02 84 48 51 97
28 55 53 09 48	86 28 30 02 35	71 30 32 06 47	93 74 21 86 33	49 90 21 69 74
89 83 40 69 80	97 96 47 59 97	56 33 24 87 36	17 18 16 90 46	75 27 28 52 13
33 20 96 05 68	93 41 69 96 07	97 50 81 79 59	42 37 13 81 83	82 42 85 04 31
10 89 07 76 21	40 24 74 36 42	40 33 04 46 24	35 63 02 31 61	34 59 43 36 96
91 50 27 78 37	06 06 16 25 98	17 78 80 36 85	26 41 77 63 37	71 63 94 94 33
03 45 44 66 88	97 81 26 03 89	39 46 67 21 17	98 10 39 33 15	61 63 00 25 92
89 41 58 91 63	65 99 59 97 84	90 14 79 61 55	56 16 88 87 60	32 15 99 67 43
13 43 00 97 26	16 91 21 32 41	60 22 66 72 17	31 85 33 69 07	68 49 20 43 29
71 71 00 51 72	62 03 89 26 32	35 27 99 18 25	78 12 03 09 70	50 93 19 35 56
19 28 15 00 41	92 27 73 40 38	37 11 05 75 16	98 81 99 37 29	92 20 32 39 67
56 38 30 92 30	45 51 94 69 04	00 84 14 36 37	95 66 39 01 09	21 68 40 95 79
39 27 52 89 11	00 81 06 28 48	12 08 05 75 26	03 35 63 05 77	13 81 20 67 58
73 13 28 58 01	05 06 42 24 07	60 60 29 99 93	72 93 78 04 36	25 76 01 54 03
81 60 84 51 57	12 68 46 55 89	60 09 71 87 89	70 81 10 95 91	83 79 68 20 66
05 62 98 07 85	07 79 26 69 61	67 85 72 37 41	85 79 76 48 23	61 58 87 08 05
62 97 16 29 18	52 16 16 23 56	62 95 80 97 63	32 25 34 03 36	48 84 60 37 65
31 13 63 21 08	16 01 92 58 21	48 79 74 73 72	08 64 80 91 38	07 28 66 61 59
97 38 35 34 19	89 84 05 34 47	88 09 31 54 88	97 96 86 01 69	46 13 95 65 96
32 11 78 33 82	51 99 98 44 39	12 75 10 60 36	80 66 39 94 97	42 36 31 16 94
81 99 13 37 05	08 12 60 39 23	61 73 84 89 18	26 02 04 37 95	96 18 69 06 30
45 74 00 03 05	69 99 47 26 52	48 06 30 00 18	03 30 28 55 59	66 10 71 44 05
11 84 13 69 01	88 91 28 79 50	71 42 14 96 55	98 59 96 01 36	88 77 90 45 59
14 66 12 87 22	59 45 27 08 51	85 64 23 85 41	64 72 08 59 44	67 98 56 65 56
40 25 67 87 82	84 27 17 30 37	48 69 49 02 58	98 02 50 58 11	95 39 06 35 63
44 48 97 49 43	65 45 53 41 07	14 83 46 74 11	76 66 63 60 08	90 54 33 65 84
41 94 54 06 57	48 28 01 83 84	09 11 21 91 73	97 28 44 74 06	22 30 95 69 72
07 12 15 58 84	93 18 31 83 45	54 52 62 29 91	53 58 54 66 05	47 19 63 92 75
64 27 90 43 52	18 26 32 96 83	50 58 45 27 57	14 96 39 64 85	73 87 96 76 23
80 71 86 41 03	45 62 63 40 88	35 69 34 10 94	32 22 52 04 74	69 63 21 83 41
27 06 08 09 92	26 22 59 28 27	38 58 22 14 79	24 32 12 38 42	33 56 90 92 57
54 68 97 20 54	33 26 74 03 30	74 22 19 13 48	30 28 01 92 49	56 61 52 27 03
02 92 65 68 99	05 53 15 26 70	04 69 22 64 07	04 73 25 74 82	78 35 22 21 88
83 52 57 78 62	98 61 70 48 22	68 50 64 55 75	42 70 32 09 60	58 70 61 43 97
82 82 76 31 33	85 13 41 38 10	16 47 61 43 77	83 27 19 70 41	34 78 77 60 25
38 61 34 09 49	04 41 66 09 76	20 50 73 40 95	24 77 95 73 20	47 42 80 61 03
01 01 11 88 38	03 10 16 82 24	39 58 20 12 39	82 77 02 18 88	33 11 49 15 16
21 66 14 38 28	54 08 18 07 04	92 17 63 36 75	33 14 11 11 78	97 30 53 62 38
32 29 30 69 59	68 50 33 31 47	15 64 88 75 27	04 51 41 61 96	86 62 93 66 71
04 52 21 65 47	39 90 89 86 77	46 86 86 88 86	50 09 13 24 91	54 80 67 78 66
38 64 50 07 36	56 50 45 94 25	48 28 48 30 51	60 73 73 03 87	68 47 37 10 84
48 33 50 83 53	59 77 64 59 90	58 92 62 50 18	93 09 45 89 06	13 26 98 86 29

FIG. 54.—Random number tables.

Technique

As mentioned above, activity sampling involves the making of visits at random intervals to assess the work being performed. To ensure that the visits are statistically random, random-number tables can be used. An example is shown in Fig. 54 which would read sequentially, either vertically or horizontally. Thus, a timing for each hour of the day (reading vertically down the first column) might read:

9·28
10·30
11·00 (nil)
12·35
1·01
2·10
3·05
4·04
5·05

The work activities observed at these different times are *entered on analysis sheets* like that shown in Fig. 55.

Where the study is being made of a number of workers, the different columns would be completed for the type of work being performed by different workers.

WORK OPERATION: Shorthand Typist															Period of Study: 16 – 23rd June					
DATE							DATE							DATE						
Time	T.	S.	F.	Te.	U.	O.	Time	T.	S.	F.	Te.	U.	O.	Time	T.	S.	F.	Te.	U.	O.
9.29	✓																			
10.00																				
11.06		✓																			

T = Typing   S = Shorthand   F = Filing   Te = Telephone   U = Unoccupied   O = Other

FIG. 55.—A work activity analysis sheet.

Ultimately, it will yield analytical totals of different kinds of work being performed by individual workers, so that

(a) work can be re-distributed to make the best use of staff;

(b) work can be re-cycled so that staff do not waste time waiting for it;

(c) figures are provided of time spent on different work activities, which then assist work measurement.

Regarding (c), the final analysis after activity sampling might be as shown in Fig. 56.

No. of Observations		% of Total	Minutes	Work Volume	Work Unit Time
Activity A	40	53	1,113	2,671	0·41
Activity B	11	15	315	1,102	0·30
Activity C	10	13	273	992	0·27
Away from desk	3	4	84		
Idle (no work)	6	8	168		
Personal	5	7	147		
	75	100	2,100		

(5 clerks on 7 hour day = Total of 2,100 minutes together)

FIG. 56.—Final analysis after activity sampling.

It will be noticed that the Work Volume is inserted from measurement of the number of units of work, and that the last column, headed "Work Unit Time," is in reality arrived at by dividing Minutes by Work Volume. This does not give control in itself, although if the measurements are performed when good staff are employed and in normal circumstances, the last column can thus become the standard to give control in the future.

Confidence limits of samples

With any method of sampling, the greater the number of samples examined, the greater the confidence will there be in the findings being representative. Various formulae have been developed, so that

1. the percentage of error can be decided, and
2. the least number of samples to take can be established.

A popular formula for use here is:

$$\text{Number of observations } (n) = \frac{4p(100 - p)}{L^2}$$

where p = estimated proportional work activity
and L = limit of accuracy (or confidence limit).

1. Thus, supposing, to take a simple example, an activity sampling is being made of a shorthand typist, and on a rough check, it is found that she spends 60 per cent of her time on typing, and it is wished to obtain a 90 per cent degree of accuracy in the sampling, then the number of samples to be taken would be

$$n = \frac{4 \times 60(100 - 60)}{100} = 96 \text{ observations.}$$

2. If the circumstances were that the estimated time of the activity being investigated was as high as 75 per cent of total time, and the degree of confidence required was as high as ±3 per cent, then the formula becomes

$$n = \frac{4 \times 75(100 - 75)}{9} = 833 \text{ observations.}$$

3. But it may be that the activity being investigated was only 5 per cent of total time ($p = 5$), and a ±1 per cent degree of confidence was required; then the formula becomes

$$n = \frac{4 \times 5(100 - 5)}{1} = 1,900 \text{ observations.}$$

It will be noticed that to use this formula, it is necessary first of all to have a rough estimate of p—the estimated proportional work activity being studied. Obviously, where the *total* work content is being investigated, the formula is not of such great use.

1. To increase the degree of confidence means increasing the number of observations.
2. The smaller the volume of n the smaller the number of observations.

It is important that the period of the observations should be spread over the whole of the work cycle, otherwise it might be very biased.

To use the Random Numbers table in fig. 54:

Select 53 random numbers in the range 1–2,100, to cover activity sampling over Monday to Friday, 9.00 a.m. to 1.00 p.m., and 2.00 p.m. to 5.00 p.m. = 35 hours, or 2,100 minutes.

(*i*) Refer to the table, taking four digits (two adjacent columns), and record those under 2,100 only.
(*ii*) Continue until 53 have been selected.
(*iii*) Rearrange these in numerical order, *e.g.*, 0185
              0345
              0443, etc.
(*iv*) Treat these numbers as minutes and convert to hours and minutes, *e.g.*, 0185 = 3.05 hours
              0345 = 5.45 hours
              0443 = 7.23 hours
(*v*) Convert these times into inspection times by adding them to the starting time of Monday 9.00 a.m.
       e.g., 10.85 a.m. Monday
           12.45 p.m. Monday
           13.43 p.m. Monday, etc.

Advantages of technique

A great advantage of activity sampling is the fact that any junior can perform it, provided a senior has decided on the design of the recording-form, on the activities to be studied, and on the random interval times.

It has great flexibility, so that it can be used in connection with machine use, staff activities, organisation, or work measurement.

Provided the observers are unobtrusive, staff are said to be less self-conscious than with a continuous observation, but as with all O. & M. approaches, it will depend on the general climate of opinion in making the inquiry and particularly on the tact of those carrying it out.

It has been found feasible to use the technique for analysing work under as many as forty different headings.

The greater the frequency of observations required, the greater will be the work of subsequent analysis, and punched cards and even computers can assist in giving the final analyses required.

Limitations

Like all scientific methods, the results of activity sampling can be no better than the premises on which they are based, *i.e.*, the number of samplings, their representative character, and the precision of the recordings.

Secondly, the technique is not likely to tell how well different work activities are being performed. If some external standards are available, it may help in measurement of work, but otherwise, it only gives some indication of *proportions* of work done—or not done.

While by averaging, it is possible to use the technique to set up standards for work measurement, it must be remembered that to be reliable, rating of the workers is also required.

CHECK LIST

1. What is the purpose of using activity sampling?
2. What is the estimated proportion of activity we are investigating?
3. How many observations should be made?
4. What degree of confidence is required?
5. Have we made a preliminary survey of all work factors (*e.g.*, machines)?
6. Do the times (or days, months) represent characteristic performance?
7. Have we fully discussed it with the staff beforehand?
8. Why is activity sampling preferred to simple time study?
9. Are we using statistical random numbers?

10. Would an employee self-recording method be better?
11. How long a period should it spread over—to be representative?
12. Will several observers be required (perhaps of different machines)?
13. How will the results be used?
14. Have human aspects of organisation been taken into account?
15. If used for work measurement—can "should take" time be evolved as well?
16. What are the possible limitations of using this technique?
17. If it requires thousands of observations, have we checked the value of "p" after a few hundred?
18. If idle time is revealed, have we investigated causes?
19. Are the activities recorded really purposeful behaviour of the workers?
20. Is it worth all the time and effort involved?

Appendix I

STATIONERY

B.S. 1411: 1947	Printers' cards and blanks (terms and sizes).
B.S. 917: 1949	Commercial envelopes (terms and sizes).
B.S. 1808: 1951	Sizes and recommended layout of commercial forms.
B.S. 2699: 1956	Method for determining the absorbency of blotting paper.
B.S. 1808: 1970	(Part 1), 1967 (Part 2) Sizes and recommended layout of commercial forms —letterheads, purchase orders, advice notes, invoices and statements.
B.S. 3003: 1964	Glossary of paper, stationery and allied terms— various classes of paper and board, technical terms.
B.S. 4000: 1968	Sizes of papers and boards.
B.S. 4264: 1967	Envelopes for commercial, official, and professional use (terms and sizes).

FILING

B.S. 1153: 1955	Recommendations for the storage of microfilm.
B.S. 1371: 1956	Microfilm, readers and reels—dimensions and features of readers and microfilm; guidance on arrangement of images, sequence of pages, etc.
B.S. 3700: 1964	Preparation of indexes for books, periodicals and other publications, hazards of storage, use of microfilms.
B.S. 1749: 1969	Alphabetical arrangement—guide on alphabetical classification.
B.S. 1467: 1972	Dimensions of folders and films for correspondence filing—folders, letter files, arch files, box files, and transfer cases.

MACHINES AND FURNITURE

B.S. 3044: 1958	Anthropometric design of chairs and tables.
B.S. 3079: 1959	Anthropometric design of chairs and tables.
B.S. 2481: 1961	Specifications for typewriters—layout of keyboard for ease of typing.
B.S. 3404: 1961	Office chairs for machine operators.
B.S. 1909: 1963	Specification for adding machines.
B.S. 3738: 1964	Specification for dictating machines (all types).
B.S. 3861: 1965	Electrical safety of office machines:

Part 1: 1965—General requirements and tests for earthed equipment.
Part 2: 1968—Requirements for machines presenting special hazards.

| B.S. 3893: 1965 | Office desks, tables and seats—includes most of recommendations in previous three B.S.S. |

DATA PROCESSING

B.S. 3174: 1959	Alpha-numerical punching codes for data processing cards.
B.S. 2641: 1955	Glossary of terms relating to digital computers.
B.S. 3527: 1962	Glossary of terms used in automatic data processing —specialised terms (100 pages) (at present under revision).
B.S. 3880: 1971	(Part 3), B.S. 4730: 1971 Specification for alpha-numeric punching (tape).
B.S. 3880: 1971	(Part 3) Representation on one inch punched tape of 6 and 7 bit coded character sets for data interchange.
B.S. 4636: 1971	(Part 3), B.S. 4730: 1971 Specification for alpha-numeric punching (cards).

O.R. AND STATISTICS

B.S. 600: 1935	Application of statistical methods to industrial standardisation and quality control.
B.S. 600R: 1942	Quality control charts.
B.S. 1100: 1945	Office aids to the factory (Parts 1, 2, 3, 4, 5, 8, 9, 10).
B.S. 1313: 1947	Fraction defective charts for quality control.
B.S. 1638: 1950	Report on the selection of ranges of type and size (preferred numbers).
B.S. 1957: 1953	Presentation of numerical values (fineness of expression, rounding of numbers).

B.S. 2045: 1953   Preferred numbers.
B.S. 2564: 1955   Control chart technique.
B.S. 2635: 1955   Drafting specifications based on limiting number of
                  defectives permitted in small samples.
B.S. 2846: 1957   Reduction and presentation of experimental results.

MISCELLANEOUS
B.S. 3138: 1969   Work study.
B.S. 3723: 1968   Specification for dividend, and interest warrants and
                  related tax vouchers—layout, content, dimensions
                  and requirements.
                  I. Revenue and postal authorities.

Documentation standards

B.S. 1360: 1947   Personal stationery.
B.S. 2489: 1954   Sequence of measurements for printed matter.
B.S. 1153: 1955   Recommendations for the storage of microfilm (at
                  present under revision).
B.S. 1311: 1955   Sizes of manufacturers' trade and technical literature.
B.S. 1219: 1958   Recommendations for the proof correction and copy
                  preparation.
B.S. 3176: 1959   Printed matter and stationery: A and B series of
                  trimmed sizes.
B.S. 1896: 1960   Recommendations for sizes of sensitised photographic
                  papers and materials for document reproduction.
B.S. 1000C: Guide to the Universal Decimal Classification
   1963   (UDC).
B.S. 3700: 1964   Preparation of indexes for books, periodicals and
                  other publications.
B.S. 4187: 1967   Microfiches (sheets of film). Metric units.
B.S. 4191: 1967   Essential characteristics of 35 mm microfilm reading
                  apparatus.

This list is supplied by permission of the British Standards Institution.
Copies of any of them are obtainable from their Sales Branch at
101 Pentonville Road, London N1 9ND.

Appendix II

BIBLIOGRAPHY

PART 1: INTRODUCTION
Developments in office management (Batty) Heinemann
Case studies in business administration (Deverell) Macmillan

PART 2: OFFICE EFFICIENCY
Clerical job grading and merit rating (I.A.M.)
Office staff—selection, supervision and training (Pepperell) Ind. Society
Job evaluation (B.I.M.)
Improving office efficiency (Management Check List No. 26) B.I.M.
Office management (Denyer) Macdonald and Evans

PART 3: ELEMENTS OF MANAGEMENT
Dynamic administration (Follett) Pitman
Industrial organisation: theory and practice (Woodward) O.U.P.
Management: its nature and significance (Brech) Pitman
Modern management: principles and practice (Carlson) O.E.C.D.
Business administration and management (Deverell) Gee
Students guide to principles of management (Denyer) Zeus Press

PART 4: O. & M.
Organisation charts (Mason) I.A.M.
Work study in the office (Cemach) Maclaren and Sons
The practice of O and M (H.M.S.O.)
The design of forms in government departments (H.M.S.O.)
Work study (Currie) Pitman
Applications of O. and M. (Milward) Macdonald and Evans

PART 5: OPERATIONAL RESEARCH
A manager's guide to O.R. (Rivett and Achoff) Wiley, N.Y.
A network analysis for planning and scheduling (Battersby) Macmillan
An introduction to critical path analysis (Lockyer) Pitman

PART 6: E.D.P.
Introduction to computers (London) Faber and Faber
Management information services (I.C.M.A.) Gee
Computers in business studies (Lucas) Macdonald and Evans
Mechanised accounting (Ashton) Macdonald and Evans
Case studies in business data processing (Purchall and Walker) Macmillan

PART 7: CONTROL OF WORK
Clerical work measurement (Harmer) H.M.S.O.
Work measurement in typewriting (Burke and Watts) Pitman
Measurement and control of indirect work (Whitmore) Heinemann

Appendix III

INDEX OF CASE STUDIES

INDEX